COMPARATIVE FEMINIST STUDIES SERIES
Chandra Talpade Mohanty, Series Editor

PUBLISHED BY PALGRAVE MACMILLAN:

Sexuality, Obscenity, Community: Women, Muslims, and the Hindu Public in Colonial India
  by Charu Gupta

Twenty-First-Century Feminist Classrooms: Pedagogies of Identity and Difference
  edited by Amie A. Macdonald and Susan Sánchez-Casal

Reading across Borders: Storytelling and Knowledges of Resistance
  by Shari Stone-Mediatore

Made in India: Decolonizations, Queer Sexualities, Trans/national Projects
  by Suparna Bhaskaran

Dialogue and Difference: Feminisms Challenge Globalization
  edited by Marguerite Waller and Sylvia Marcos

Engendering Human Rights: Cultural and Socio-Economic Realities in Africa
  edited by Obioma Nnaemeka and Joy Ezeilo

Women's Sexualities and Masculinities in a Globalizing Asia
  edited by Saskia E. Wieringa, Evelyn Blackwood, and Abha Bhaiya

Gender, Race, and Nationalism in Contemporary Black Politics
  by Nikol G. Alexander-Floyd

Gender, Identity, and Imperialism: Women Development Workers in Pakistan
  by Nancy Cook

Transnational Feminism in Film and Media
  edited by Katarzyna Marciniak, Anikó Imre, and Áine O'Healy

Gendered Citizenships: Transnational Perspectives on Knowledge Production, Political Activism, and Culture
  edited by Kia Lilly Caldwell, Kathleen Coll, Tracy Fisher, Renya K. Ramirez, and Lok Siu

Visions of Struggle in Women's Filmmaking in the Mediterranean
  edited by Flavia Laviosa; Foreword by Laura Mulvey

Islam, Women, and Violence in Kashmir: Between India and Pakistan
  by Nyla Ali Khan

Gender Epistemologies and Eurasian Borderlands
   by Madina Tlostanova

"Neoliberalization" as Betrayal: State, Feminism, and a Women's Education Program in India
   by Shubhra Sharma

Transnational Borderlands in Women's Global Networks: The Making of Cultural Resistance
   edited by Clara Román-Odio and Marta Sierra

Transnational Borderlands in Women's Global Networks

The Making of Cultural Resistance

Edited by

Clara Román-Odio
and
Marta Sierra

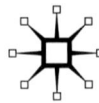

TRANSNATIONAL BORDERLANDS IN WOMEN'S GLOBAL NETWORKS
Copyright © Clara Román-Odio and Marta Sierra, 2011.
All rights reserved.

First published in 2011 by
PALGRAVE MACMILLAN®
in the United States—a division of St. Martin's Press LLC,
175 Fifth Avenue, New York, NY 10010.

Where this book is distributed in the UK, Europe and the rest of the world, this is by Palgrave Macmillan, a division of Macmillan Publishers Limited, registered in England, company number 785998, of Houndmills, Basingstoke, Hampshire RG21 6XS.

Palgrave Macmillan is the global academic imprint of the above companies and has companies and representatives throughout the world.

Palgrave® and Macmillan® are registered trademarks in the United States, the United Kingdom, Europe and other countries.

ISBN: 978–0–230–10981–0

Library of Congress Cataloging-in-Publication Data
    Transnational borderlands in women's global networks : the making of cultural resistance / Clara Román-Odio, Marta Sierra, editors.
        p. cm.—(Comparative feminist studies)
    Includes bibliographical references.
    ISBN 978–0–230–10981–0
    1. Women—Social networks. 2. Feminism. 3. Transnationalism. I. Román-Odio, Clara, 1960– II. Sierra, Marta, 1968–

HQ1885.T73 2011
303.48′208209051—dc22   2010043775

A catalogue record of the book is available from the British Library.

Design by Newgen Imaging Systems (P) Ltd., Chennai, India.

First edition: June 2011

10 9 8 7 6 5 4 3 2 1

Printed in the United States of America.

Contents

List of Figures   vii
Series Editor's Foreword   ix
Acknowledgments   xiii

Part I   Introduction

Introduction: Transnational Borderlands in Women's Global Networks: The Making of Cultural Resistance   3
Clara Román-Odio and Marta Sierra

Part II   Globalization, Transnationalisms, and the Politics of Representation in the Borderlands

One   Transnational Feminism, Globalization, and the Politics of Representation in Chicana Visual Art   23
Clara Román-Odio

Two   Markings on the Walls: Writing in Opposition in Alicia Gaspar de Alba's *Desert Blood*   45
Irene Mata

Three   Global Patagonia: Belén Gache's Nomadic Writings   77
Marta Sierra

Four   Family Imaginaries and Postmemory in Chilean Narrative: Andrea Jeftanovic's *Escenario de guerra* and Lina Meruane's *Cercada*   99
Bernardita Llanos

Five   Iraqi Women, Jewish Men, and Global Noises in Two Texts by Ya'qub Balbul   119
Orit Bashkin

Part III   Transnational Decentering of Human/Women's Rights

Six   Race, Gender, and Human Rights: A Glimpse into the Transnational Feminist Organization of Afro-Brazilian Women   141
Jessica Franklin

Seven	Shaping Political Discourse on Women's Rights: The Role of Women in the Amendment of Gender Policies in Turkey *Gul Aldikacti Marshall*	165
Eight	Trouble in the Global Village: A Snapshot of LGBT Community in Eastern Europe *Anna Kłosowska*	179

Part IV Pedagogies of Crossing and Dissent

Nine	*The Vagina Monologues*: Theoretical, Geopolitical, and Pedagogical Concerns *Kimberly A. Williams*	203
Ten	The Long Table Model: Bringing Transnational Feminist Debates to a Small Midwestern University *Katy Strzepek, Beatrice Jacobson, and Katherine Van Blair*	221

Notes on Contributors	241
Index	245

Figures

1.1	*California Fashions Slaves* © Alma Lopez, 1997	29
1.2	*Virgen de los Caminos* 1994 @ Smithsonian American Art Museum	32
1.3	*Virgen de las Red-Hot Tortillas* © Consuelo Jimenez-Underwood	34
1.4	*Shrine to Guadalupe* © Marion C. Martinez, 2005	36
1.5	*Virgen de las Calles* © Ester Hernández	39
3.1	Usuhaia Prison (hallways) where the installation took place	79
3.2	*Diary of the Cannibal Moon* (video still). Usuhaia Prison (exterior). Behind, the Cinco Hermanos mountains	87
3.3	*Diary of the Cannibal Moon* (video still). Photograph taken from inside a prison's cell	88
3.4	*Diary of the Cannibal Moon*. Promotional image for the installation	91

Series Editor's Foreword

As I write, we have witnessed historic people's revolutions in Tunisia, and Egypt, and are witnessing the rise of social movements against autocratic rulers and neoliberal economic policies in other parts of the Arab world, most notably Libya. And as many of us are glued to the media and hungry for news, we hear very little about women's roles in these movements, women's leadership in organizing the community resistance in Tahrir Square (Egypt), women's visions, dreams, and strategic organizing skills in the revolutions. And yet, we see images of women confronting armed police, organizing picket lines, reeling from being beaten by militias, and video taping and blogging at great risk to themselves. The last two months have profoundly changed the landscape of democratic and social justice struggles in the Arab world, and while women are perhaps less visible than we would like, gender politics remain at the center of these human rights struggles. Perhaps we need better lenses, better feminist analytics to "see" women's participation and leadership in these revolutions. The mobilization of transnational organizing and knowledge networks is readily acknowledged in the current anti-authoritarian social movements, and women's broad based participation in creating sustainable infrastructures is evident to some of us. But, many of us still ask "where are the women?" *Transnational Borderlands in Women's Global Networks: The Making of Cultural Resistance* provides some provisional answers to this question. As a whole the book provides innovative feminist theoretical and methodological lenses that allow us to "see" and analyze transnational forms of cultural resistance. *Transnational Borderlands* is thus a perfect fit for the CFS series.

The Comparative Feminist Studies (CFS) series is designed to foreground writing, organizing, and reflection on feminist trajectories across the historical and cultural borders of nation-states. It takes up fundamental analytic and political issues involved in the cross-cultural production of knowledge about women and feminism, examining the politics of scholarship and knowledge in relation to feminist organizing and social justice movements. Drawing on feminist thinking in a number of fields, the CFS series targets innovative, comparative feminist scholarship, pedagogical and curricular strategies, and community organizing and political education. It explores a comparative feminist praxis that addresses some of the most urgent questions facing progressive critical thinkers and activists today.

Over the decades, feminists across the globe have been variously successful at addressing fundamental issues of oppression and liberation. In our search for gender justice in the early twenty first century, however, we inherit a number of the challenges our mothers and grandmothers faced. But there are also new challenges to face as we attempt to make sense of a world indelibly marked by the failure of postcolonial (and advanced) capitalist and communist nation-states to provide for the social, economic, spiritual, and psychic needs of the majority of the world's population. In the year 2011, globalization has come to represent the interests of corporations and the free market rather than self-determination and freedom from political, cultural, and economic domination for all the world's peoples. The project of U.S. Empire building, the rise of Islamophobia in the United States and Europe, alongside the dominance of corporate capitalism and neoliberalism kills, disenfranchises, and impoverishes women everywhere. Militarization, environmental degradation, heterosexist State practices, religious fundamentalisms, sustained migrations of peoples across the borders of nations and geopolitical regions, environmental crises, and the exploitation of women's labor by capital all pose profound challenges for feminists at this time. Neoliberal economic policies and discourses of development and progress mark yet another form of colonial/imperial governance, masking the exercise of power over peoples lives through claims of empowerment. Recovering and remembering insurgent histories, and seeking new understandings of political subjectivities and citizenship have never been so important, at a time marked by social amnesia, global consumer culture, and the worldwide mobilization of fascist notions of "national security."

These are some of the very challenges the CFS series is designed to address. The series takes as its fundamental premise the need for feminist engagement with global as well as local ideological, historical, economic, and political processes, and the urgency of transnational dialogue in building an ethical culture capable of withstanding and transforming the commodified and exploitative practices of global governance structures, culture, and economics. Individual volumes in the CFS series provide systemic and challenging interventions into the (still) largely Euro-Western feminist studies knowledge base, while simultaneously highlighting the work that can and needs to be done to envision and enact cross-cultural, multiracial feminist solidarity.

Transnational Borderlands is a book about the intricate connections between local and global sites that women occupy in transnational networks—sometimes in highly visible ways, sometimes not. The book illustrates in subtle and complex ways what Egyptian feminist Nawal el Saadawi said of the revolution in Egypt and the gathering in Tahrir Square: women are everywhere, and we are here to stay! In the introduction, editors Clara Roman-Odio and Marta Sierra describe the project of the book in this way: "Trans*national Borderlands* examines the impact transnational feminist methodologies have in conceptualizing women's place in the global sphere and in understanding emancipatory ways of connecting knowledge, location and subjectivity" (p. 1). Drawing on literary, cinematic, and cultural texts, on art, organizing strategies, knowledge systems, and grassroots networks, the essays offer innovative and challenging ways to recognize and understand women's place in transnational justice work. The volume is organized around analyses of (1) transformations in literature and art, (2) in social movements, and struggles over human rights, and citizenship, and (3) radical antihegemonic pedagogies that theorize and enact transnational border crossings. Anchored in the theorizations of feminists of color, anticolonial theorists, and transnational feminist methodologies, the text offers new conceptualizations of "borderlands" linking questions of subjectivity, citizenship, political economy, and cultural production to women's agency in the Global South and North. A volume that will be of interest to scholars and activists alike—one that helps us "see" what we so often miss in the grand narratives of revolutions, social movements, and knowledge paradigms.

CHANDRA TALPADE MOHANTY
Series Editor
Ithaca, New York

Acknowledgments

The genesis of this book is a vigorous interinstitutional collaboration seeded under the auspices of the Great Lakes College Association and Kenyon College. The conference "Transnational Dialogues: Decentering the Academic Debate on Global Feminisms" that took place at Kenyon College in 2008 sought to engage a group of faculty in a dialogue that would challenge academic exclusions of transnational feminist debates from our curricula and students' common preconceptions about first-/third-world dichotomies, western/nonwestern women, and developed/developing countries. It was with these early ideas and with the enthusiastic encouragement of many colleagues and friends that we drafted a collaborative project that eventually brought this volume to fruition. We would like to call out the special and invaluable contributions of several individuals whose perspectives and commitment to transnational feminist methodologies have guided our efforts, especially Chandra T. Mohanty and Jacqui M. Alexander for their extraordinary leadership in the "Teaching Transnational Feminisms" summer seminar (Kenyon College, May 2009) and Kum-Kum Bhavnani for her outstanding presentation "Shaping Transnational Feminisms, Shifting Development" (Kenyon College, September 2008). We extend our immense appreciation to all our contributors for their enduring enthusiasm and hard work. We especially thank Palgrave's *Comparative Feminist Studies* series and their editors and staff for their ongoing assistance and support, along with the feedback from Palgrave Macmillan's anonymous evaluators. The complete project was made possible by several grants and sponsors, including the GLCA Academic Innovation Fund: Single and Multi-College Initiatives, Faculty Lectureships from Kenyon College, and the Teachers Teaching Teachers Kenyon College grant. We also want to thank Kenyon College for its unyielding support every step of the way. Our largest debts are to our families, Alan Hirsch and Alejandro Hirsch-Sierra, Mauricio Odio, and Camila and Catalina Odio for their steadying love and support.

Part I

Introduction

Introduction

Transnational Borderlands in Women's Global Networks: The Making of Cultural Resistance

Clara Román-Odio and Marta Sierra

This book began with a shared interest in the location of women in the present era of globalization. It is a book about place: those hidden, sometimes visible, and more or less noticeable places women occupy both in small localities and transnational networks. It analyzes the constructions of language, art, and knowledge women inhabit and the empowerment they seek in collective efforts, shaped either as concrete or imagined alliances of shared fears and dreams. It is about how women migrate and transform those habitats and the ways in which women build common borderlands that resist the constraints of such locations. *Transnational Borderlands* examines the impact transnational feminist methodologies have in conceptualizing women's place in the global sphere and in understanding emancipating ways of connecting knowledge, location, and subjectivity. As such, this book explores the reconfigurations of transnational discourses and social agendas at three levels: transformations in literature and art, social changes related to rights and citizenship, and pedagogies that transform educators and students as agents of change. We approach transnational feminist practices as theories that conceptualize location, not as a fixed category that reifies identity politics, but as the product of intersections of class, race, ethnicity, sexuality, age, religion, and gender. "Location is, then, discontinuous, multiply constituted and traversed by diverse social formations," Caren Kaplan states, and "does not simply *reflect* identity: identities are formed through the mediating activities of places, locations, and positions" (emphasis in the original, 185). Further, we believe discourses on globalization are key in reconfiguring such notions of location.

Globalization entails the intensification of processes of reciprocal dependencies that began with the internationalization and transnationalization of global relations since the European expansion, beginning in the sixteenth century. However, a more complex interaction among scattered networks of production, circulation, and consumption developed as a consequence of the spread of global capitalism and the deterritorialization of nation-states, the growth of international institutions and organizations, the impact of demographic changes, and the expansion of global media and communication technologies (Brysk and Shafir 2004; García Canclini 2008; Kim-Puri 2005; Sassen 2003, 2007). As Néstor García Canclini contends in *La globalización imaginada* [*The Imagined Globalization*], globalization involves, as well, a number of metaphors and narratives that are divergent and contradictory. For instance, some proponents consider globalization either as a homogenizing force directly related to the influences of neoliberalism, while others see it as heterogeneous and scattered processes, where no overarching connections or explanations are possible (García Canclini 48). Hence, García Canclini draws two important conclusions from these divergent views. First, globalization is not a scientific paradigm with a clear and coherent object of study. And second, it can't be considered a political or cultural paradigm since fragmentation constitutes its primary structural feature (49). The essays in this volume demonstrate that the fragmentary, scattered nature of globalization opens up borderland spaces where "Third World," "marginalized," or "minority" populations can create, within hegemonic discourses, local and global interventions.

The distinction between the material and imagined conditions of globalization is crucial for the scope of this volume. For instance, as citizens of an "imagined global community," we think ourselves in situations of immediate copresence and interaction, a fallacy that conceals negative implications of globalization, such as new forms of lack of communication and social exclusion (García Canclini, 65). However, as Canclini also highlights, the imaginary constitutes a crucial function in elucidating and resisting material conditions of globalization. In a similar vein, we believe the imaginary, as expressed in literary and visual productions as well as in social and pedagogical narratives, brings to fore how Western cultural hegemonies are built and how strategic constructions of location in transnational networks resist such homogenizing paradigms. A primary objective of *Transnational Borderlands* is to address imaginary formations from transnational feminist perspectives that are historically and culturally grounded, and avoiding in this way cultural relativism or, what Kaplan calls "a transnational 'fiesta' or difference that mystifies and codifies power relations" (1994, 141).

Transnational feminist methodologies emerge from a critique to postmodern practices and center-periphery models to explain hegemony. In *Scattered Hegemonies: Theorizing Feminist Transnational*

Practices, Inderpal Grewal and Kaplan analyze the cultures of modernity as produced in diverse locations (1994, 5). By locating postmodern practices within a complex and dynamic model of social, economic, and political relations, Grewal and Kaplan offer a productive model to feminist analyses and their critique of Western hegemonies. In their words:

> If feminist movements cannot understand the dynamic of these materials conditions, they will be unable to construct an effective opposition to current economic and cultural hegemonies that are taking new global forms. Without an analysis of transnational scattered hegemonies that reveal themselves in gender relations, feminist movements will remain isolated and prone to reproducing the universalizing gesture of dominant Western cultures. (17)

The effective opposition for which the authors advocate is only viable from a transnational perspective, which becomes instrumental through methodologies that "rearticulate the histories of how people in different locations and circumstances are linked by the spread of and resistance to modern capitalist social formations even as their experiences of these phenomena are not at all the same or equal" (5).

In addition to reviewing modernist and postmodernist legacies, the critique of racial and imperialist implications of feminist discourses has been pivotal within transnational methodologies. Chandra Mohanty shows how Western feminist texts exercise power through discursive homogenizations of Third World women. For when described in terms of underdevelopment, oppressive traditions, high illiteracy, rural and urban poverty, and so forth, Third World women are robbed of their historical and political agency (2003, 20). Using a radical transnational feminist approach, Mohanty appropriates the notion of Third World women and deconstructs Western feminist reductionism by asking: "Who/what is the Third World? Do Third World women make up any kind of constituency? On what basis? Can we assume that Third World women's political struggles are necessarily 'feminist'?" (44). In so doing, Mohanty claims that a political, not an essentialist, definition of Third World women explains how communities of women who share histories and struggles against racism, sexism, colonialism, imperialism, and monopoly capital operate (46). Borrowing Benedict Anderson's term, she further proposes an imagined community, "'imagined' not because it is not 'real' but because it suggests potential alliances and collaborations across divisive boundaries" (46). Thus, for Mohanty, Third World women share political, rather than biological, or even cultural bases for alliance. Neither color, sex, nor culture constitutes the ground for struggle, but rather the way women think about race, class, and gender and the political links they choose to make among and between struggles (46). In other words, the opposition to systemic forms of domination brings together these imagined communities of women with diverse histories and social locations. Within the United States women of color become an important sociopolitical designation, which Mohanty deliberately links to Third World women.[1]

A third approach to transnational feminist methodologies argues that traditionally, development studies have been overly structural and economic-based, as supported by international aid agencies such as the World Bank. Bhavnani, Foran, and Kurian propose instead a new paradigm—Women, Culture, and Development (WCD)—that places Third World women at the center of development and global processes. Using Raymond Williams's notion of *lived experience*, they view culture in terms of agency, subjectivity, consciousness, and emotion. In Bhavnani's words, the WCD paradigm

> brings women's agency into the foreground (side by side with, and within, the cultural, social, political, and economic domain) as a means for understanding how inequalities are challenged and reproduced. In integrating production and reproduction alongside women's agency, the WCD approach interrogates issues of ethnicity, gender, religion, sexuality, and livelihood simultaneously, thereby providing a nuanced examination to social processes. (2003, 8)

As Bhavnani's *The Shape of Water* illustrates, structures of development are grounded in women's lives. In this documentary specific histories and locations tell the stories of how women meet and confront the multiple challenges of poverty, unemployment, limited access to land, legal and social discriminations, sexual abuse, and other forms of violence in remarkable and effective ways (2). Thus, as a critique to discourses of modernism and postmodernism, Western racist and imperialist feminisms, and development studies, transnational feminist methodologies call for a new understanding of location that includes the "historical, geographical, cultural, psychic and imaginative boundaries which provide the ground for political definition and self-definition" (Mohanty, cited in Kaplan 1994, 149).

Chicana theorist and writer Gloria Anzaldúa's concept of borderlands constitutes an excellent example of transnational feminisms' novel way of understanding location. Anzaldúa and Cherríe Moraga's *This Bridge Called My Back: Writings by Radical Women of Color*, the groundbreaking first anthology by women of color published in the United States in 1981, contests Western cultureless feminisms by affirming location. One of Anzaldúa's major contributions to contemporary feminist theory, *Borderlands/La Frontera: The New Mestiza Consciousness* (1987), theorizes this radical understanding of location as borderlands, "the land in the middle." The term refers to a specific geographic locale, the U.S-Mexico border, and the specific history of American citizens of Mexican descent. Anzaldúa distinguishes between borderlands, conceived as a territorial and cultural category, and the spiritual result of residing in that location she calls *nepantla*.[2] Borderlands is also a metaphor for "liminal stages of transition," which describes how identity becomes an ongoing activity and a framework for a complex composition that melds disparate selves and the collective dreams and experiences that are held together by memory. Hence, borderlands points to "disassociations of identity, identity breakdowns and buildups, and to intercultural impingement" (Anzaldúa 1993, 110). In this process, conventional labeling and epistemic categories are challenged, which explains why, for Anzaldúa, borderlands become a way and quest for decolonization, a counternarrative to globalization, a technology for border crossing, and an alternative epistemological approach to dominant ideologies. The notion of borderlands is also crucial in understanding what Walter Mignolo calls the "colonial difference," which responds to hegemonic discourses in a world that continues to be divided between "developed" and "underdeveloped," "primitive" and "civilized" sectors (2000, x). Mignolo's borderlands emerge from an intense ideological battlefield that produces "subalternization of knowledge and legitimation of the colonial difference" (12). To illustrate, Mignolo redefines Anzaldúa's project of borderlands as an example of the fractured enunciations of subaltern knowledge, or what he calls "border thinking." In his words, border thinking entails a fractured enunciation, "enacted from a subaltern perspective as a response to the hegemonic discourse and perspective. Thus, border thinking is more than a hybrid enunciation. It is a fractured enunciation in dialogic situations with the territorial and hegemonic cosmology (e.g., ideology, perspective)" (x).

By using the aforementioned theoretical perspectives, this volume engages the reader in a critical reflection about subaltern knowledge production and how it disrupts what Mignolo refers to as the global designs of coloniality and modernity. It foregrounds how transnational feminist methodologies force us to rethink borderlands as spaces for symbolic productions that transgress material relations of power and privilege. Furthermore, this book offers a transdisciplinary space for reflection, which examines the impact feminist methodologies have in transcending comparative studies' assumptions on national territories and languages, essential identities and locations. Emerging from transnational borderlands, the cultural productions addressed in this volume challenge the scattered hegemonies built within colonial and modern legacies, as well as current processes of globalization, while emphasizing the creative ways in which knowledge is rearticulated within diverse communities and women's networks.

Our study establishes a dialogue with previous works that focus on the roles women play in global processes. In *Women, Migration and Citizenship. Making Local, National and Transnational Connections*, authors Evangelia Tastsoglou and Alexandra Dobrowolsky also employ the notion of borderlands to study global migration processes and their impact on modern notions of citizenship. Borderlands typically "but not only, found at national borders" are, for these authors, physical spaces where "women problematize common categories of identity in terms of gender, race, ethnicity, and nation, and develop extended forms of identification and networking across multiple borders" (2006, 6). The transnational and borderland perspective adopted by Tastsoglou and Dobrowolsky is key in decentering feminist methodologies as they demonstrate that migrant women are not simply victims of global processes (5). Instead, their study shows how, located in the borderlands, women navigate multiple social and economic spaces and negotiate local and global "dimensions of belonging" (4). By conducting a nuanced analysis of the changing definitions of citizenship and nation-state under the influences of global migrations, this work sheds light on a global dynamic that is transforming gender roles traditionally associated with the local and global binary. By contrast, the essays in *Transnational Borderlands* explore cultural dimensions of borderlands that move beyond the spatial, demographic, and economic aspects found in Tastsoglou and Dobrowolsky's study. We demonstrate that women's global networks utilize the symbolic and material dimensions of borderlands to decenter world systems. In other words, we understand borderlands not only as a spatial category but also as a "global connectivity discourse" that links people across national borders through transnational imaginaries and narratives (Ramamurthy 2003, 527). Our study avails itself of transnational feminist methodologies to unravel the politics of knowledge embedded in these narratives through borderland epistemological approaches. We attest to the need of finding commonalities between different local and global realities from a "noncolonizing feminist solidarity across borders" (Mohanty 2003, 224). From this perspective,

Transnational Borderlands enables new methodological and critical spaces for feminist cross-cultural work that lead us to reexamine cultural, political, and pedagogical hegemonies.

The first section of *Transnational Borderlands*, "Globalization, Transnationalisms, and the Politics of Representation in the Borderlands," addresses the contradictory impact of globalization in the configuration of literary, visual, and critical discourses. The essays included here employ transnational feminist methodologies that reconceptualize the connections between subjectivity, location, and language. They consider examples of how oppositional agency, created through visual art and literature, make visible scattered hegemonies, challenge literary and artistic cannons, and reclaim a feminist voice traditionally silenced in Western imperialist discourses. By exploring artistic and literary works from Iraq, South America, and the United States, this group of essays exemplifies how transnational feminisms impact critical readings in art and literature from an interdisciplinary approach. In addition, they propose transnational feminist frameworks as invaluable tools for understanding cultural productions and reconfigurations of subjectivities within the power asymmetries that arise from different global processes. In sum, this section examines the ways in which artists and writers intervene in such networks and create new spaces for critical production.

As feminists of color were the first ones within the United States to formulate and practice transnational approaches, the first section of this book is devoted to the use of transnational feminist methodologies in Chicana art and literature. Chicana critic Chela Sandoval coined the phrase "U.S. Third World feminism" to describe the coalitional movement of women of color that challenged the construction of U.S. feminism as a universal category. By addressing how a discourse on difference was constructed, U.S. Third World feminism signaled a new global consciousness that disputed the distinctions of nation-state, First-Third World, and north-south (2000, 191). Clara Román-Odio's essay examines connections between U.S. Third World feminism, globalization, and recent developments in transnational feminisms. A focal emphasis of the essay is the notion of *oppositional consciousness*, which, as postulated by Sandoval, constitutes a mobile strategy whereby the transcultural, transgendered, transsexual, and transnational are activated in order to defy ideology and equalize power on behalf of the colonized (62–63). Visual art by Ester Hernández, Consuelo Jiménez Underwood, Alma Lopez, and Marion C. Martinez is used to illustrate the method of *oppositional consciousness*. The analysis demonstrates that Chicana art is indeed a powerful symbolic representation that contests the unified view of globalization as an impenetrable process that contains and dominates local practices of cultural resistance. By turning the *mestiza* body into the site where neocolonial ideologies are played out, this group of artists is able to rupture systemic forms of domination and inscribe Chicana into history.

Irene Mata analyzes Alicia Gaspar de Alba's novel *Desert Blood* within the context of the femicides and the *maquiladora* industry in the México-United States border. By situating the violence that takes place on the border under the light of transnational systems of power, Gaspar de Alba interweaves historical information into a story that connects globalization to the femicides. Unlike prevailing interpretations of the Juárez murders, Mata reads *Desert Blood* as an example of an oppositional narrative in which the protagonist, a queer *mestiza*, embodies the opportunities that divergent thinking offers in the analysis of transnational capital interests. In effect, she deciphers "markings on the walls," metaphors for the crimes, as well as systems of power, that commodify the female body in and outside of the *maquila*. The women in the assembly plants become commodities— disassembled for their labor and for their sexuality. As Mata's analysis demonstrates, Gaspar de Alba's narrative illustrates the possibilities of writing from the borderlands to create new paradigms that can fully incorporate the stories of border crossers, or what the author calls "citizen warriors," committed to revealing and dismantling the structures of power that have drastically altered life in the area.

At the turn of the twenty-first century and under the influences of neoliberalism and globalization, the depiction of Patagonia as a borderland connecting national and global imaginations of place is particularly relevant. Marta Sierra examines how constructions of territoriality in Argentina are destabilized under the influence of transnational cultural dialogues, as exemplified by the works of writer and visual artist Belén Gache. In the context of the First Biennial of the Ends of the World that took place in Tierra del Fuego in 2007, Gache's *Diary of the Cannibal Moon* constitutes a critique of asymmetrical relations of power that are embedded in local and global spatialities. Sierra's essay borrows methodologies from transnational feminisms in order to reflect on the connections between spatiality and power within transnational networks. Her piece demonstrates how Gache reworks the Patagonian landscape as a place of national and global tensions, an opportunity to redefine territoriality, and a liminal space or borderlands that includes previously marginalized voices in the shaping of a spatial memory for the country. As such,

Gache's works establish a dialogue with transnational feminist projects and their critique of the effects of globalization.

In "Family Imaginaries and Post-memory in Chilean Narrative: Andrea Jeftanovic's *Escenario de guerra* and Lina Meruane's *Cercada*," Bernardita Llanos discusses how post-memory narrative representations produce social critiques to dictatorial states and international militarism. Llanos posits that, following the model of coming-to-age narratives, the novels by Jeftanovic and Meruane enact a memory field and reconstruct "family imaginaries" that contest neoliberal culture as a form of neocolonial amnesia. Within this context, post-memory becomes a tool for reconstructing transnational fractured memories and traumatic experiences, which in the case of Jeftanovic and Meruane refer to issues of internal displacement, exile, and censorship in Europe and Chile. A main contribution of this essay is the discussion of a nomadic, diasporic, and transnational memory as an interpretative tool for re-creating historical narratives. Llanos links this form of memory to the issue of women's rights in the climate of disillusionment and political skepticism in Chile. In so doing, this essay brings to fore the key role women have had in re-creating communal memories present in national and transnational narratives. In this way, the reconstruction of "family imaginaries" becomes a crucial tool to contest a politics of oblivion that is embedded in pervasive social and political practices in post-dictatorial Chile.

Orit Bashkin's essay explores the works of Iraqi Jewish intellectual Ya'qub Balbul in the context of Iraqi's independence (1931–41). Balbul's collection of short stories published in 1938, *al-Jamra al-ula* [The First Ember], reflects a number of gender debates taking place in Iraq as the country is slowly seeking integration to the global economy in the 1930s. Bashkin demonstrates that the acceptance of a Western lifestyle among middle and upper classes was supplemented with a strong redefinition of Arab traditions, as transregional social and cultural networks linked Iraqis to other Middle Eastern countries such as Turkey, Egypt, Lebanon, and Iran. The "global noises" referenced in her title were key in reformulating national models about masculinity and gender. Balbul's stories depict the central role the representation of women and the domestic sphere had in this process. Grounding her analysis in a complex transnational perspective that integrates gender, religion, and nation, Bashkin explores the ways in which narrative structures in Balbul's stories reflect the cultural transformations Iraq underwent during the 1930s and 1940s and how gender was crucial in redefining modern identities in the country.

The second section of *Transnational Borderlands*, "Transnational Decentering of Human/Women's Rights," analyzes the history and most recent reconfigurations of human/women's rights in Brazil, Turkey, and Eastern Europe. Globalization and the transnational flows of people, norms, and information have been instrumental in decentering discourses and practices on rights. As shown by Brysk and Shafir, globalization places into question the modern concept of citizenship that, since the Enlightenment, linked the notions of territory and nation-state to principles of universalism and rationality available to "citizens." This conceptualization, however, denied minority groups such as women, gays, lesbians, or immigrants the rights and privileges of citizenship, as this notion "coincided not with humankind but with particular membership" (Brysk and Shafir 2004, 16). Nonetheless, in the present era of globalization, a "differentiated citizenship" emerges—one that Kymlicka defines as "bestowed not only on individual, as is done in the liberal model, but on groups as well" (quoted in Shafir, 17). As Grewal demonstrates, women have benefited from such a shift, as novel notions of citizenship have produced changes in the discourse of human rights, which have been reframed as women's rights (2005, 126).

In *Globalizing Women. Transnational Feminist Networks*, Valentine M. Moghadam examines globalization as a gendered process. Transnational feminist networks are, according to Moghadam, organizational expressions of a transnational women's movement, a global feminism that is guided by a set of ideas and goals responding to and resisting "growing inequalities, the exploitation of female labor, and patriarchal fundamentalisms" (2005, x). This movement unites "globalizing women" from several countries around a common agenda, including women's rights, reproductive health and rights, violence against women, peace and antimilitarism, and feminist economics. Indeed, divergences between First and Third World feminisms began to narrow in the mid-1980s as a result of the rise of neoliberalism and the growth of fundamentalist movements that sought to recuperate traditional norms and codes and put pressure on states to observe public morality and to tighten controls over women (Moghadam 2005, 7–8). Such new economic and political realities led to a convergence of feminist perspectives across the globe: "for many First World feminists, economic issues and development policies became increasingly important, and for many Third World feminists, increased attention was now directed to women's legal status, autonomy, and rights" (8). This transnational civil society has been crucial for women and other minorities as they enact transnational forms of activism, as the cases of Brazil, Turkey, and Eastern Europe, analyzed in this section, demonstrate. Within this understanding of citizenship, Jessica Franklin's essay explores the ways in which Afro-Brazilian women challenge pervasive racial and gender hierarchies in Brazil by drawing on a universal human rights paradigm and gender equality platforms. Franklin examines the significance of increased alliances within Brazilian feminist movements and the extensive participation of these black feminists in international policy forums, including the 1995 UN Conference on Women and the 2001 UN Conference against Racism. The author demonstrates that Afro-Brazilian women have exposed various historical, civil, and political barriers, including pervasive colonial logics of white superiority and deeply ingrained patterns of racial and sexual discrimination masked by the myth of racial democracy as articulated by Gilberto Freyre. Afro-Brazilian feminists have overcome alienation within the country's black and feminist movements by developing autonomous organizations, rebuilding fractured relations with domestic social movements, and effectively conveying their message transnationally. The international human rights framework is a critical instrument for the movement. However, Franklin also shows that, despite over two decades of democratic rule, black women are yet to receive full membership in the Brazilian political arena.

Gul Aldikacti Marshall's essay examines how Turkey's efforts to join the European Union pressed the country to make changes in policies regarding human and women's rights. Conditionality for membership to the European Union opened spaces for women's activism to have a significant impact on policy amendments. Through a series of interviews, as well as a review of examples of grassroots women's movements, the author illustrates how women's activism constitutes an ongoing discursive struggle to redefine some of the most discriminatory laws in Turkey. The author demonstrates the crucial influence of these groups in shaping the laws, which now signals a more egalitarian legal approach to men's and women's status and conduct. Even when in the public sphere such activism has been considered tangential when compared to the pressures of the European Union, women's groups have shifted the hegemonic patriarchal legal discourse. Above all, Marshall's study makes a significant contribution to the understanding of women's activism as a discursive struggle that questions the ideology of masculinity and femininity entrenched in the culture. The author validates the notion that shaping political discourse involves multiple actors that contest the power of dominant groups. Furthermore, feminist movements in Turkey underscore women's effective engagement in negotiating social and political power.

Following Mohanty's call for decentering the history of feminisms, Anna Kłosowska's essay focuses on lesbian, gay, bisexual, and transgender (LGBT) rights movements in northeastern Europe (Poland, Lithuania, Latvia, Estonia, and Belarus). The author combines personal testimonies, press articles, sociological data, art, and literary criticism to create a snapshot of the LGBT community twenty years after the fall of communism and the rise of Eastern European nation-states. Kłosowska employs a rich theoretical corpus that includes Mohanty's radical transnational feminism, Gilles Deleuze and Félix Guattari's notion of pluralism, Jacques Rancière's dissensus model of effective democracy, and Timothy Melley's analysis of post–World War II rise of conspiracy theory to analyze discursive struggles taking place between religious and governmental organizations and the LGBT movement. A central aspect of Kłosowska's essay is the discussion of how conspiracy theories have impacted LGBT rights' movements. The author demonstrates how the LGBT community has been perceived as a foreign perversion, a characterization that represents the mindset associated with nationalist, populist, and religious family values in Eastern European mainstream society. By examining discourses, instrumentalities, technologies, and power differences, this essay demonstrates that the discourse on homophobia in northeastern Europe is a complex struggle that manifests in ideological clashes and establishes a *third term* through which ideological differences can be communicated. The essays by Franklin, Marshall, and Kłosowska demonstrate that transnational feminist networks are distinctive in their calls for gender justice, the bridging of the divide between First and Third World feminisms, and in their use of an innovative organizational form that is premised on commonality and solidarity (Moghadam 2005, 20).

The last section of *Transnational Borderlands*, "Pedagogies of Crossing and Dissent," addresses how transnational feminisms advocate for teaching strategies that deconstruct social, racial, and generic boundaries.[3] For instance, bell hooks pleads for "engaged pedagogies" by encouraging teachers to oppose the "assembly-line approach to learning" (1994, 13). In a similar vein, Jacqui Alexander states the need for "pedagogies of crossing" that "put us in conversation, not domination, with a range of relational knowledges" (2005, 109). This pedagogy demystifies the boundaries between the academy and the community and "brings self-conscious positionality (a sense of place and space) to the knowledges we produce, the contradictory oppositions we occupy, and the internal systems of rewards and privileges we derive from those very positions" (112). Transnational feminist pedagogies construct teaching communities that take into account the material effects of teaching; in other words, communities where both students and teachers become agents of change as they challenge "the way institutionalized systems of domination (race, sex, nationalist imperialism) have, since the origin of public education, used schooling to reinforce dominator values" (hooks 2003, 1). *Transnational Borderlands* echoes these uses of transnational feminist pedagogies and the teaching and learning communities for which they advocate.

In her essay "*The Vagina Monologues*: Theoretical, Pedagogical and Geopolitical Concerns," Kimberly A. Williams explores the pedagogical possibilities and pitfalls inherent in using Eve Ensler's *The Vagina Monologues* and its attendant antiviolence organization, V-Day, as an example of transnational feminist antiviolence organizing and activism. While acknowledging the importance of the play and V-Day in antiviolence fund-raising efforts and in generating awareness of the global ubiquity of gender-based violence, Williams argues that the play, as well as the global antiviolence movement that has grown up around it, relies almost exclusively on U.S.-based feminist epistemologies, subjectivities, and theoretical perspectives that are embedded within an American nationalist discourse that positions the west/north—including western/northern feminists—as the "rescuers" of poor, brown women. She contends that U.S. feminism's embeddedness in American nationalism affects how and why the play is used, both formally and informally, as a pedagogical tool in U.S. women's studies' classrooms. She concludes that *The Vagina Monologues* has the potential to serve as an important antiracist pedagogical tool through which women's studies' students can learn to engage in critically productive transnational feminist critique that avoids ethnocentrism, but feminist teachers who use the play must be willing to incorporate analyses of capitalism, the historical legacies of colonialism, and the contemporary consequences of U.S. imperialism to acknowledge U.S. feminism's position as part and parcel of American nationalism.

The case study included in this volume represents our commitment to challenge new forms of domestication of differences of gender, race, or class in academia and to transform classrooms and educational institutions in democratic spaces to effect social justice. Following the model Lois Weaver labeled "The Long Table," an experimental public forum where participating artists sat at a dinner table to discuss issues related to human rights, violence, or the politics of representations, authors Katy Strzepek, Beatrice Jacobson, and Katherine Van Blair describe examples of a feminist pedagogy that opens up a "long table" for the discussion of transnational feminisms at St. Ambrose University. Their account is quite telling. Faculty of a diocesan Catholic school in Davenport, Iowa, aided by the Ambrose Women for Social Justice (WSJ), implemented curricular and institutional changes that created a space for a transnational dialogue—a "long table" where discussions spanned from Iowa to Beijing, Argentina, Ecuador, Ireland, and Africa. In addition to curricular changes that intended the internationalization of the women's studies curriculum, this project implemented a number of guest lectures and service activities that involved the entire community and sought to connect activism and teaching. Strzepek, Jacobson, and Van Blair demonstrate the impact on transnational feminisms in radical pedagogies that implement connections that go beyond the classroom and breach the gap between academia and society. More important, their work gives a powerful example of how a transnational feminist discourse and praxis propose dislocations of place that challenge the global-local binary.

Transnational Borderlands illustrates the impact of transnational methodologies and feminist practices in creating what Alexander calls "pedagogies of crossing," which gather "subordinated knowledges that are produced in the context of the practices of marginalization" in order to deconstruct the mechanisms of exclusion and marginalization embedded in knowledge production (2005, 7). As the essays in this volume demonstrate, global processes offer unique opportunities for the formation of borderland spaces to reshape individual and collective experiences of marginalization. Our project is to engage in a critical feminism that, as Mohanty describes it, produces sites of empowerment for minority groups within the complex intersections of local and global networks. Borders, both as material and symbolic experiences, are the crucial points where imaginations of place and subjectivity can be shifted. The feminist practices and discourses explored in this book are built within and around transnational hegemonies, and as such, *Transnational Borderlands* exemplifies the efforts of a "feminism without borders": a feminism that claims back those contradictory positionalities women and other minority groups have historically occupied. As a methodology, critical practice, and pedagogic endeavor, this book offers challenges and possibilities for living within the constraining and emancipatory potential of border crossing.

Notes

1. In Mohanty's words: "This term designates a political constituency, not a biological or even sociological one. It is a sociopolitical designation for people of African, Caribbean, Asian, and Latin American descent, and Native people of the United States. It also refers to 'new immigrants' to the United States in the last three decades: Arab, Korean, Thai, Laotian, and so on. What seems to constitute 'women of color or Third World women' as a viable oppositional alliance is a common context of struggle rather than color or racial identification. Similarly, it is Third World women's oppositional political relation to sexist, racist, and imperialistic structures that constitutes our potential commonality" (49).
2. The Mesoamerican concept of *nepantla*, a Nahuatl word referencing to "the land in the middle," was originally used by Nahuatl-speaking people in the sixteenth century to define their situation vis-à-vis the Spanish colonizer. According to the legend, Fray Diego Duran, a Dominican missionary who was writing an ethnographic history of the Nahuatl speakers, asked one of them what he thought about the difficult cultural situation created for them by the Spanish invasion. The informant is said to have responded: "Estamos en nepantla," that is, "We are in-between." According to Anzaldúa, the state of being in *nepantla*... "prompts you to shift into a new perception of yourself and of the world. Nothing is fixed. The pulse of existence, the heart of the universe is fluid. Identity, like a river, is always changing, always in transition, always in *nepantla*" ("Now let us shift...the path of conocimiento...inner work, public acts," 556).
3. Carolyn Zerbe Enns and Ada L. Sinacore analyze the role and impact of "diversity feminisms" in the classroom, where they include transnational feminisms within the group of postmodern, women-of-color, antiracist, lesbian, third-wave, and global feminisms. The authors explain how transnational feminisms contest second-wave feminisms and their disregard of issues of race, social class, generational difference, and sexual orientation. Sinacore and Zerbe Enns summarize their pedagogical implications as an emphasis of how different intersections in power relations shape groups of knowledge. See "Diversity Feminisms: Postmodern, Women-of-Color, Antiracist, Lesbian, Third-Wave and Global Perspectives," *Teaching and Social Justice. Integrating Multicultural and Feminist Theories in the Classroom*, 41–68.

Works Cited

Alexander, M. J. 2005. *Pedagogies of Crossing. Meditations on Feminism, Sexual Politics, Memoir, and the Sacred.* Durham and London: Duke University Press.

Anzaldúa, G. 1993. "Border Arte: *Nepantla*, el Lugar de la Frontera." *La Frontera/The Border: Art about the Mexican/United States Border Experience*. San Diego: Centro Cultural de La Raza/Museum of Contemporary Art. 107–23.

———. 2002. "Now let us shift…the path of conocimiento…inner work, public acts." *This Bridge We Call Home: Radical Visions of Transformation*. Eds. Gloria E. Anzaldúa and Analouise Keating. New York: Routledge. 540–78.

Anzaldúa, G., and C. Moraga, eds. 1981. *This Bridge Called My Back: Writing by Radical Women of Color*. Watertown, MA: Persephone Press.

Bhavnani, Kum-Kum, John Foran, and Priya Kurian. 2003. *Feminist Futures: Re-imagining Women, Culture and Development*. New York: Zed Books.

Brysk, Alison and Gershon Shafir. 2004. "Introduction: Globalization and the Citizenship Gap." Eds. Alison Brysk and Gershon Shafir. *People Out of Place. Globalization, Human Rights, and the Citizenship Gap*. London: Routledge. 3–9.

García Canclini, Nestor. 2008. *La globalización imaginada*. 4th edition. Barcelona: Paidós.

Grewal, Inderpal. 2005. "'Women's Rights as Human Rights': The Transnational Production of Global Feminist Subjects." *Transnational America. Feminisms, Diasporas, Neoliberalisms*. Durham and London: Duke University Press. 121–57.

Grewal, Inderpal, and Caren Kaplan. 1994. *Scattered Hegemonies. Postmodernity and Transnational Feminist Practices*. Minneapolis and London: Minnesota University Press.

hooks, bell. 1994. *Teaching to Transgress. Education as the Practice of Freedom*. New York and London: Routledge.

———. 2003. *Teaching Community. A Pedagogy of Hope*. New York and London: Routledge.

Kaplan, Caren. 1994. "The Politics of Location as Transnational Feminist Practice." Eds. Inderpal Grewal and Karen Caplan. *Scattered Hegemonies. Postmodernity and Transnational Feminist Practices*. Minneapolis and London: Minnesota University Press. 137–52.

———. 2000. "Postmodern Geographies. Feminist Politics of Location." *Questions of Travel. Postmodern Discourses of Displacement*. 3rd ed. Durham and London: Duke University Press. 143–87.

Kim-Puri, H. J. 2005. "Conceptualizing Gender-Sexuality-State-Nation: An Introduction." *Gender and Society*, 19(2) 137–59.

Mignolo, W. 2000. *Coloniality, Subaltern Knowledges, and Border Thinking: Local Histories/Global Designs*. Princeton, NJ: Princeton University Press.

Moghadam, Valentine M. 2005. *Globalizing Women. Transnational Feminist Networks*. Baltimore and London: Johns Hopkins University Press.

Mohanty, Chandra Talpade. 2003. *Feminism without Borders. Decolonizing Theory, Practicing Solidarity.* Durham and London: Duke University Press.
Ramamurthy, Priti. 2003. "Material Consumers, Fabricating Subjects: Perplexity, Global Connectivity Discourses and Transnational Feminist Research." *Cultural Anthropology*, 18 (4):524–50.
Sandoval, Chela. 2000. *Methodology of the Oppressed.* Minneapolis: Minnesota University Press.
Sassen, Saskia. 2003. *Los espectros de la globalización.* Trans. Irene Merzari. Buenos Aires: Fondo de Cultura Económica.
———. 2007. *Una sociología de la globalización.* Trans. María Victoria Rodil. Buenos Aires: Katz editores.
Tastsoglou, Evangelia, and Alexandra Dobrowolsky. 2006. *Women, Migration and Citizenship. Making Local, National and Transnational Connections.* Hampshire, England: Ashgate.
Zerbe Enns, Carolyn, and Ada Sinacore. 2005. *Teaching and Social Justice, Integrating* Multicultural and Feminist Theories in the Classroom. Washington, DC: American Psychological Association.

Part II

Globalization, Transnationalisms, and the Politics of Representation in the Borderlands

Chapter One

Transnational Feminism, Globalization, and the Politics of Representation in Chicana Visual Art

Clara Román-Odio

Recent publications on transnational feminisms emphasize that mainstream academia lacks a focus on transnational movements—that is, the ideas and conditions that cross national borders and affect women's lives and concerns.[1] For instance, Caren Kaplan argues that until recently there were only two ways of addressing international issues in the women's studies classroom: "The first method, popular since the 1970s, was to point to the similarities among women around the world and across time periods" (2002, xvii). Focusing on topics such as motherhood and family structure, this method did not recognize the intersections of race/class/gender and nationality in the analysis of women's experiences. The second approach was ethnocentric, for it viewed Western culture as modern and other cultures as "needing to catch up to the West in Western terms" (xvii). The development approach proved to be important in setting up questions about poverty, education, and health, but it also proved that modernization need not also bring with it the empowerment of women (Bhavnani et al. 2003).

From this realization, feminists came to the understanding that the framework for the analysis of women's lives had to change, once again, to include an international system of states that is profoundly gendered (Kim-Puri 2005, 137). To address this new construct, feminists from all over the globe are using interdisciplinary approaches to consider asymmetries and inequalities that arise from new forms of globalization. Within the United States, feminists of color who had experienced firsthand race and class biases of early women's movements were the first ones to use these transnational approaches to assess political, economical, and cultural shifts affecting women's lives.[2]

According to Chicana theorist Chela Sandoval, in the 1970s U.S. feminists of color, coming from a similar position in relation to racial, gender, sexual, class, and cultural subordinations, became politically allied in a transnational feminist movement that came to be known as U.S. *Third World feminism*. Sandoval points out that the very name of the movement signaled a new global consciousness that challenged the distinctions of nation-state, First-Third World, north-south: "U.S. third world feminism refers to a deliberate politics organized to point out the so-called third world *in* the first world" (Sandoval 2000, 191). In this chapter I will analyze artwork by four contemporary Chicana visual artists who, using the politics and methodologies of this feminist movement, challenge new forms of colonialism and aggressive capitalism arising from the growth and acceleration of economic and information networks that operate globally. The analysis will show that, contrary to the prevailing view, capitalist globalization is not a unified, impenetrable process that contains and dominates local practices of cultural resistance, but rather a fragmentary process to which Chicana artists speak back in order to create liberating spaces for resistance. I have chosen artwork by Ester Hernández, Consuelo Jiménez Underwood, Alma Lopez, and Marion C. Martinez because their works illustrate the influence of the global market on local artistic productions, which use new themes and materials, as well a new spatiality of resistance, to create their own histories of colonization, dislocation, and marginalization.

U.S. feminists of color who were active across diverse social movements from 1968 to 1990 practiced a method of oppositional consciousness that Sandoval named *differential consciousness*: "Differential consciousness is the expression of the new subject position called for by Althusser—it permits functioning within, yet beyond the demands of dominant ideology" (2000, 43–44). *Differential consciousness*—also referred to as "*la conciencia de la mestiza*" (Gloria Anzaldúa), "outsider/ within" (Patricia Hill Collins), "the house of difference" (Audre Lorde) and "in-appropriated otherness" (Trin Minh-ha)—represents a strategy of oppositional ideology that seeks to transform power relations through a process of shifting location, where the subject is both within and outside dominant ideology (152–53). The method was used by U.S. feminists of color as a strategy to seek empowerment and to unmask gender, sexual, racial, and social inequalities within the United States by highlighting the multiple axes of oppression for women of color.[3] For Chicanas in particular, the tropes of transculturalism, global-local tensions, and the border became dominant, and *mestizaje* emerged as a thematic and formal marker of identity. The Chicana body became a site from which a history of dislocation, violence, and economic exploitation emerged.[4] Yet, from the Chicana body also emerged an alternative way of knowledge, represented by Gloria Anzaldúa's new *mestiza* consciousness, as well as by a feminist spirituality standing over and against the patriarchal Indo, Hispanic, Anglo nation-state.[5]

The method of oppositional consciousness found expression in what Sandoval called "the methodology of the oppressed." This methodology was developed to challenge dominant ideologies via five technologies of resistance, including the reading of cultural signs (or what Sandoval calls "semiotics"); deconstructing such signs or separating their material forms from their dominant meanings; appropriating and transforming dominant ideological forms (in Sandoval's terminology "meta-ideologizing"); a moral commitment to equality (or "democratics"); and what Sandoval calls "differential movement," the reappropriation of space and boundaries to impress dominant powers, where the self shifts in order to survive and according to the requisite of power (Sandoval 1994, 89). These technologies of resistance were used as cognitive, material strategies to reinterpret, deconstruct, redefine, and transform cultural signs that had controlled or limited the agency of the oppressed.

The artwork we will analyze here exemplifies the methodology of the oppressed and connects to a group of Chicana visual artists—including Ester Hernández, Consuelo Jiménez Underwood, Alma Lopez, Yolanda Lopez, Marion Martinez, and Santa Barraza, among others—who have engaged with the iconography of the Virgin of Guadalupe with the aim of equalizing gender power, countering racism, and helping to galvanize the political feminist spirit of the Chicana social movement. Their sign-readings, deconstructions, and ideological reappropriations are vital to their ethical commitments and political agendas. In their own ways, these artists seek to make visible subjects who have been erased or devalued by mainstream America. They engage in re-creating the self and in mapping their own identities. They debate and produce new conceptualizations of Azltán (the Chicano imaginary homeland) in response to the entrenched sexism of the Chicano Movement.[6] They explore spiritualism as a method of transmutation. And they find in transnational debates ammunition and insight to fight for human and women's rights. Moreover, they practice what Sandoval and Guisela Latorre call "artivism," "a hybrid neologism that signifies work created by individuals who see an organic relationship between art and activism" (2008, 82). And they recognize, as technoculture scholars Constance Penley and Andrew Ross do, that cultural technologies are powerful and persuasive means of social agency and that, far from neutral, they are the result of social processes and power relations (1991, xii–xiii).

For instance, Ester Hernández ruptures ideology by turning the *mestiza* body into a site where the material conditions of neocolonial histories are played out.[7] Jiménez Underwood deploys tactics that resist conflating the local and the national to dismantle narratives that render invisible poor and immigrant populations in the borderlands. Marion Martinez's "tech-media" art locates the damaging effects of capitalist globalization within the United States by making visible the politics of racialization in the Southwest. Santa Barraza reappropriates pre-Columbian *códices*, colors, and designs to stir historical memory and to reconnect with a cultural ideology that has been suppressed, for it is rooted in the Mexican past. And Lopez traverses the global-local nexus to deconstruct multiple systems of oppression that arise from new forms of globalization, using love as oppositional consciousness.[8]

The origins, components, and capacity of globalization to reorganize social order continue to be debatable. Some critics locate its roots in the sixteenth century at the dawn of capitalist expansion and Western modernity (Chesnaux 1989, Wallerstein 1989). Others place it in the mid-twentieth century, when technology enabled the articulation of markets at a planetary scale (Albrow 1997, Giddens 1999, Ortiz 1997). The economic, communicative, and migratory dimensions of globalizations are further discussed by other authors, who assert that globalization promotes a new conception of space and time (Giddens 1999, Sassen 1998). In *La globalización imaginada*, Néstor García Canclini draws two important conclusions from these divergent views with respect to the meaning and reach of globalization: first, that globalization is not a scientific paradigm with a clear and coherent object of study; and second, that it cannot be considered a political or cultural paradigm since it does not follow a single or unique mode of development. More than a social order or a single process, globalization—states García Canclini—is the result of multiple movements, in part contradictory, with open results. Hence, for García Canclini there isn't a unitary theory of globalization, and this arises from the fact that fragmentation is a structural feature of globalizing processes: "Para decirlo más claro, lo que suele llamarse globalización se presenta como un conjunto de procesos de homogeneización, y a la vez, de fragmentamiento articulado del mundo, que reordenan las diferencias y las desigualdades sin suprimirlas." [To say it more clearly, what is normally called globalization constitutes multiple processes of both homogenization and articulated fragmentation of the world, which reorder differences and inequalities without suppressing them (49, my translation)]. Moreover, for García Canclini the imaginary is a crucial aspect of globalization inasmuch as metaphors and narratives are producers of knowledge, which, in the critic's words: "intentan captar lo que se vuelve fugitivo en el desorden global, lo que no se deja delimitar por las fronteras sino que las atraviesa, o cree que las atraviesa y las ve reaparecer un poco más adelante, en las barreras de la discriminación" [attempt to capture what becomes fugitive in the global disorder, that which does not allow to be delimited by borders but goes through them, or believes to go through them and see them reappear some time later, in the barriers of discrimination (58, my translation)]. The artistic examples that will be examined in this chapter will illustrate these modes of thinking about globalization and transnationalism.

I use the term *globalization* following García Canclini's theoretical perspective and the position of Kim-Puri, for whom the term refers to a complex phenomenon that includes a range of economic, political, and cultural changes: "the proliferation of capital, the international flows of finance and investments, the predominance of multinational corporations, the emergence of supranational forms of governance, the spread of cultural homogeneity and the rapid compression of time and space" (2005, 140). A remarkable outcome of these processes is the integration of the world economy for the benefit of "those who matter," whereby an enormous portion of humanity remains trapped in extreme poverty, lacking basic social warranties and rights. Even so, Kim-Puri calls for a more nuanced understanding of globalization or of the meanings and maps of the global flow, where the local is not synonymous with third world or conflated with the national. She sees globalization as gendered, racialized, sexualized processes that create an impact on marginalized groups (140) and warns us that an uncritical understanding of capitalist globalization as indomitable, universal, and omnipresent renders global dominance as fixed and unchanged, and the local as contained and dominated by capital globalization. In Kim-Puri's words:

> In this way of framing capitalist globalization, the local is often synonymous with the Third World or other areas external to and separated from the West (e.g., Japan, Singapore, Russia, and Eastern European nations), and the local is conflated with the national. This approach locates the pernicious effects of capitalist globalization only in the Third World and masks inequalities that are deepened within the West itself, particularly against the poor and the immigrant populations. (140)

Feminist sociologists such as Kim-Puri reveal the fractures, multiple origins, and complex effects of globalization by focusing on local forms of cultural resistance. As we will see in the following analysis, Chicana visual artists create a cultural politics of resistance by highlighting the asymmetries and inequalities of global capital and the ways globalization helps to sustain such conditions within the United States. They structure their artworks around the referent of the lost or colonized territory and manipulate the Mesoamerican concept of *nepantla*, a Nahuatl word referring to "the land in the middle," to challenge globalization and the racialization of the urban space.[9]

Originally, the word *nepantla* was used by Nahuatl-speaking people in the sixteenth century to define their situation vis-à-vis the Spanish colonizer. According to legend, Fray Diego Durán, a Dominican missionary who was writing an ethnographic history of the Nahuatl speakers, asked one of them what he thought about the difficult cultural situation created for them by the Spanish invasion. The informant is said to have responded: "Estamos en nepantla," that is, "We are in-between." In *Borderlands/La Frontera*, Gloria Anzaldúa suggests that *nepantla* points to disassociations of identity, to identity breakdowns and buildups, and to intercultural impingement. Border crossing, which emerges from the state of being in *nepantla*, represents the Chicana alternative epistemological approach to dominant ideologies. Using the border as an organizing trope, the artists we will examine travel with "mental nepantilism," accepting their interstitial existence and committing to social action through the construction of "a new activist subject who can reinscribe Chicana History into the record" (Anzaldúa 1999, 9). Like Anzaldúa, they inscribe a borderlands that refers to a specific geographic locale—the U.S-Mexico border—with a specific history, American citizens of Mexican descent, and interject a counternarrative that challenges the appropriation of the land and the people—mostly women—by the global market.

In *California Fashions Slaves*, 1997 (figure 1.1), Alma Lopez uses Photoshop to create a digital composition that makes visible the political-economic conditions of Mexican-American women, working in one of the largest and most exploitative multinational industries of the globe: the garment industry in urban Los Angeles.

Through a topography of displacement, Lopez inscribes a multilayered history of territories and protagonists: the invisible female Mexican-American workers normally hidden behind the skyscrapers of Los Angeles; the original 1848 map marking the border between the United States and Mexico; a Mexican man running from the border patrol; the Virgin of Guadalupe standing over the inscription

Feminism, Globalization, Representation

Figure 1.1 *California Fashions Slaves* © Alma Lopez, 1997

1848 and being pointed to by an arrow that alludes to the U.S. foreign policy of "Manifest Destiny"; and in the background the lunar Aztec deity *Coyolxauhqui*. The combination of these visual elements creates a paradoxical decentralizing narrative. On the one hand, Lopez pays homage to her mother, who worked in a multinational garment shop and is represented sewing a piece that reminds us of the mantle of the Virgin (Prado 2000, 8). On the other hand, the ghostly image of female workers in the background points to the garment industry, a primary force responsible for the feminization of poverty in Los Angeles. On this issue Jo-Ann Mort explains:

> The Los Angeles garment industry is largely nonunion. It is like a sponge that soaks up available labor and thrives especially on illegal immigrants who—in this anti-immigrant climate—are more dependent on their bosses. They produce the goods in what has become a $13.3 billion-plus industry in Southern California. Virtually none of the legislation either to tighten or to discourage illegal immigration will do anything for the tens of thousands of illegal immigrants who

already work in the Los Angeles area garment shops. About two-thirds of the sewing shops in L.A. are sweatshops, many operating in full view of anyone who cares to look, especially in the downtown garment district in the shadow of the Convention Center. (1999, 197)

The profitable garment industry, evidently sustained by a super-exploitation of female workers, is marked by the word "gold." Gold also was the primary goal of the "Manifest Destiny" policy that led to the U.S.-Mexican War. Regarding how *California Fashions* interjects into the official history of the war, Lopez explains:

> The piece belongs to the series *1848 Chicanos in the U.S. after the Signing of the Treaty of Guadalupe*. The space portrayed was created after the Treaty. The U.S. Manifest Destiny myth of conquest has attempted to erase, to make invisible those who were/are in that land and I make them visible. So it is a counter-narrative that has a political theme. (2008, personal communication)

The U.S. Manifest Destiny myth of conquest refers to the Anglos' moral and divine mission to conquer the land all the way to the Western frontier for the sake of progress and civilization. On December 27, 1845, John O'Sullivan, the editor of *The Review*, summarized this ideology as follows:

> ...Our Manifest Destiny [is] to overspread and to possess the whole continent, which providence has given us for the development of the great experiment of liberty....In everything which makes a people great, the supremacy of the Anglo-American is the most prominent factor of this age. (Martinez 2008, 27)

Lopez debunks this ideological framework, which continues to operate in today's globalized economy, by revealing Los Angeles-gendered poverty and discrimination resulting from the Anglo project of progress and civilization. Moreover, as Alicia Gaspar de Alba argues in "There Is No Place Like Aztlán," for third-world people living in the United States, place means more than geographic location:

> For Third World people in the United States, place means race, religion, community, and [as we shall see later] body, as well. Central to all these practices is the concept of *homeland*, the idea that the land of the artist's place of birth or the place of origin of the artist's people/group/race, as well as the history and cultural beliefs and practices of the land—all inform the content and theme of the art. (2004, 114)

This understanding of place is crucial in *California Fashions Slaves*. For instance, the iconography of the Virgin of Guadalupe contrasts with the image of *Coyolxauhqui*, the warrior Aztec goddess of the moon. In doing so, Lopez resists equating unequivocally the notion of the Sacred Mother with the Virgin of Guadalupe. Instead, we find the Sacred Mother as women, young women, warriors, virgins, cultural ancestral mothers, women with many roles to play: the *Tonantzin-Guadalupe-Coalicue-Coyolxauhqui-Real Chicana* mothers of the community, who are also women. This opening up of the Sacred Mother icon to include a multilayered Chicana identity rejects patriarchal manipulations of the Virgin of Guadalupe image and represents an appropriation and transformation of a dominant ideological form.

Similarly, the paradoxical representation of space and cultural signs in *California Fashions* makes the spectator aware of the visibility and invisibility of borders within and across nation-states that have sustained social, racial, and gender domination. Lopez makes visible the invisible face of globalization, as well as an alternative narrative that retraces the social and spiritual suppression of the Mexican-American community. As a new *mestiza* mythmaker, Lopez takes inventory of past and present history, "puts history through a sieve" (Anzaldúa 1999, 104), documents the struggle, and shapes a new myth in which the Virgin of Guadalupe, the rising Aztec warrior goddess, and the mothers and women of the community demand political awareness and social change. Lopez's "digital artivism" provides access to a myriad of cultures, histories, languages, and worldviews. As Sandoval and Latorre claim, regarding the role of Chicana artivism, Lopez uses Anzaldúa's new *mestiza* consciousness to express "a consciousness aware of conflicting and meshing identities and uses these to create new angles of vision to challenge oppressive modes of thinking" (2008, 83). In so doing, Lopez denounces capitalistic exploitation arising from globalization and Anglo-American neocolonialism, while betting on a new idea of citizenship that affirms the diversity and difference of the borderlands experience.

Consuelo Jiménez Underwood, a contemporary Chicana fiber artist, also refers to the borderlands experience by exploring connections between place, culture, and personal identity. The daughter of migrant agricultural workers—a Chicana mother and a father of Huichol Indian descent—her weavings and textile/fiber artworks unearth the Indian in the Chicano. Underwood does not create textiles in the traditional sense, but uses textiles to express personal ideas the same way that a painter or sculptor might, by combining traditional textile materials with those not commonly used (barbed wire, plastic-coated wire, and safety pins). As Laura Pérez explains, her choice of materials and methods is not at all gratuitous, given that "her multimedia, loom-based art work powerfully undermines contemporary gendered and racialized distinctions between art and craft that demote weaving to a 'feminine' or 'third-world' artistically undeveloped 'craft'" (2007, 163). In this way, Underwood legitimates the art of weaving and her politics of representation.

Figure 1.2 *Virgen de los Caminos* 1994 @ Smithsonian American Art Museum

In *Virgen de los Caminos* (Virgin of the Roads) (figure 1.2) the artist reflects the struggles of Mexicans crossing the U.S.-Mexican border.

In the center of the quilt, she embroidered the Virgin of Guadalupe, to whom the travelers pray as they make the dangerous crossing. The barbed wire symbolizes the literal and truly painful border between the two countries that separates insiders from outsiders. The word *caution* and the image of a running family appear throughout the background but are stitched in nearly invisible white thread, suggesting that undocumented immigrants are invisible in the eyes of U.S. citizens. The narrative of the border depicted in *Virgen* points to issues of migration and displacement as two major, often tragic, consequences of globalization.

Another salient theme in Underwood's artwork is the pervasiveness of indigenous cultures, represented through images of tortillas, chilies, and cactuses, standing for immemorial eating habits of precolonial populations. For instance, in *Virgen de las Red-Hot Tortillas* (figure 1.3), the artist paints huge red tortillas over a typical plastic tablecloth of the Mexican-American kitchen. To many Mexicans and Mexican-Americans in the United States, tortillas are a personal signifier of culture and connection to family. But in this case, they are juxtaposed over a green, painted map of the North American continent.

In *Virgen de las Red-Hot Tortillas*, the artist combines a political commentary about national territories while addressing spirituality as a form of cultural resistance. Hence, to the lower left in blue, there is painted a chili; to the upper right, a blue arrow pointing to the north. The confluence of these elements maps the migratory path of Mexican and Mexican-Americans who cross the border seeking their livelihood in the United States. An opposing north-south movement is marked by a yellow tape measure hanging down beyond the frame at the right side and a green tape measure at the other side ending two-thirds to the end of the tablecloth. This north-south cartography brings to memory the U.S. Manifest Destiny myth of conquest and the 1848 Treaty of Guadalupe by virtue of which Mexican citizens who chose to remain in the north of Mexico lost their citizenship, their country, their land, and eventually their language. Tentatively secure with a safety pin, the tape measures visually represent the artificiality of the modern nation-state concept. Moreover, as a Chicana *mestiza*, Underwood is aware of the multiple positionalities, contradictions, and ambiguities of her borderland existence. This "nepantilism" enables her to destabilize the idea of culture as monolithic and static. She resists stasis by pointing to a spirituality that is *transfronteriza*—beyond and without borders. Hence, the Hispanic "Virgen" of the title crosses with the

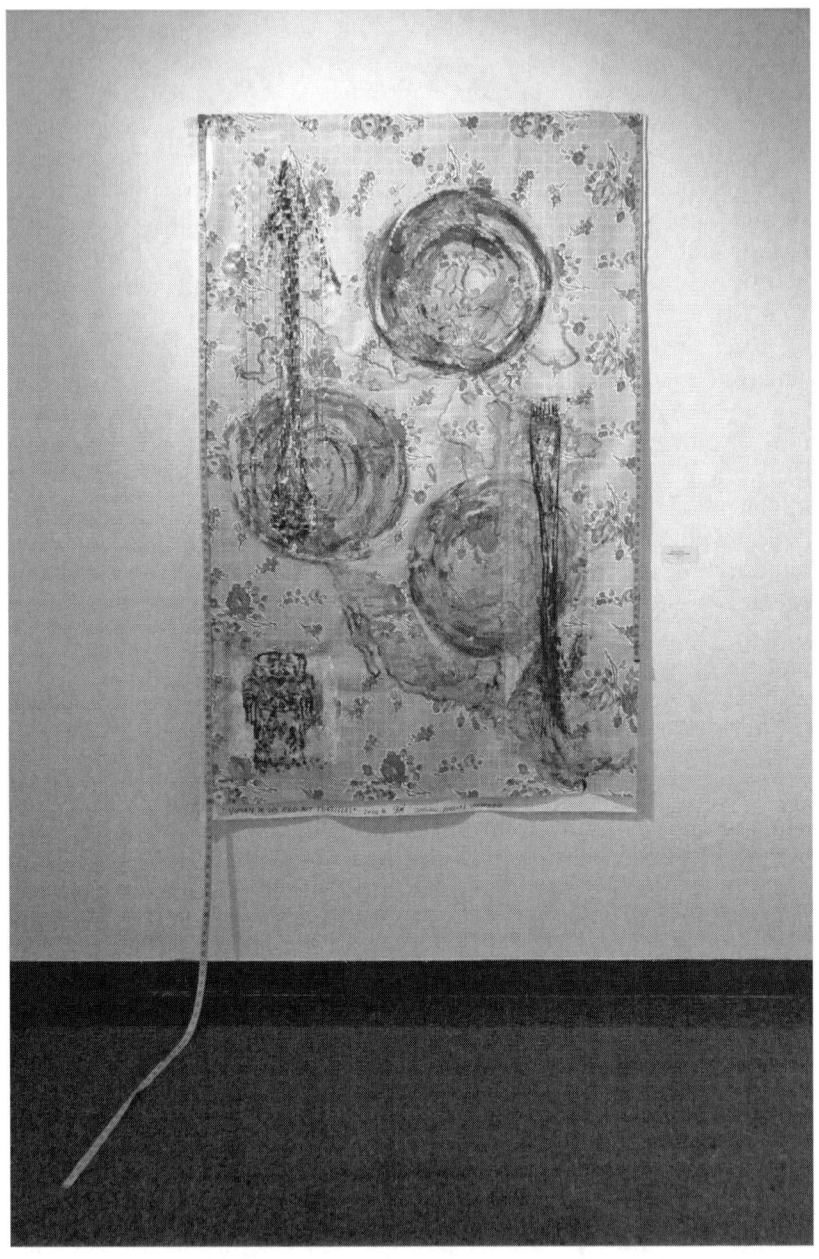

Figure 1.3 *Virgen de las Red-Hot Tortillas* © Consuelo Jimenez-Underwood

Aztec goddess *Coatlicue*, mother of all creation and the gods, which is stamped at the lower-right side of the work. The multilingual title of the piece enacts the methodology of the *mestiza* language, staging her artwork within the larger context of the continent and its layered histories. In doing so, Underwood's art deploys tactics that resist conflating the local and the national. She celebrates the local by embracing the spiritual and material elements that have dignified and nurtured Indo-Hispanic cultures for more than 500 years. Yet, she does it, not with nostalgia, but with a clear awareness of the global present that fantasizes with a homogenous mass of Western, white, first-world citizens. Hence, Underwood's affirmation of the local becomes a strategy to dismantle the narrative of the global, which tends to render invisible the poor and immigrant populations.

Another Chicana artist, Marion C. Martinez, restructures the referents of the land and borderlands with an innovative art that she herself characterizes as "Mixed Tech Media" (www.marionmartinez.com/home.php). Martinez was born in Española, New Mexico, one of the poorest states of the nation, and was raised in Los Luceros, an agricultural community, mainly Latino, located just miles from Los Alamos National Laboratory (LANL). New Mexico became a depository of radioactive waste on July 16, 1945, when the LANL scientists detonated the first atomic bomb in the Trinity Test Site. As Catherine S. Ramirez explains, "Martinez's works point directly to New Mexico's history as a dumping ground for high-tech trash" (2004, 67–8). New Mexico also has a long tradition of Indo-Hispanic folk art where saints and popular expressions of devotional piety are prevalent. A native of New Mexico, Martinez grew up Catholic, was educated in a parish school, and served her community as a family psychotherapist for twenty years. Her spirituality was and continues to be a fundamental part of her life and work. Hence, in a computer board circuit she sees a central connection between human work and divine energy, "pure God energy" (72). Martinez identifies herself as a feminist who celebrates the divine feminine that inhabits within all of us (2008, personal communication). Thus, her frequent reference to the Virgin of Guadalupe is not only spiritually authentic but also intentionally transforming—a kind of social therapy seeking to liberate Hispanic women from the "primitivism" and isolation to which racist and sexist stereotypes pigeonhole them. Ramirez considers her art futuristic, for it "locates Hispanas in narratives of science and technology, and, at the same time, inserts science and technology into narratives of and about Hispanas" (76).

In *Shrine to Guadalupe*, 2005 (figure 1.4), the artist combines Indo-Hispanic folk art with e-waste materials—in this case, a computer circuit board—to create a wall-hanging shrine to the Virgin of Guadalupe.

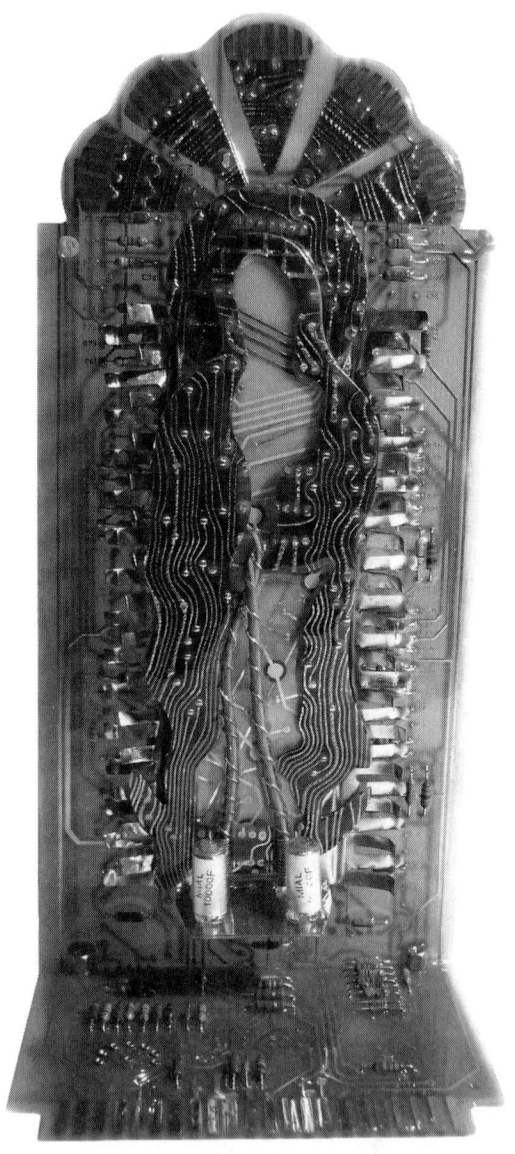

Figure 1.4 *Shrine to Guadalupe* © Marion C. Martinez, 2005

This image affirms, on the one hand, a cultural identity associated with the spiritual Hispanic and, on the other, displays the mechanization and digitalization promoted by capitalism and globalization. Gender stereotypes are also questioned here, since the artist appropriates a "masculinized" technology to reinscribe a devotional practice that has been perceived primarily as feminine. The image reminds us as well that many of these circuit boards are made in *maquiladoras* by the small and flexible fingers of women who survive brutally oppressive working conditions.[10] As the artist explained to a reporter from the *Albuquerque Journal*, *Shrine to Guadalupe* was intended to question the way we handle electronic waste: "Among other things, my work makes a stand about recycling technology" (Van Cleve 2001, F1–F2). It is a known fact that e-waste constitutes a huge global problem that primarily affects the so-called "third world countries" such as China, India, and Nigeria. In "E-Waste Dumping on the Poor." Michael Zhao documents that U.S. citizens alone dump 400 million electronic products every year. In 2005 this population generated 2.6 million tons of e-waste (http://www.youtube.com/watch?v=EXzsqTFwV3Q). The majority of this waste is exported to third-world countries in order to generate super profits from a waste that contaminates foreign territories and their people. The same capitalistic and racist logic that keeps the "dark" population of the globe in the "primitive" and "underdeveloped" end of the spectrum and the "white" population in the "civilized" and "developed" end, operates within the dark and poor communities of the United States. Martinez's art re-creates the way communities experience these kinds of borders within the United States. As stated by feminist geographer Doreen Massey, Martinez makes evident that "the global is everywhere and already, in one way or another, implicated in the local" (1994, 120). More specifically, Martinez's artwork pointedly locates the damaging effects of capitalist globalization within the United States by making visible the politics of racialization in the Southwest United States. In doing so, the artist challenges the artificial first-third-world binary that globalization promotes while using e-waste materials to remake a message that speaks of hope and beauty in the midst of human and environmental degradation.

Transnational identities and borders are also central in the visual art of Ester Hernández, a Chicana from the San Francisco Bay area. An artist of Yaqui and Mexican descent, Hernández is best known for her depiction of women through pastels and prints and her involvement in many of the most important U.S. historical movements that began in the late 1960s, including the feminist, farm workers, and international environmental movements. Her images are linked both to the artist's personal and spiritual experience as the daughter of an immigrant family from the San Joaquin Valley of California and to a new political consciousness that is aligned with transnational issues and concerns. For instance, in *La Virgen de las Calles* (figure 1.5) Hernández makes visible the cross-cultural transnational body of the Chicana *mestiza*.

Her garments—jeans, a sweatshirt, and tennis shoes—signify the spread of cultural homogeneity throughout the globe, while her *rebozo*, with the stars and colors of the Mexican flag, points once again to the local—the Virgin of Guadalupe. Her brownness marks the skin color of the Chicana *mestiza*, invisible in the eyes of U.S. citizens, while her flowers point to the miracle of Tepeyac—the roses in the hill and in Juan Diego's *tilma*—now for sale. Hernández explains her intentions in creating this image as follows:

> This pastel pays tribute to what I consider heroic women who with great sacrifice, dignity, strength, and perseverance, work to better the lives of their families and themselves. They work day and night to educate their children because they know this is the greatest gift a parent can give a child. The woman depicted here wears a traditional native *rebozo*—shawl with the stars and colors of the Mexican flag. This subtly connects her with the *Virgen de Guadalupe*. She is, nevertheless, postmodern with her sweatshirt, athletic shoes, and denim pants, creatively and independently making a living for herself, living her life in two worlds; traversing the traditional as well as the contemporary neither here nor there but somewhere in between, a new reality. She presents an image of someone who has traversed many translucent borders and has re-created herself in the mode of Do or Die. She has left her family, her home, her country, her language. She has adapted in her role as a woman. This image also celebrates an entrepreneurial spirit in so many immigrant women to survive with dignity. The mother in this drawing represents all the women who immigrate to our country (lest we forget that we are a nation of immigrants) for freedom, land, better wages, and to escape war, repression, and poverty. Growing global, social and economic and environment issues have greatly accelerated migration. In some ways, it's about the meaning of home; about finding a place where you, me, and everybody can feel that they are safe and accepted. I have met many recent (newcomer) immigrant women and, without exception, they were kind and gentle people, but the forces that drove them to migrate were ruthless. (2009, lecture)

Through the tropes of immigration and transnationalism, *La Virgen de las Calles* engages the spectator in a transnational discourse of location for, as Kaplan reminds us, "the 'local' is not really

Figure 1.5 *Virgen de las Calles* © Ester Hernández

about a specific intrinsic territory but the construction of bundles or clusters of identities in and through the cultures of transnational capitalism" (2000, 159–60). In this case, Hernández is able to grasp in this image the local in a dialectical relation with the global, destabilizing master narratives of race, class, nation, and culture. Furthermore, by juxtaposing the image of a U.S.–Mexican-American woman with the Spanish language in the title, Hernández makes a larger cultural critique, signaling how the dominant group enforces domination through language. *La Virgen de las Calles* leads us as well to Anzaldúa's interpretation of the Virgin of Guadalupe, since, for Anzaldúa, the religious icon functions as a bridge, as a third term that unites opposites, breaks down dichotomies, and pushes through dualistic thought (1999, 52). Hence, Hernández's pastel illustrates Anzaldúa's new *mestiza* consciousness, manifesting a borderlands subjectivity: postmodern, yet traditional; proletarian, yet spiritual; global and transnational, yet strategically made to signal an essence in order to mobilize racial, class, and gendered hierarchies of the nation-state. Moreover, *La Virgen de las Calles* epitomizes Pérez-Torres's argument that "critical mestizaje locates how people live their lives in and through their bodies as well as in and through ideology" (Pérez-Torres 2006, xii), for here, as the artist states, the immigrant *mestiza* has traversed many translucent borders to re-create herself in the mode of "Do or Die."

Hence, in common with the practices of Gloria Anzaldúa and other Latina writers living in the United States, these visual artists strive to make visible the experience of borderlands subjects, who struggle against global economic, political, and cultural hegemonies in the United States. In doing so, they turn the borderlands into a site for a transformative practice in which hegemonic discourses about nation, cultural identity, race, and spirituality are appropriated and transformed as part of a moral commitment to equality. These visual artists use a myriad of materials and methods to defy a notion of globalization that marginalizes the poor and the immigrant through their racialization. They offer an alternative narrative that challenges the conflation of the local and the national, emphasizing the various forms of domination that borders, within and across nation-states, help to sustain. Their multilayered narratives of location speak of a new Aztlán: an inclusive global/local community that, immersed in the cultures of transnational capitalism, is able to grasp their citizens in all their complexity and difference.

In conclusion, as Aili Tripp suggests, when we look through the transnational lens, we can see "national and local movements creating waves of feminism with their own dynamic and pace that did not necessarily correspond to Western trends" (2006, 54). U.S. *third world feminism* represents one of these feminist waves, not a deviation from the normalized category we call "U.S. feminism," but a movement of its own that, as the artwork examined here illustrates, explores the global-local nexus to deconstruct multiple systems of oppression that arise from globalization. As new *mestizas*, these visual artists speak back to globalization as a gendered, racialized process and produce a politics of representation that inscribe culture in terms of agency, subjectivity, consciousness, and emotion. As the "globalizing women" that Valentine M. Moghadam describes in *Globalizing Women: Transnational Feminist Networks*, their ideas and goals respond to, and resist, "growing inequalities, the exploitation of female labor, and patriarchal fundamentalisms" (2005, x). In sum, these Chicana artists make evident that letting the actors speak from their peculiar intercultural experiences can contribute to regain power through a differential consciousness that seeks to unmask the multiple axis of oppression for U.S. women of color.

Notes

1. To mention a few examples: *Feminism without Borders, Gender in a Transnational World, Globalizing Women: Transnational Feminist Networks,* and *Transnational America: Feminisms, Diasporas, Neoliberalism.*
2. The 1981 publication *This Bridge Called My Back: Writing by Radical Women of Color* can attest to the networking of U.S. feminists of color of this generation.
3. As Marta Cotera says, U.S. history of suffrage is a good point of departure to understand some of the political strategies that Anglo feminists used to bar the way to universal suffrage for U.S. women of color.
4. For an example in visual art, see my article "Transnational Alliances, U.S. Third World Feminism and Chicana *Mestizaje* in Ester Hernández's Visual Art" in *Latino Studies* 7(3) (2009). An earlier interpretation was published as "La Virgen de Guadalupe y el feminismo transnacional de Ester Hernández."
5. Laura Pérez's book *Chicana Art* highlights the broad and influential contributions of Chicana visual artists to a new understanding of spirituality. For an example in literature, see my essay "Disrobed: The Virgin of Guadalupe and Social Activism in Chicanas' Writing."
6. Aztlán is the Chicano imaginary homeland that came into being in 1848 with the Treaty of Guadalupe, by virtue of which Mexican citizens who chose to remain in the north of Mexico lost their citizenship, their country, their land, and eventually their language.

7. For instance, in Hernández's dry point etching *Libertad* (1976), the artist represents herself chipping away the Statue of Liberty, unearthing the native people who inhabit the Americas but who still remain invisible to the neocolonial perspective. In a personal interview, she states: "This is, what I consider, a humorous dry point etching that I created while a student at Berkeley and it was 1976 and the U.S. was celebrating the American Bicentennial. Being such a good citizen, I felt I had to contribute something from my perspective. It was just a little reminder that we must not forget that the Americas were/are inhabited by mestizo/Native peoples. Beneath the surface of this modern day icon, the ancient Mayan stele reminds us of the rather recent arrival of a European world" (personal communication, 2007). Another example is her aqua-tint etching *La Virgen de Guadalupe Defendiendo los Derechos de los Xicanos* (1975), where Hernández exhibits her new capacity to read and renovate signs through the *mestiza* body of a mixed-race Madonna: a body arising from the hyphens of the Indo-Asian-Hispanic-American blood. The image defies, among other things, the one-drop rule that still informs dominant U.S. constructions of a binary racial identity.
8. For the use of love as oppositional consciousness in Alma López's imagery, see my chapter "Queering the Sacred: Love as Oppositional Consciousness in Alma López's Visual Art" forthcoming in *Our Lady of Controversy: Alma López's Irreverent Apparitions* (UT Press 2011). For a discussion about the making of transnational identities for U.S. Latinas, see Daniel Mato's essay "On the Making of Transnational Identities."
9. See Gloria Anzaldúa's reinterpretation of *nepantlism* in *Borderlands* pp. 99–113. Another useful exploration of the terms is in Miguel Leóon-Portilla's *Endangered Cultures* pp. 10–18.
10. I would like to thank my colleague Mary Castañeda for suggesting the connection between this image and *maquiladoras*, where these technologies are produced by female workers who are severely exploited.

Works Cited

Albrow, M. 1997. *The Global Age*. Stanford: Stanford University Press.
Anzaldúa, G. 1999. *Borderlands/La Frontera: The New Mestiza*. 2nd ed. Introduction by Sonia Saldívar-Hull. San Francisco: Aunt Lute Books.
Anzaldúa, G. and C. Moraga, ed. 1981. *This Bridge Called My Back: Writing by Radical Women of Color*. Watertown, MA: Persephone Press.
Bhavnani, K., J. Foran, and P. Kurian. 2003. *Feminist Futures: Reimagining Women, Culture and Development*. New York: Zed Books.
Chesnaux, J. 1989. *La modernité-monde*. Paris: La Découverté.
Cotera, M. 1997. "Feminism: The Chicano and Anglo Versions—A Historical Analysis." *Chicana Feminist Thought: The Basic Historical Writings*. New York: Routledge.

García-Canclini, N. 2008. *La globalización imaginada*. 4th ed. Buenos Aires: Paidós.
Gaspar de Alba, A. 2004. "There Is No Place Like Aztlán." *The New Centennial Review* 42(2):103–40.
Grewal, I. 2005. *Transnational America: Feminisms, Diasporas, Neoliberalism*. Durham: Duke University Press.
Grewal, I. and C. Kaplan, eds. 2002. *An Introduction to Women's Studies: Gender in a Transnational World*. New York: McGraw-Hill.
Giddens, A. 1999. *La tercera vía: la renovación de la social democracia*. Madrid: Taurus.
Kaplan, C. 2000. *Question of Travel. Postmodern Discourses of Displacement*. Durham: Duke University Press.
Kim-Puri, H. J. 2005. "Conceptualizing Gender-Sexuality-State-Nation: An Introduction." *Gender and Society* 19(2):137–59.
León-Portilla, M. 1990. *Endangered Cultures*. Dallas: Southern Methodist University Press.
López, Alma. 2011. "Visual Art." *Our Lady of Controversy: Alma López's Irreverent Apparitions*. Texas: University of Texas Press.
Martinez, E. 2008. "Betita." *500 Years of Chicana Women's History: Años de la Mujer Chicana*. New Brunswick, NJ: Rutgers University Press.
Mato, D. 1998. "On the Making of Transnational Identities in the Age of Globalization: The U.S. Latina/A Latin American Case." *Cultural Studies* 12(4):598–620.
Massey, D. 1994. "Double Articulation: A Place in the World." *Displacements. Cultural Identities in Question*. Bloomington: Indiana University Press. 111–21.
Moghadam, V. 2005. *Globalizing Women: Transnational Feminist Networks*. Baltimore: Johns Hopkins Univ. Press.
Mohanty, C. 2003. *Feminism without Borders: Decolonizing Theory, Practicing Solidarity*. Duke University Press.
Mort, J. A. 1999. "They Want to Kill Us for a Little Money": Sweatshop Workers Speak Out." *No Sweat: Fashion, Free Trade and the Rights of Garment Workers*, ed. Andrew Ross. New York: Verso. 193–7.
Ortiz, R. 1997. *Mundialización y cultura*. Buenos Aires: Aliznza.
Penley, Constance and Andrew Ross, eds. 1991. *Technoculture*. Minneapolis: University of Minnesota.
Pérez, L. 2007. *Chicana Art: The Politics of Spiritual and Aesthetic Altarities*. Durham: Duke University Press.
Pérez,-Torres, R. 2006. *Critical Uses of Race in Chicano Culture*. Minneapolis: Minnesota University Press.
Prado Saldívaar, R. 2000. "Goddesses, Sirenas, Lupes y Angel Cholas: The Works of Alma López." *Aztlán* 25(1):195–201.
Ramirez, C. 2004. "Deus Ex Machina: Tradition, Technology, and the Chicanafuturist Art of Marion C. Martinez." *Aztlán: A Journal of Chicano Studies* 29(2):55–92.

Román-Odio, C. 2009. "Transnational Alliances, U.S. Third World Feminism and Chicana *Mestizaje* in Ester Hernádez's Visual Art." *Latino Studies* 7(3):f317–35.

———. 2008. "Disrobed: The Virgin of Guadalupe and Social Activism in Chicanas' Writing." *Pembroke Magazine, Hispanic Latino(a) Feature* (Liliana Wendorff, Guest Editor) 40: 187–200.

———. 2007. "La Virgen de Guadalupe y el feminismo transnacional de Ester Hernández." *Confluencias en Mexico: Palabra y Género.* Patricia González, Gómez Cásseres and Alicia V. Ramírez Olivares, eds. 299–315. Fomento editorial, Benemérita Universidad Autónoma de Puebla.

Sandoval, C. 2000. *Methodology of the Oppressed.* Minneapolis: Minnesota University Press.

———. 1994. "Re-entering Cyberspace: Science of Resistance." *Disposition* 19(46):75–93.

Sandoval, C., and G. Latorre. "Chicana/o Artivism: Judy Baca's Digital Work with Youth of Color." *Learning Race and Ethnicity.* Anna Everett, ed. Cambridge: MIT Press.

Sassen, S. 1998. "Ciudades en la economía global: enfoques teóricos y methodológicos." *Eure* 24(71):5–25.

Tripp, A. and Ferree, M. 2006. *Global Feminism: Transnational Women's Activism, Organizing, and Human Rights.* New York: New York University Press.

Van Cleve, E. 2001. Modern Art. *Albuquerque Journal.* Feb. 18, F1–2.

Wallerstein, I. 1989. *The Modern World System, vol. III. The Second Era of Great Expansion of Capitalist World Economy. 1730–1840.* San Diego: Academic Press.

Zhao, Michael. 2007. "E-Waste: Dumping on the Poor." DVD video.

Chapter Two

Markings on the Walls: Writing in Opposition in Alicia Gaspar de Alba's Desert Blood

Irene Mata

In recent years various cultural productions have been created that attempt to make sense of the violence being perpetrated on the bodies of women in Ciudad Juárez. From films starring U.S. actors like Jennifer Lopez and Minnie Driver, to independently produced documentaries, writers and directors have focused their attention on the murders often referred to as the "maquiladora murders."[1] Some of these productions sensationalize the violence, while others are more interested in raising public awareness without necessarily overdramatizing the violence. One of the best received of these productions is Alicia Gaspar de Alba's *Desert Blood*.[2] The novel, published in 2005, combines research and conjecture in a mystery story that illustrates the complex web of networks at play in the violence occurring in the border city. What distinguishes Gaspar de Alba's novel from other fictionalized accounts is the ways in which it goes further than simply addressing the violence of the border. Unlike works that offer uncomplicated resolutions, Gaspar de Alba's novel moves beyond the quest for answers and provides a literary example of an oppositional narrative that demonstrates the opportunities divergent thinking offers in the analysis of transnational systems of power.

Many have critiqued the tendency of U.S. cultural productions to perpetuate the ideology of the "savior from the North" that reinforces the racist portrayal of the Mexican people as inept. The notion that the community needs to be "rescued" is one that infantilizes the country and places the United States in the continual role of guardian. For example, the films *Bordertown* and *The Virgin of Juárez* position their U.S. protagonists as the agents of change that bring with them the necessary knowledge to seek answers in Juárez. Such a patronizing practice reinscribes colonial strategies of the past and does little to advance the community's cause. At first glance, Gaspar de Alba's novel can also be critiqued for the way in which Ivon, a Chicana protagonist born on the U.S. side of the border, is placed at the center of the narrative. *Desert Blood*'s protagonist, however, is a much more complex character, whose story traverses an intricate web of transnational structures of power. She is a border crosser, to borrow Gloria Anzaldúa's term, who has experienced both sides of the border.[3] In this essay I will demonstrate that *Desert Blood*'s protagonist, Ivon Villa, embodies the strategy of reading signs and symbols, which Chela Sandoval has identified as a "methodology of the oppressed," by employing a transnationalist feminist analysis of global networks of oppression. Read through an analytical framework that privileges a differential mode of consciousness, the novel becomes an example of the power of writing in creating alternative paradigms for challenging the social inequality of globalization processes.

Gaspar de Alba's *Desert Blood* illustrates the possibilities the imaginary holds in creating cultural productions that critique processes of modernity and globalization. The novel's narrator uncovers the social, economic, and political relations that have created a location where the violence of colonial and imperial histories, neoliberal processes, and patriarchal structures intersect. Read through a transnational feminist lens that theorizes location beyond just a physical space, like the one proposed by Caren Kaplan's scholarship on the politics of location, the character of Ivon Villa comes to embody an identity formed through diverse social formations based on a specific border area location. Her positionality as a border crosser situates Kaplan's theories of location in the transnational space of the Mexico-U.S. border area in order to illustrate the impact that neoliberal labor practices have had on women. The text also builds on Anzaldúa's theorizing of the border through its treatment of current industrial development in the Juárez-El Paso area, its impact on a border-crossing community, and resistance by those often framed as "underdeveloped." Gaspar de Alba's novel provides a fictionalized account of the dangers of mass industrialization projects—one that is historically and culturally grounded—that deconstructs the celebratory rhetoric of globalization and challenges hegemonic narratives of violence against women. The text reminds us of the importance of reading narratives through a transnational feminist perspective in order to identify resistance and opposition to postmodern practices.

In her influential text *Methodology of the Oppressed*, Sandoval maps out the strategies that have aided the survival of subaltern groups under various systems of oppression. Her theories illustrate the importance that technologies of recognition and signification have played in the creation of alternative modes of thought and inquiry. In mapping out her ideas, Sandoval explains that the methodology of the oppressed is made up of five techniques: "the technologies of semiotics, deconstruction, meta-ideologizing, democratics and differential movement" (2000, 146). The technology of semiotics, or reading of signs, leads to the deconstructing of these signs as a strategy of resistance. Meta-ideologizing challenges dominant cultural forms through the appropriation of existing ideologies, or what Sandoval terms the "*ideologization of ideology* itself" (108). The technology of democratics brings together the previous techniques for the purpose of egalitarian social change. The fifth technology, differential movement, allows for the operating, maneuvering, and progression of the other four technologies that make up the methodology of the oppressed. These techniques, or "oppositional technologies of power," allow for a decentering of power that makes possible the movement toward a transnational social justice that is based on an understanding and respect of difference. With Ivon, Gaspar de Alba creates an example of a transnational feminist character able to use her positionality as a border crosser and her ability to employ the different technologies of oppositional thinking in an effort to make sense of the violence occurring in Ciudad Juárez. Sandoval's methodology of the oppressed facilitates an analysis of the complex processes of globalization that have altered this border city.

The protagonist of the novel is a queer Chicana academic who returns to her hometown of El Paso to adopt the baby of Cecilia, a young *maquiladora* worker living across the border in Juárez, Mexico. Upon her return, Ivon discovers that in her absence, life on the border has become much more dangerous for poor women. Set in 1998, the number of women violently murdered and dumped in the desert is over 100, and Ivon is astounded by her ignorance of the violence occurring in her hometown. Once in El Paso, Ivon discovers that Cecilia and her unborn child have been brutally murdered. While devastated by the death of Celilia and the baby she had begun to think of as her own, it is the disappearance of her younger sister, Irene, that creates the impetus for Ivon's investigation into the violence occurring in Juárez. The story interweaves a quest for answers with research in an attempt to understand the changes that industrialization has brought to the border.

Gendered Violence: Connecting Labor, Industrialization, and Globalization

Because the murders began in the early nineties during a period of continuing mass industrialization of the border and a year after the signing of the North American Free Trade Agreement (NAFTA), it is difficult to separate an analysis of the femicides in Juárez from the material and social changes that have taken place during this time. In her essay on the labor structure of the *maquilas*, Melissa M. Wright points out that "[a]fter the passage of NAFTA in 1994, the maquila industry grew by 29 percent throughout the country, with the highest growth rates occurring in Ciudad Juárez" (2001, 97). Of even more significance is the fact that prior to the early 1990s, "female homicides averaged a scant handful of cases annually—far lower than in U.S. cities of similar size" (Nathan 2002, 2). The growth of the *maquila* industry in Juárez has led to a substantial increase in population and has drastically changed the dynamics of the city.[4]

The *maquiladoras* in Juárez are part of a government program administered by the Mexican Border Industrialization Program (BIP) that began in 1965, one year after the Bracero Program, which provided almost 200,000 jobs for Mexican migrant workers, came to an end.[5] The Mexican economy was unprepared to absorb those displaced workers into the labor force, and so the "BIP's founders hoped that the jobs the program brought to the border cities would help absorb the growing surplus labor pool" (Tiano 1994, 19). Originally, the Mexican government restricted the foreign ownership of *maquiladoras*—limiting the amount of stock ownership to 49 percent and restricting land ownership to Mexican citizens, forcing foreign investors to rent the land upon which the assembly plants were built. In March 1971, however, these conditions changed through an executive decree that greatly increased foreign investors' power and control over the *maquilas*.[6] Leading Mexican migration expert Jorge A. Bustamante indicates the impact of the executive act by drawing attention to the increasing number of *maquiladoras* in Mexico: in 1965 there were 12 in existence; by 1971 the number had climbed to 209; and by 1974 the number of *maquiladoras* had reached 516.[7] The Mexican government's main objectives in the promotion of the *maquiladora* were aimed at improving the border economy, and by extension, strengthening the national economic structure.[8] Bustamanete makes clear that "[in] drawing up [the] objectives, it was added that the maquiladoras should not be considered a sign of dependency"

(1983, 242). He also points out that "the concept of the maquiladoras, as it was presented by the government of Mexico on May 2, 1971...did not include the proposal that such predominance be given to female labor" (252). The maquiladora industry, however, grew in a way that was not envisioned by the original planners, resulting in massive economic and social upheavals, one of which is the increased violence against women.

Maquila work is a gendered form of labor that is part of the new global economy, one based on intense industrialization and the collaboration between the state and the supranational corporation. In her essay on the industrial development of Puerto Rico, Palmira N. Ríos notes that the role of developing nations within the new global economy has been redefined, positioning them as manufacturers "of goods for the world market," and creating what Ríos refers to as the "global assembly line" (1995, 126–27). The majority of the manufacturing assembly work is being done by women, who now "constitute the principal new sources of labor in today's economy" (127). María Patricia Fernández-Kelly, like Ríos, points to several characteristics that make female workers a "particular kind of labor reserve," attractive to industries not only because of lower wages, but also because,

> [a]ccording to maquiladora managers and promoters, women are hired because of their putative higher levels of skill and performance; because of the quality of their handwork; because of their willingness to comply with monotonous, repetitive and highly exhausting work assignments; and because of their docility, which discourages organizing effort by union leaders. (1983b, 219)

While there is no scientific basis for such assumptions, the gender typing of labor works to "feminize" *maquiladora* employment and further benefits industries. What makes women more vulnerable laborers is not only their economic circumstance, but also their subordination as women in the patriarchal hierarchy of the state—a hierarchy that has been transformed "to meet the requirements of global competition" (Fernández-Kelly and Sassen 1995, 114). The industry, with the help of the state, replicates the cultural hierarchy that places women on the bottom in order to generate higher profits.

The gendering of assembly work not only situates women within the lower strata of the global assembly line, but it also invites several labor practices that specifically exploit female workers. In Puerto Rican industrialization, Ríos finds that gender typing concentrates women within a few industries and causes the occupational distribution of men and women (133, 137). Aihwa Ong's work on Asian labor relations points to a similar practice in the separation of labor by transnational firms. Ong highlights the "institutionalization of race, gender, and age inequalities in industrial enterprises...reflected by daily practices" (1997, 71). While neither the work of Ong nor Ríos is situated in Mexico, their findings apply directly to the labor practices in the *maquiladoras*. Like the female laborers in Puerto Rico, *maquiladora* women are employed primarily as operatives or in clerical positions in manufacturing establishments, while the professional or administration jobs are reserved for men. The working conditions of the *maquiladoras* echo the "industrial labor relations...[that] often elaborate and reinvent principles of male and racial superiority" and that Ong sees occurring in Japan, Malaysia, and China (71). The *maquiladoras* in Juárez are most often managed and supervised by male workers, and American supervisors and engineers hold the highest positions.[9] Women who work in the assembly plants are positioned in entry-level positions, with few if any opportunities for advancement, and most significant, are placed in a subordinate position to the male supervisors who wield significant power. The gender hierarchies re-created in the workplace generate further opportunities for the exploitation of women. Fernández-Kelly writes that "[i]n general, women are particularly vulnerable to advances made by men who have a superior status in the professional, economic, and educational hierarchy" (1983b, 141).

The labor structure within the "*maquila* culture" not only exploits the female worker and places her in a position of inferiority to the male worker, but also encourages widespread sexual harassment, leaving many young women exposed and vulnerable.[10] The women are often hired based not only on their appearance, but also on their youth and inexperience, providing the *maquiladoras* with a labor pool that can be exploited easily—both economically and physically—by management and industries. Many of the women employed by the *maquiladoras* know they are replaceable, and their need for employment keeps them from either turning down male workers' advances or reporting the harassment, resulting in what Fernández-Kelly refers to as a "factory harem mentality."[11] In effect, the women in the assembly plants become commodities—disassembled for their labor and for their sexuality.[12] The commodification of the female body in the workplace affects the way she is viewed and treated in and outside of the *maquila* because the sexual exploitation of the *maquila* worker does not remain within the confines of the workplace.

Young women who work for the *maquiladoras* are often represented in the media as loose and immoral, sexualizing the women in such a way that they are no longer seen as victims; instead, they become accomplices in their own victimization. In looking at the theoretical construct of femicide, Julia Monárrez Fragoso points out that the social phenomena of crimes against women and girls are "tied to the patriarchal system that predisposes, to a greater or lesser degree, that women be murdered. Be it for the simple act of being women, or for not being one 'adequately'" (2002, 3). A perfect example of this mentality is the attitude of Arturo Gonzales Rascon, former attorney general of Chihuahua. Rascon publicly suggested that the Juárez victims had "put themselves in harm's way by dressing provocatively and frequenting unsavory after-hours nightclubs" (Stowers 2001, 5). The fact that the attorney general—the man responsible for the law enforcement agencies of the state—so willingly blames the victims is indicative of the society's attitude toward the *maquiladora* workers. The tolerance of different forms of violence against women is what allows femicide to take place with impunity.[13] The structural changes brought about by the *maquila* industry have led to a higher level of tolerance for violence in the industrialized area. In her essay "Serial Sexual Femicide in Ciudad Juárez: 1993–2001" Monarrez Fragoso argues that

> there is a direct proportional correlation between the structural changes that take place in a society and a direct proportion to the level of tolerance manifested by the collective to it and its level of violence. All of the factors and all of the policies that end the lives of women are tolerated by the state and other institutions. (2)

By allowing the exploitation of women to go unpunished, the state, through its agencies and institutions (law, legislative, etc.) has, in effect, accepted and reinforced the idea that it is permissible to violate the rights of women. Strengthening the connection between state and the corporations, Fragoso points out that the industry's rhetoric of "consume and dispose cycle" is the same discourse used by authorities in discussing the murders of the women (6).

In "Toward a Planetary Civil Society," the first chapter from her book *meXicana Encounters*, Rosa Linda Fregoso (2003) critically analyzes the connection between the *maquiladoras*, the state, and the Juarez killings. Fregoso offers a formidable critique of cultural productions that blames the industrialization of the border region for the killings within a discourse of globalism. While it is true that critical theories of globalization frequently overemphasize the global and ignore the local, an analysis of globalization and neoliberal practices that considers not only the supranational but also the state can provide a deeper understanding of the changes being experienced in the local. By situating the *maquiladora* industry within the larger structure of state-motivated globalization projects—projects that have drastically altered the material and social conditions of Juárez—the state becomes directly implicated in the exploitation and oppression of its people.[14]

In the past decade, various cultural productions have attempted to document the violence on the border. Among the many films produced, Lourdes Portillo's 2001 documentary *Señorita Extraviada* remains one of the most important because of its transnational framework and feminist methodology. While not perfect or as "up-to-date" as more current cultural productions dealing with the femicides, the documentary informs viewers about the murders while also demonstrating the power that oppositional aesthetics offers in providing alternative narratives. Like other filmmakers, Portillo is interested in visually documenting the violence being perpetrated against women and making connections between the industrialization of the border and the femicides, but her work is much more consciously situated within the community through her reliance on interviews from activists, victims, and the victims' families.

One of the most significant aspects of the documentary is the point of view Portillo offers her viewers. Instead of relying on the official state narratives offered, she turns to community members to share their own accounts of the violence in Juárez. In the film, Portillo includes captions that translate the words of those being interviewed for a non-Spanish–speaking audience, but does not impose commentary on the words of the interviewees. She provides the outlet for those she interviews to voice their own opinions without mediating their meaning for the viewer. Portillo does intersplice several visual images that support the narratives of the victims' families. In her decision to provide those most affected with a platform for their stories, Portillo employs a transnational feminist methodology that offers alternative narratives and speaks back to power. The testimony of community members disputes the rhetoric of modernization that positions industrialization projects as benefiting the "underdeveloped."

Señorita Extraviada visually documents the changes Juárez has undergone because of the *maquiladora* industry and challenges the celebratory rhetoric of globalization processes. Portillo makes the connection between the *maquilas* and the migration to Juárez and the subsequent pressure on the city's infrastructure. Portillo explains that "as a model of globalization, Ciudad Juárez is spinning out of control." By beginning her conversation on the industrialization of the city with statistics that tie that industrialization project to the U.S.-owned factories and the profits that these transnational corporations make, Portillo is implicating the United States and its industries in the problems being encountered by the residents of Juárez. Through the ties she establishes between the *maquila* industry and the rising violence against women, she also holds U.S. transnational corporations accountable for some of the femicides. The *maquiladora* can be viewed as a site where the multiple forms of oppression come together—a combination of both the local and the global. It is into this space of industrialized chaos that the novel brings its readers. Gaspar de Alba positions her narrative as a recognition and critique of the multiple, and very mobile, structures of power currently operating in Juárez.

Queering the Detective Genre

When analyzing *Desert Blood*, it also becomes important to situate the genre of the novel in a larger literary context. As many critics have argued in the past, the conventions of the traditional detective novel are often based on the need to restore social order through the solving of a crime or mystery. It is a popular genre, and when writing the novel, Gaspar de Alba chose to fictionalize her research in order " 'to inform the broadest audience...so more people would read it" (qtd. in Ayala 2008). The detective novel holds appeal to a wider readership, as evidenced by the ways in which publishing houses like St. Martin's Press and Putnam Publishing promote Latino crime writers, and the fact that Arte Publico, *Desert Blood*'s publisher, reports that "the mystery/crime novel is one of their best-selling lines" (Ponce 1998, 44+). However, unlike the more hegemonic detective novels, the text does not attempt to simply solve a crime, but instead uses the kidnapping of Irene as a way of uncovering a history of violence and transnational corruption being silenced by official channels.[15]

Gaspar de Alba's narrative is not just about the disentangling of a mystery. The text becomes an example of what literary critic Ralph E. Rodriguez argues when he writes that

> Chicana/o authors have used the detective novel to understand the shifting political, social, cultural, and identitarian terrain of the postnationalist period. The criminality that pervades the detective novel speaks to the alienation, criminalization, and violence surrounding Mexican Americans, both in large cities and along the border. (2005, 5)

While the novel never proposes a solution to all of the crimes being committed, it tries to make sense of the violence against young women. It provides a literary illustration of the conditions women in the border area must labor under and the impunity with which they are murdered. The text challenges the silence that has surrounded the violence, offering Gaspar de Alba's conjectures to further the action in the story, but rejects a simple narrative closure. At the end of the novel, although Irene is rescued and the reader is provided with answers to some questions, there is no satisfactory restoring of the social order. The reader comes to understand that the story is not just about Irene, but also about the community on both sides of the border. As such, the chaos of the border continues, and the corruption of the border government is more evident than ever. Gaspar de Alba employs the strategies of the detective novel in ways that challenge the hegemonic narrative structure of detective fiction and instead pushes for analysis of the crime that is based on a critique of multiple structures of power that cannot simply be dismantled. The tangled network of corruption and injustice makes the restoring of social order an impossible task. By rejecting a traditional solution to the crimes, Gaspar de Alba expands the conventions of the detective novel and illustrates the oppositional possibilities of the genre.[16] *Desert Blood* also pushes the boundaries of the genre through Gaspar de Alba's decision to place at the center of the narrative a queer Chicana. As Lucha Corpi's character—Gloria Damasco—has proven, female detectives are as adept at solving crime as the traditionally male detective. With Ivon Villa, Gaspar de Alba further challenges the literary tradition, one that has heavily favored the representation of the sleuth as male. The character of Ivon, however, challenges the heteronormativity of the genre and makes visible a member of the Chicana/o community often invisible in mainstream media. Not only does the text blur the conventional structure of the detective novel; by positioning a queer woman of color in the role of knowledge interpreter, the text confronts any racist, sexist, or homophobic ideologies the reader might harbor. In her essay on Barbara Wilson's *Gaudi Afternoon*, Susan Elizabeth Sweeney argues that

> lesbian crime fiction makes the investigator's relationship to her society even more ambiguous and problematic. Indeed, it extends the critique of binary gender roles (heterosexual woman versus heterosexual man), already present in other feminist detective novels, by adding a third term: "lesbian." (1999, 125)

While Wilson's character Cassandra Reilly is white and Sweeny is not writing specifically about Gaspar de Alba's text, the argument does function to explain the role the lesbian detective plays in disrupting the rigid structures of the genre.

The fact that Gaspar de Alba's lesbian character is a woman of color upsets the literary paradigm of the detective novel even further. In his analysis of Michael Nava's gay Chicano detective, Henry Rios, Rodriguez also comments on the importance that Henry's sexuality plays in the unfolding of the narrative. He writes, "In addition, it is only in queering the forces of family, home, race, and sexuality that one can disarticulate them from the naturalizing, heteronormative logic that underwrites them, that makes them seem necessary rather than contingent or constructed" (35). By queering the narrative, Gaspar de Alba provides the reader with a different way of looking at the violence in Juárez and advocates for a reading of the border that takes into account the complexities of transnational networks of exploitation, resistance, and activism. Gaspar de Alba not only queers her protagonist, but also imparts Ivon with a *mestiza consciousness*, which is what facilitates Ivon's mobility through numerous spaces. Gloria Anzaldúa (1987) theorizes the *mestiza consciousness* as a form of border consciousness that refuses paradigms based on binaries of difference. Instead, a *mestiza consciousness* allows the border crosser the ability to transcend duality in order to reach a different level of perception through which to view the world.

The notion of the *mestiza consciousness* is based on the understanding that borders are constructed and are policed on both an ideological and physical level. As such, borders can be denaturalized and crossed, although often under threat of repercussions. For Anzaldúa, the borderland is a space of constant movement and transition that can be traversed by those who recognize its vagueness. As one who is a border crosser, both in the metaphorical and geographic sense, Ivon is one of the *atravesados*, those who inhabit the borderlands, "the squint-eyed, the perverse, the queer, the troublesome...in short, those who cross over, pass over, or go through the confines of the 'normal' "(3). She is a Chicana whose queerness positions her outside of the heteronormative construction of sexuality; but instead of allowing her marginalized position to hamper her, Ivon uses it to develop a *mestiza consciousness*, one that allows her to see beneath the surface and draw connections not easily recognized. While her sexuality is not at the focus of the novel's story line, its importance in the narrative cannot be overlooked, as a close reading of the story illustrates.[17] Ivon's character embodies the intersection of race, gender, and sexuality in the character of the queer detective. She is not the typical private dick, but instead uses her multiple subject positions to maneuver through the interstitial spaces of the borderlands.

Industrialization, Violence, and Border Crossings

Gaspar de Alba begins *Desert Blood* by linking the murder of the young woman and the *maquila* industry in an effort to inform her reader of the effects the industry has had on the lives of women on the border. The novel opens with a harrowing description of a young woman being dragged behind a car, her body viciously brutalized. From the very beginning, Gaspar de Alba confronts the reader with a violence that seems too horrific to be real. As the narrator describes the death of the young woman at the hands of several men, the connection to the *maquiladoras* is established. The nameless young woman recognizes one man "from the factory" and, as she is being repeatedly stabbed, begins to see her body as "a bag of water and bones," using the words the factory nurse had once employed in describing her (1–2). The reducing of the young woman to "a bag of water and bones" illustrates the objectification of the woman and the lack of worth her body commands. The fact that it was a nurse at the *maquila* who uses this rhetoric becomes important as the novel attempts to connect the violence against young women to the ways in which the *maquila* industry reduces female workers into objects to be exploited and discarded.[18] It also debunks the myth of "sisterhood" and points to the ways in which gender solidarity does not always survive in the face of capitalist interests.

Throughout the novel, the history of the *maquilas* is interwoven into the narrative. The characters of Father Francis and Ivon's cousin Ximena are fellow border crossers who act as unofficial historians to provide the background of the industry in Juárez and bear witness to the drastic changes in migration to the city and the consequences of this population growth. As a priest from El Paso, Father Francis uses his ability to move between the border cities to better understand what is happening with the young women of the area and offers an alternative narrative of the events. Although he might be an agent of a patriarchal conservative religious order, he does use his authority as a representative of the Catholic Church to gain access to spaces normally restricted to the public.[19] Father Francis is also a literary representation of the type of community activism that has organized to combat the violence in the border area. In the novel he is the founder of Contra el Silence [Against the Silence] a nonprofit that performs *rastreos*—sweeps for bodies in the desert—advocates for the missing young women, and "picket[s] the courthouses and the offices of [local newspapers] protesting the silence of the authorities and the media on these murders" (40). Ximena relies on her resources as a social worker to help not only at-risk youth in El Paso, but also young women who labor in the *maquilas* in Juárez.

Although agents of traditional religious and state institutions, both of these characters work outside of the laws that regulate the movement of people on the border.[20] A disillusioned Catholic priest and a drunk-driving social worker might not normally be seen as valuable allies in more traditional narratives, but these two characters represent the possibilities that exist when differences are embraced and connections are made across boundaries. For Sandoval, through the "compassionate inclusion of our differences and the self-conscious understanding that each difference is valid in its context, we are awakened to a new realm of methodological, theoretical, political, and feminist activity" (2000, 67). The characters initially function to mediate the adoption of Cecilia's child by Ivon, but end up providing Ivon with access to alternative spaces and the information necessary to analyze the events occurring on the border. Their position as border crossers working for the rights of subjugated groups allows their characters the ability to observe and document a history from the margins, one that provides Ivon and the reader with a narrative of industrialization and violence that challenges the state's strategies of negation and disaggregation. More important, Father Francis and Ximena represent the possibilities of transnational activist networks to function in opposition to the exploitation of workers under global systems of power.

Aided with the knowledge acquired from Ximena and Father Francis, along with more traditional research, Ivon begins her investigation into the murder of Cecilia and later the disappearance of Irene. The more she discovers through her combination of formal and informal sources, the more suspicious she becomes and she, too, starts to question the efficiency of the official investigation and the meaning behind the lack of answers. This questioning is vital, as Sandoval reminds one that the "enactment of differential social movement...necessarily creates new modes of resistance, new questions and answers that supersede those that went before" (152). When discussing the arrest of the Egyptian who is credited as the mastermind behind the murders—in real life, Omar Latif Sharif

Sharif—the character of Rubí Reyna, a local journalist, discusses with Ivon the power of the *maquila* industry on the border: "In Juárez, only two institutions have power: the government and the maquiladoras. Even the police are nothing but pawns" (242). Ivon's access to alternative information leads her to ponder the very complicated relationship:

> The government and the *maquiladoras*. Were they two separate suits, one of spades, one of diamonds, say? Or were they just two different face cards in the same suit? If they were different suits, they'd stack up separately, but these two had something in common. What was it? The U.S.-educated rich men who ran both of them? (242)

Through Ivon's musings, Gaspar de Alba voices the concerns of many individuals who have questioned the corruption of the government and Mexico's dependence on foreign investments. By employing the symbolism of playing cards, Gaspar de Alba is alluding to the idea that there is a higher force controlling the players in this game of life and death. The ultimate losers end up being the women whose bodies are being used to advance the game. The text illustrates the manner in which Ivon's differential mode of consciousness leads her to identify the ways in which the interests of capital are protected at the expense of women's lives. It also provides a more nuanced account of the violence that poses a danger to more than just one group of women.

When Ivon begins her search for Irene, she comes to understand that the violence is not only occurring to women from Juárez. In Father Francis's office, Ivon notices that "one side of the room was paneled in corkboard, crowded with layers of colored index cards and photographs of young women" (178). Irene's picture has joined this wall of pictures identified by the sign in the middle of the board, "*The Missing Girls from El Paso*" (178). The wall makes the victims visible, but more importantly, visually challenges the misconception that only Mexican women or *maquiladora* workers are being killed in Juárez.[21] Father Francis contradicts this narrative, telling Ivon about the seven women from the U.S. side of the border whose bodies had been discovered in various locations of the desert (40). Irene becomes one of the many that have disappeared, and Ivon's investigation begins to draw connections between the men who abducted her sister and those who have abducted other young women. The reader discovers that Irene has become a victim of an international ring of snuff filmmakers who violate young women for an online audience. The answer of "who" kidnapped Irene, however, is not so simple. In the story line, Gaspar de Alba incorporates various theories surrounding the femicides of Juárez while positioning them as occurring under transnational structures of power.

In *Señorita Extraviada*, Portillo presents interviews that draw a connection between the Juárez police department and the murders. In a screening of her film at a Human Rights Watch film festival that took place in New York, Portillo reported another commonly circulated theory about the murders to the audience during the Q & A session: "A 'web' of murderers...are [reportedly] capturing and killing girls in order to make highly profitable 'snuff films'" (Nathan 2002, 5). Cultural critics like Fregoso see the murders as part of a state-run campaign of terror. Other sources, like *Frontera NorteSur*, have pointed to stories on the growing drug cartel movement and noted the close proximity of sites where the bodies of victims have been found in the *narco-traficantes*' areas of activity.[22] The online news service has also reported a connection between the murders of some of the women, the computer school named ECCO, and the school's proximity to shoe stores.[23] Julia Monárrez Fragoso sees the serial femicides as part of a backlash against women because of their newfound independence in the *maquilas*. Others believe the victims are murdered by "Juniors," the sons of the rich families in Juárez, who kill women as a form of sport, while some believe the women are victims of satanic rituals.

Desert Blood does not try to advance just one theory, but instead positions the border area as a transnational space of chaos where all of these theories are possible. Here is an interconnected system that depends on a corrupt police force, wealthy elites who run the government, the quest for profit, and the availability of disposable bodies. Instead, the fictionalized narrative gives Gaspar de Alba the freedom to put forth a theory that makes visible the possible reasons why young women are being murdered on the border. By including several theories, the text incorporates multiple modes of analysis into the narrative and relies on a technology of resistance that rejects a simplistic analysis of the murders. In providing a story line that connects the various conjectures, the text implicates all of the different actors, making them all complicit, and provides readers who might know little about the murders with a sense of how complicated the situation in Juárez has become.[24] As a result, Ivon develops into a translator for the audience, one that helps navigate the various spaces the novel traverses.

Writing in Opposition

Ivon's ability to rescue her sister and unravel the mystery around Irene's kidnapping is directly related to her positionality as a queer Chicana academic. She inhabits the liminal space between insider and outsider. As a woman of color, she is suspect in academia; as an out lesbian, she is rejected by many in her community; and as a Chicana, she doesn't belong within the construct of national citizen. Her position as outsider functions well in placing her in the role of detective, a role predicated on being "on the outside, being the alienated other" (Rodriguez 2005, 6). Furthermore, as a queer Chicana constantly having to make a space for herself, Ivon's everyday existence is based on an oppositional consciousness that allows her to identify and navigate through various structures of oppression, an ability Anzaldúa referred to as *la facultad*. Part of a *mestiza consciousness*, Anzaldúa identifies *la facultad* as the capacity to see beneath the surface, "an acute awareness mediated by the part of the psyche that does not speak, that communicates in images and symbols" (38). For Anzaldúa, it is those who have been marginalized and pushed out that have developed such a skill in order to survive. Gaspar de Alba's protagonist has developed *la facultad*, or the first technology of the "methodology of the oppressed," and it is her ability to decode and decipher the signs around her that lead her to the solution of Irene's kidnapping.

In her conception of a "methodology of the oppressed," Sandoval provides us with the theoretical framework through which to decipher the meaning of the dominant-order signs and advocates for a literacy of ideology that allows for a navigation through meaning in order to reach a differential consciousness. In this consciousness, "the differential represents the variant" (57), Sandoval argues:

> Under conditions of colonization, poverty, racism, gender, or sexual subordination, dominated populations are often held away from the comforts of dominant ideology, or ripped out of legitimized social narratives, in a process of power that places such constituencies in a very different position from which to view objects-in-reality than other kinds of citizen-subjects. (104)

In the novel Ivon's positionality as a queer Chicana functions as a productive location from which to approach and interpret the violence against women in Juárez. In fact, it is her initial quest to adopt a child with her partner that brings Ivon back to the border. Ivon's decision to become Mapi, "a combination of Mami and Papi, because [she] was going to be a little of each," challenges the mother/father binary of the heteronormative family on both an ideological and semantic level (20). As a lesbian, Ivon redefines the meaning of parenthood and rejects the rhetoric that characterizes the "traditional" family.[25] Gaspar de Alba's resignification of parenthood allows a point of entry into the mystery that follows.

From the beginning of the novel, Ivon is presented as a strong woman who, while negotiating the difficulties of inhabiting multiple identities, is aware of her sense of self. An independent, queer Chicana, her body is marked by her gender, race, and sexuality. Early on in her description of Ivon, Gaspar de Alba gives the reader a clue into the importance that signs and symbols will play in the novel by making Ivon's body a canvas on which to project meaning. We discover that "Ivon had gotten a labrys tattooed on the back of her neck her first year of grad school at Iowa" (14). The introduction of the tattoo makes the audience aware of the fact that Ivon openly and unapologetically embraces her sexuality. While the labrys is known as a weapon or harvesting tool used in the past, today it is "a lesbian and feminist symbol of strength and self-sufficiency" (Ellis 2004). It is also significant that Ivon gets the tattoo during her first year in graduate school, an academic time many women of color find trying to say the least. For this population, the quest for an advanced degree comes with the challenges of navigating a system of institutionalized sexism, racism, classism, and homophobia. Here is where many begin to develop the skills Sandoval argues are part of a differential consciousness of marginalized people, including "the ability to perceive and decode dominant-order sign systems in order to move among them with a certain literacy, thus ensuring their survival" (182). It is in graduate school that Ivon learns to employ an oppositional consciousness in order to survive academia and conduct meaningful work. In the novel she becomes a literary embodiment of Sandoval's idea of a "repoliticized citizen-warrior" (178).

Ivon's academic background, combined with her knowledge of the border area and her positionality as a border crosser, is what positions her as a reader and decoder of signs. A visiting professor at Saint Ignatius College in L.A., she is in the process of writing her dissertation. Gaspar de Alba strongly connects Ivon's research to the investigation she undertakes in El Paso. The telling title of her dissertation is "Marx Meets the Women's Room: The Representation of Class and Gender in Bathroom Graffiti (Three Case Studies)." She explains to the dean

> that public bathrooms are a type of exhibition space in which the bodies of women and the graffiti they write and draw on the walls—a

closed discursive system of words and images—can be read semiotically to analyze the social construction of class and gender identity in what Marx called "the community of women." (17–18)

While at first it is easy to dismiss the subject matter, as the dean originally does, the importance of Ivon's ability to read text not normally valued plays a large role in the development of the narrative. Ivon's capacity to recognize the graffiti found in bathrooms as a form of expression through a class and race framework illustrates her recognition of this type of writing as the participation of individuals in a form of public discourse.[26] Like a detective reading a mystery from the outside, Ivon reads the graffiti from a position in the margins, a place from where alternate meaning can be uncovered. Beyond just seeing the bathroom graffiti as a simple form of vandalism, Gaspar de Alba represents this informal arrangement of writing as a valid structure of communication.[27] Her dissertation also provides her with a Marxist analytical framework through which to interpret signs, a framing that will prove vital to her analysis of the industrialized border area.

Unlike the popular representations of academics as alienated individuals whose work belongs only to those who inhabit the ivory towers of academia, Ivon is able to use her training in reading signs as a way to reconnect to the community from which she has been separated. She rejects the constructed boundaries between academia and the community, not an easy feat considering the extent to which these borders have been naturalized, and combines her knowledge of both. Through the praxis of differential thinking, she uncovers information about the murders in Juárez and Irene's disappearance that others had overlooked. Posting flyers and asking questions regarding her sister, Ivon finds herself visiting some of her old haunts and taking on the role of detective. These are bars and clubs she had once frequented with her former lover Raquel. It is her past queer relationship that allows Ivon access to locales she might not have discovered on her own, and it is this history that provides Ivon with the knowledge necessary to reenter these spaces. Ivon knows that in these bars, which many would consider unsavory, information is spread and shared. Like the graffiti she studies in Los Angeles, the bars and clubs in Juárez provide alternative venues for communication and offer her valuable clues.

Ivon is not disappointed by her visits to the Juárez establishments. As other "brown gumshoe tales," to use Ralph Rodriguez's phrase, the narrative positions the bars as existing outside of the mainstream.[28] In a later visit to the bars and clubs in Juárez, we see that while Ivon's history with these spaces allows her to comfortably navigate them, her Mormon cousin William is extremely uncomfortable and judgmental.[29] While Ivon might be a strong and independent woman, her patriarchal family has a difficult time envisioning her alone across the border, and William, who stands in stark contrast to Ivon, is forced to accompany her. For William, there is no value to be found in these alternative spaces. His attitude illustrates the fact that just because one crosses the physical border does not mean one is a "border crosser."[30] During her first visit to the Kentucky club, Ivon finds herself reading the graffiti on the walls of a bathroom stall:

> Someone had scrawled that old saying of Mexican president Porfirio Díaz: *Poor Mexico, so far from God, so close to the United States.* Underneath it, somebody else had written in red nail polish and shaky lettering, *Poor Juárez, so close to Hell, so far from Jesus.* (98)

The use of red nail polish to write on the wall is a vivid employment of a color that symbolizes everything from danger to blood. The polish is also a tool used in the emphasis of feminine beauty, but unlike lipstick, is longer lasting and not easily wiped away. Also, the phrase is written in "shaky lettering," indicating that it was done in a hurry. With all of the graffiti in the bathroom, it seems unlikely that the writer feared being caught writing on the stall, but the content of the phrase written might be what caused the hurried communication.[31] The positioning of the phrase under Díaz's words bemoaning the proximity of Mexico to the United States functions to situate the current situation in Juárez within a longer history of U.S. imperialism in Mexico. By emphasizing the location of the city closer to "Hell," the writer of the graffiti draws a connection to the position of Juárez on the border next to the United States. In the phrase, the United States is equated with "Hell," a reference that becomes clearer as the mystery unravels. Ivon doesn't understand the connection at first, but sees reading the graffiti as a part of her work and decides to incorporate it into her dissertation project. As a case study, she hopes to use the graffiti as a way of understanding what is going on in her hometown.

Her second visit to the Kentucky club is much more urgent, as it occurs after Irene's disappearance. Once in the club, she heads to the bathroom, hoping to find new graffiti and any clue to Irene's whereabouts. In the bathroom stall,

> she saw some fresh graffiti on the wall, couldn't find the one she was looking for, and then she saw it, but it said something else now: *Poor Juarez, so far from the Truth, so close to Jesus.* The old version, she

could still see traces of it—*tan cerca al infierno, tan lejos de Jesús*—had been scratched out with something sharp. So far from the Truth. Talk about understatement. (186–87)

In this version of graffiti, the Truth is capitalized, indicating an absolute, not an abstraction. The reference to the Truth being found close to Jesus is an important clue Ivon is not able to decipher at this point. However, she recognizes the fact that the new graffiti is relevant and decides to engage the writer. She returns to the bathroom before leaving the bar and writes on the stall: "*She drew a circle around so far from the Truth and then an arrow pointing to a question: Do you know the truth? Call me.* She wrote her cell phone number" (188). Instead of simply decoding the meaning behind the writing on the wall, Ivon actively participates in the dialogue taking place on this unlikely canvas. With Irene's disappearance, Ivon's detective work, like her dissertation, becomes personal.

The last bar Ivon and William visit is the Casa Colorada, a strip bar off the regular tourist areas. Here, she again finds messages written on the wall.

> She took a quick look at the graffiti, thinking maybe someone was leaving clues on the walls of women's toilets.... Over the screw holes where a toilet paper holder might have been fastened once, inside a box decorated with stars, was the statement: *Aqui no hay cholas ni maqui-locas.* And in tiny letters at the bottom edge of the door: *El nuevo gobernador le chupa la verga a la migra.* (211)

The phrase "Aqui no hay cholas ni maqui-locas" [No *cholas* or *maqui-locas* here] at first glance seems quite ubiquitous. A more literal reading of the text, however, illustrates the ways in which the discourse of blaming the victims has permeated this informal public discourse. A *chola* is commonly seen as a gang member, someone involved in violent and illegal activities. The meaning of *maqui-loca* is more nuanced, as Ivon points out, when she questions the definition of them as "maquiladora workers who become Americanized and turn into whores" and instead wonders if "that [is] just the way people perceive them because they have jobs outside the home" (211). The rhetoric of blaming women for their victimization is not new, but has been much more vocalized in the public discourse surrounding the murders.[32] While it is easy to see the words as a further indictment of blame, one can also read the phrase as a strategy of survival the dancers in the Casa Colorada employ to disassociate themselves from the women they believe are targets for violence. As Father Francis explains to Ivon, "if [the public] see a picture of someone that to them looks like a prostitute, they won't have sympathy for her. They'll just think she was a bad girl and she got what she deserved" (179). As dancers in a bar, these women are already positioned outside of the mainstream construction of a "good" girl, and one can read the graffiti as an attempt to define one's self against girls who are more "bad," thereby deflecting the violence.[33]

Unlike the clearly visible first phrase, the second sentence is written in much smaller letters and located in an area not visible with a simple glance. Even though the meaning of the phrase is not immediately clear, the positioning of the text and the size of writing, and the fact that Ivon has to work harder to find it, points to the importance it plays in the future story line. Of significance is the statement the phrase makes about the corruption taking place at the high level of state power and the connection to the U.S. Border Patrol. By claiming that the governor of the state is sexually servicing the Border Patrol, the sentence makes clear that the local government is not only in a relationship with *la migra*, an agency whose authority is supposed to be restricted to the U.S. border, but that this relationship places the Mexican government in a position of subservience. The reader is made aware that the abuse of power the U.S. agency enjoys is not limited to one side of the border only, but that it is able to permeate the life of Mexicans in their own country.[34]

Connecting the Dots

Ivon's synthesis of gathered information is moved along as the investigation comes to a dramatic peak when she, too, is kidnapped. After participating in a *rastreo* and sleeping with her former lover, Raquel, Irene leaves Juárez but is apprehended at the border under the false pretense of driving a stolen vehicle and is taken into custody by Border Patrol agent Jeremy Wilcox, or JW. As they are driving in the desert, Ivon begins to make sense of the graffiti and the coins that had been found on the bodies of several victims. In attempting to provoke JW into giving away more information, she tells him about the writing she saw in Casa Colorada: "'You know, they're writing graffiti about you in the red-light district, something about how the Border Patrol sucks the Chihuahua governor's cock'" (285). She deliberately inverts the translation of the original quote and teases him about the need to rape women with rolls of coins because he lacks a real penis in order to infuriate JW and threaten his masculinity. The roll of coins used to rape the women becomes an allegory for the abuse of Juárez women by transnational structures of power. Gaspar de Alba takes the liberty of adding to the story line the finding of coins on the bodies of the victims. The coins are supposed to "signify the value of the victims in the corporate machine; the poor brown women who are the main target of these murders, are...as expendable as pennies in the border economy" (v). The addition of the pennies comes to signify the nebulous connections between the violence against young women and the capitalist interests of transnational corporations.

In the culminating action of the story, Ivon finds herself being taken by JW to the location where Irene is being held and where young women are being murdered on film for profit. The location is not in Mexico but across the border in El Paso. For Ivon, "Everything fell into place. ASARCO—the American Smelting and Refining Company—was a copper refinery, a factory close to Cristo Rey" (286). Mount Cristo Rey is the location of a forty-foot statue of Christ, an important borderland landmark. Earlier in the novel, Gaspar de Alba describes the statue as a "huge white-robed limestone Christ stretch[ing] its crucified arms out like a holy bridge between the First World and the Third, like a mirage of faith across the desert" (236). A symbol of hope and faith, the statue instead becomes a silent witness to the atrocities taking place in its shadow. By "meta-ideologizing" the meaning of the Christ figure, the text implicates this "holy bridge" in the violence on the border. It is at this point that Ivon is able to connect the dots. She unravels the various clues and realizes that JW is running a snuff film business and that some of the women being murdered are being tortured on film for profit.

Gaspar de Alba's choice to end the mystery of Irene's kidnapping at ASARCO is significant because of the relationship of the plant to the border area. The plant is mentioned many times throughout the novel. On her first morning back home, Ivon notices, "that the smog hovering over the border was thicker than usual, like a heavy brown pall that stretched across the valley. Toxic fumes from ASARCO, she thought" (27). The city of El Paso has documented a long history of environmental law violations, including lead contamination of the surrounding community (Joint Resolution). For over a century, residents of both El Paso and Juárez have "been exposed to high levels of air pollutants, contaminated soil, and a contaminated Rio Grande River, which has resulted in the development of serious health conditions," all because of ASARCO's smelting operations (Joint Resolution 2). Later, while in captivity, Irene "thought she saw ASARCO in the distance" (174). By incorporating ASARCO into the narrative, Gaspar de Alba emphasizes the danger the refinery poses to the residents of the border area. As a result, the text situates the current crisis on the border within a long history of capitalist greed overruling the well-being of the border's citizens. The connections between the interests of capital on both sides of the border go beyond the corporate to the individual when the reader discovers that JW is not only a U.S. Border Patrol agent, but is, in fact, a chief detention enforcement officer. In making JW one of the masterminds of the murder ring, Gaspar de Alba is alluding to the crooked law enforcement that exists on both sides of the border and the ways in which corruption does not recognize the constructed boundaries of the transnational border.

Conclusion

The end of the novel finds Irene reunited with her family and the mystery of her kidnapping solved, but the crimes being committed are not so easily explained. After the ordeal, Ivon's questions continue:

> This wasn't a case of whodunit, but rather of who was allowing these crimes to happen? Whose interests were being served? Who was covering it up? Who was profiting from the deaths of all these women? (332)

These questions have no answers, and the novel does not attempt to find solutions. Instead it endeavors to challenge the silence around the violence against women of the border. The novel positions Ivon, Ximena, Father Francis, Rubí Reyna, and the community of activists on both sides of the border as subjects defying the transnational order that positions human beings as collateral damage in the quest for profits. They become part of a transnational group of "citizen-warriors" committed to revealing and dismantling the structures of power that have drastically altered life on the border. Gaspar de Alba's protagonist ends up embodying the possibilities of a differential mode of consciousness. As Sandoval reminds us:

> With the transnationalization of capitalism, when elected officials are no longer leaders of singular nation-states but nexuses for multinational interests, it also becomes possible for citizen-subjects to become activists for a new decolonizing global terrain, a psychic terrain that can unite them with similarly positioned citizens-subjects within and across national borders into new, post-Western-empire alliances. (183)

Studying the violence on the border through an oppositional consciousness allows for a real disruption of ideologies that position women as disposable objects of capitalism and places the interests of capital above the value of human life. The characters illustrate the opportunities that arise when global structures of power are resisted and opposed.

Finally, Ivon gets the child she initially returned to her hometown to adopt. She is unable to adopt Cecilia's baby, but she does adopt the child of another impoverished *maquila* worker, Elsa. Elsa was impregnated without her knowledge, and the drugs she received very well could have caused her ovarian cancer. The boy, Jorgito, is an underdeveloped three-year-old whose mother is dying from ovarian cancer and is desperate to find him a home. The importance of Jorgito in the novel is not the closure he gives to the narrative, but the questions that he raises. Jorgito is the product of an experiment conducted in a *maquiladora* and comes to embody the violence being perpetrated on the bodies of young women.[35] Elsa's pregnancy is the result of the complete lack of value placed on poor workers, who are used for their labor, both reproductive and productive. While Ivon might now be the Mapi she envisioned, the story of Elsa and the other women will always be a part of her. Through Jorgito, that history will continue to remain visible. In the end, the corruption remains unchecked, Irene may never fully recover from her ordeal, and Ivon is left knowing that while she saved her sister, many other women will remain unprotected. The reader is denied a happy ending and instead leaves the book with more questions than answers.

Alicia Gaspar de Alba's *Desert Blood* offers its reader a harrowing tale of murder, injustice, and transnational exploitation. The novel goes beyond the conventions of traditional detective stories and instead provides a mystery that defies an easy solution. In "Work, Immigration, Gender," Lisa Lowe writes that "cultural forms of many kinds are important media in the formation of oppositional narratives and crucial to the imagination and rearticulation of new forms of political subjectivity, collectivity, and practice" (1997, 357). The novel offers its reader examples of the possibility of divergent thinking in reading structures of power. By employing the technologies of opposition, the text makes important connections between state agents and transnational capital interests in an effort to highlight the exploitation of workers and the violence against the young women of the border area. With its representation of "repoliticized citizen-warriors," the text also presents important strategies of resistance and draws attention to the opposition taking place by members of the community. Gaspar de Alba's narrative illustrates the possibilities of writing from the margins in creating new paradigms that can more fully incorporate the stories and words of border crossers and marginalized groups.

Notes

1. Since 1994 at least 400 women have been murdered and more than 1,000 are missing in the border city of Juárez. *Frontera NorteSur* reports that at least twenty-nine cases of women who have disappeared in the city since the beginning of 2008 are currently pending and that last year the number of women murdered in Juárez reached an all-time high of eighty-six ("Mothers of" 2009). Unfortunately, with the escalating drug violence in the city, the city has become an even more dangerous place for women.
2. Most reviews focus on the importance the text holds in educating the public about the violence occurring in Juárez. For example, see Judy Maloof's review in *Latino Studies* (2006), Anita Tijerina Revilla's review in *Chicana/Latina Studies Journal* (2007), and Patricia Trujillo's review in *My SA.com Express-News (2007)*.
3. In her foundational text, *Borderlands/La Frontera: The New Mestiza*, Anzaldúa argues for a new *mestiza* consciousness, one that is based on the negotiation of multiple subjectivities. The border crosser is one who employs this consciousness in order to inhabit what seem like contradictory locations; she learns how to survive in the in-between spaces borders try to demarcate.
4. Jorge Bustamante writes that "maquiladoras operate as a magnet in the migration to the border cities, but that population attracted to the border is not absorbed by the maquiladoras" (248). The population of Ciudad Juárez in 1970 was estimated at 407,370 (227). Current estimates place the population of the city at 1.5 million people (Chamberlain 2007).
5. Sklair 1993, 46.
6. The executive decree in 1971 permitted "that the capital stock of the enterprise could be 100 percent foreign owned and that the foreign investors could obtain the right of possession over land destined for the establishment of maquiladoras for a period of thirty years, within the border fringe restricted by Article 27 of the Mexican Constitution by means of a trust relationship with a Mexican bank" (Bustamante 241).
7. Bustamante, 241.
8. The objectives were three: (l) gaining a transfer of technology through the training received by the workers of the *maquiladoras*, (2) increasing the number of jobs in the border area, and (3) improving the income of the border population (Bustamante 242).
9. Fernández-Kelly 1983b.

10. I use "maquila culture" as used by Ong when writing about the sexual violence against women in the *maquiladoras* in Nogales, "Gender and Labor Politics."
11. She writes: "ingenieros…[insist] on having only the prettiest workers under their command" or where a manager can hire a crew "formed of women all of whom had—upon his own request—eyes and hair of different color," or where a line supervisor can take "pride in boasting that every women in his line had borne him a child" (Fernández-Kelly 1983a 129–30).
12. In her discussion on industrial discourses, Ong writes that these discourses, " 'disassemble' " the female worker into eyes and fingers adapted for assembly work, at the same time reassembling other parts of their bodies according to commodified sexual images" (73).
13. Monárrez Fragoso reports that in Juárez "prevention campaigns are centered on making women responsible for any aggression they could befall, especially if it is at night or if they are walking along an empty street. Warnings were sent out about attending parties, staying out late till the morning hours, walking alone, and more important, if she was a laborer, about dressing provocatively and consuming alcoholic beverages; her guardian angel, it was said, would not always be there to take care of her" (4).
14. For example, see Susan Tiano's discussion in *Patriarchy on the Line* of the Mexican government's economic policies, like currency devaluations and the fall of worker wages, introduced in order to encourage foreign investment.
15. In the acknowledgments, Gaspar de Alba refers to the influence that Stefano Tani's work on the "anti-detective novel" played in her writing of *Desert Blood* (343). In *The Doomed Detective*, Tani maps out the changes that the traditional detective novel has undergone as a result of a postmodernism sensibility, resulting in what he terms the "anti-detective novel" and the ways in which such a narrative illuminates the conditions of postmodernism itself.
16. For more information on the ways in which Chicana/o authors use the genre of detective fiction, see Lomelí, Márquez, and Herrera-Sobek's "Trends and Themes in Chicana/o Writings in Postmodern Times," Tim Libretti's "Lucha Corpi and the Politics of Detective Fiction," and Ana Patricia Rodrigúez's "The Body in Question."
17. In several essays, while mention is made of Ivon's sexuality, it is never fully addressed in the analysis of the text. For example, in "Gender, Order, and Femicide" Volk and Schlotterbeck write that Ivon "came out" and that Gaspar de Alba is a "lesbian feminist," but no direct mention is made of Ivon's queer identity (78–79).
18. While the rhetoric being used by the young woman is that employed by the *maquila* industry, we must be careful when using this rhetoric. Alicia Schmidt Camacho reminds of the power of language when she warns of

the dangers of the fatalistic discourse that positions the murder of these young women as inevitable—such language automatically renders them disposable (2004).
19. For instance, when Ivon, Ximena, and Father Francis receive notice of Cecilia's death, he uses his status as a priest to gain them access to the body in the morgue under the claim of being the young woman's priest (49).
20. Together, Ximena and Father Francis have expedited fifty-two transnational adoptions between *maquiladora* workers who cannot afford the cost of raising a child and individuals in El Paso. All of these adoptions have involved the bribery of officials and forgery of records (37–39).
21. For an in-depth critique of the ways in which the murders have been misrepresented as happening only to *maquiladora* workers, see Rosa Linda Fregoso's *meXicana Encounters*.
22. *Frontera NorteSur*'s online news service is part of the FNS outreach program of the Center for Latin American and Border Studies of New Mexico State University.
23. Several of the victims were students of the school, while several other victims either worked in or visited the shoe stores Tres Hermanos and Zapateria Paris, which are located in the same area as the computer school ("Ten Years" 2003).
24. For more analysis on the representation of globalization in *Desert Blood*, see Rachel Adams's "At the Borders of American Crime Fiction."
25. See Cherrie Moraga's *Waiting in the Wings: Portrait of Queer Motherhood* for an in-depth discussion of radical motherhood and the redefinition of family.
26. In their analysis of bathroom graffiti, "Anonymous Expression: A Structural View of Graffiti," Gonos, Mulkern, and Poushnisky argue that "it is fruitful to treat public toilet walls as a publicly used medium of expression, the peculiar characteristic of which is the anonymity afforded the communicator, for this situation facilitates the expression of certain sentiments which are unsuitable for virtually all other media and expressive situations" (46).
27. See Green's "The Writing on the Stall" for an analysis of gender difference in the use of graffiti.
28. Rodriguez emphasizes the role that race plays in transforming the detective novel by "browning" the genre. Such a move distinguishes between the construction of traditional detectives, commonly known as gumshoes, and Chicana/o detectives.
29. As a member of a conservative religious establishment, he acts as a foil to Father Francis, another member of the clergy. The text is drawing a strong distinction between the ways in which religious individuals navigate spaces that exist outside of the church.
30. In fact, when Ivon and William are apprehended by Juárez officials, his constant attempts to assert his U.S. citizenship demonstrate his inability to function on the other side of the border. On the other hand, Ivon's

knowledge of the corruption in the system and her ability to manipulate that information save them.
31. This is consistent with Gonos, Mulkern, and Pushnisky's hypothesis that "the relative frequency of graffiti giving expression to a particular value will be greater in social milieus where the suppression of remarks carrying this value is greater" (43).
32. Like former attorney general of Chihuahua, Arturo Gonzales Rascon, who blamed the victims, former governor of the state, Francisco Barrio Terrazas, also claimed the young victims were at fault for dressing provocatively or walking in dark places. In 2009, Barrio Terrazas was appointed Mexico's ambassador to Canada ("Controversy" Feb. 26, 2009).
33. The narrative illustrates the futility of this type of strategy by including the stories of various young women who are murdered but do not fall into either category of *maqui-loca* or *chola*.
34. In their analysis of the role graffiti played in the emotional expressions of young people following the assassination of Yitzhak Rabin, the prime minister of Israel in 1995, Klingman, Shalev, and Pearlman found that writing graffiti on walls "allowed the evocation of distressing emotions within a safely contained structure...restor[ed] a sense of mastery/control distancing that eventually enhanced the release from a sense of feeling helpless" (300).
35. He can also represent hope for the next generation, for a new kind of masculinity, for a new type of citizen-subject.

Works Cited

Adams, Rachel. 2007. "At the Borders of American Crime Fiction." *Shades of the Planet: American Literature as World Literature*. Eds. Wai Chee Dimock and Lawrence Buell. Princeton University Press. 249–73.

Anzaldúa, Gloria. 1987. *Borderlands/La Frontera: The New Mestiza*. San Francisco: Aunt Lute Books.

Ayala, Elaine. 2005, 2008. "Novel Explores String of Juárez Killings." *My SA: San Antonio Express-News*. www.mysanantonio.com/life/MYSA032005_1P_desert_blood_1496b72c7.html.

Bustamante, Jorge A. 1983. "Maquiladoras: A New Face of International Capitalism on Mexico's Northern Frontier." *Women, Men and the International Division of Labor*. Eds. June Nash and María Patricia Fernández-Kelly. 2009. Albany: State University of NY Press.

Chamberlain, Lisa. 2007. "2 Cities and 4 Bridges Where Commerce Flows." *New York Times*. March 28. http://www.nytimes.com/2007/03/28/realestate/commercial/28juarez.html

"Controversy Greets New Mexican Ambassador." 2009. *The Star.Com*. February 26. www.thestar.com/News/Canada/article/593476

Ellis, Sonja J. 2004. "Ignorance Is Bliss? Undergraduate Students and Lesbian and Gay Culture." *Sheffield Hallam University Psychology Research Group Papers* http://digitalcommons.shu.ac.uk/prg papers/8.

Fernández-Kelly, Patricia María. 1983a. *For We Are Sold, I and My People: Women and Industry in Mexico's Frontier.* Albany: State University of NY Press.

———. 1983b. "Mexican Border Industrialization, Female Labor Force Participation and Migration." *Women, Men and the International Division of Labor.* Eds. June Nash and María Patricia Fernández-Kelly. Albany: State University of NY Press.

Fernández-Kelly and Saskia Sassen, 1995. "Recasting Women in the Global Economy." *Women in the Latin American Development Process.* Ed.s Christine E. Bose and Edna Acosta-Belén. Philadelphia: Temple University Press.

Fragoso, Julia Monárrez. 2002. "Serial Sexual Femicide in Ciudad Juárez: 1993–2001." *Debate Feminista*.12:25. http://www.womenontheborder.org/sex_serial_english.pdf

Fregoso, Rosa Linda. 2003. *meXicana Encounters: The Making of Social Identities on the Borderlands.* Berkeley: University of California Press.

Frontera NorteSur. www.nmsu.edu/~frontera.

Gaspar de Alba, Alicia. 2005. *Desert Blood: The Juárez Murders.* Houston: Arte PúbPublico Press.

Green, James. 2003. "The Writing on the Stall: Gender and Graffiti." *Journal of Language and Social Psychology.* 22:3 (Sept.): 282–96.

Gonos, George, Virginia Mulkern, and Nicholas Poushinsky. 1976. "Anonymous Expression: A Structural View of Graffiti." *The Journal of American Folklore.* 89(351) (Jan.–Mar.): 40–48.

"Joint Resolution of the Border Cities." *City of El Paso, Texas.* http://www.ci.el-paso.tx.us/_documents/nv101.pdf

Kaplan, Caren. 2004. "The Politics of Location as Transnational Feminist Practice." *Scattered Hegemonies: Postmodernism and Feminist Practices.* Eds. Inderpal Grewal and Karen Caplan. Minneapolis: Minnesota University Press. 137–52.

Klingman, Avigdor, Ronit Shalev, and Abigail Pearlman. 2000. "Graffiti: A Creative Means of Youth Coping with Collective Trauma." *The Arts in Psychology.* 27(5):299–307.

Libretti, Tim. 1999. "Lucha Corpi and the Politics of Detective Fiction." *Multicultural Detective Fiction: Murder from the Other Side.* Ed. Adrienne Johnson Gosselin. New York: Garland Publishing. 61–81.

Lomelí, Francisco A., Teresa Márquez, and María Herrera-Sobek. 2000. "Trends and Themes in Chicana/o Writings in Postmodern Times." *Chicano Renaissance: Contemporary Cultural Trends.* Eds. David R. Maciel, Isidro D. Ortiz, and María Herrera-Sobek. Tucson: University of Arizona Press. 285–312.

Lowe, Lisa. 1997. "Work, Immigration, Gender: New Subjects of Cultural Politics." *The Politics of Culture in the Shadow of Capital.* Eds. Lisa Lowe and David Lloyd. Durham: Duke University Press.

Maloof, Judy. 2006. "Review of Desert Blood: The Juárez Murders." *Latino Studies* 4(1–2):184–86.
Moraga, Cherríe. 1997. *Waiting in the Wings: Portrait of a Queer Motherhood*. Ithaca: Firebrand Books.
"Mothers of the Disappeared March Again…and Again." 2009. *Frontera NorteSur*. New Mexico State University, Jan. 22. http://www.nmsu.edu/~frontera/hmrt.html
Nathan, Debbie. 2002. "Missing the Story." *The Texas Observer*. Aug. 30. http://www.womenontheborder.org/Articles/Senorita_Text.pdf
Ong, Aihwa. 1997. "The Gender and Labor Politics of Postmodernity." *The Politics of Culture in the Shadow of Capital*. Eds. Lisa Lowe and David Lloyd. Durham: Duke University Press.
Ponce, Mary Helen. 1998. "Latino Sleuths: Hispanic Mystery Writers Make Crime Pay." *Hispanic*. 11(8) (May): 44+.
Portillo, Lourdes, dir. 2001. *Señorita Extraviada*. (Women Make Movies).
Ríos, Palmira N. 1995. "Gender, Industrialization, and Development Puerto Rico." *Women in the Latin American Development Process*. Eds. Christine E. Bose and Edna Acosta-Belén. Philadelphia: Temple University Press.
Rodríguez, Ana Patricia. 2007. "The Body in Question: The Latina Detective in the Lupe Solano Mystery Series." *From Bananas to Buttocks: The Latino Body in Popular Film and Culture*, ed. Myra Mendible. Austin: University of Texas Press. 243–61.
Rodriguez, Ralph E. 2005. *Brown Gumshoes: Detective Fiction and the Search for Chicana/o Identity*. Austin: University of Texas Press.
Sandoval, Chela. 2000. *Methodology of the Oppressed*. Minnneapolis: University of Minnesota Press.
Schmidt Camacho, Alicia. 2004. "Body Counts on the Mexico-U.S. Border: Feminicidio, Reification, and the Theft of Mexicana Subjectivity." *Chicana/Latina Studies: The Journal of Mujeres Activas en Letras y Cambio Social* 4(1) (Fall): 22–60.
Sklair, Leslie. 1993. *Assembling for Development: The Maquila Industry in Mexico and the United States*. San Diego: Center for U.S.-Mexican Studies.
Stowers, Carlos. 2001. "The Angels of Juárez." *Dallas Observer*. Jan. 4. http://dallasobserver.com.
Sweeney, Susan Elizabeth. 1999. "Gender-Blending, Genre-Bending, and the Rendering of Identity in Barbara Wilson's *Gaudí Afternoon*." *Multicultural Detective Fiction: Murder from the Other Side*. Ed. Adrienne Johnson Gosselin. New York: Garland Publishing. 123–41.
Tani, Stefano. 1984. *The Doomed Detective: The Contribution of the Detective Novel to Postmodern American and Italian Fiction*. Carbondale: Southern Illinois University Press.
"Ten Years of Border Femicide: Computers, Shoes, Physical Appearance and Drugs Common Threads as Juárez-Style Women's Killing Reach

Tamaulipas State." 2003. *Frontera NorteSur.* New Mexico State University, March 3. http://www.nmsu.edu/~frontera/mar03/feat2.html
Tiano, Susan. 1994. *Patriarchy on the Line: Labor, Gender, and Ideology in the Mexican Maquila Industry.* Philadelphia: Temple University Press.
Tijerina Revilla, Anita. 2007. "*Desert Blood*: An Insight to the 'Factory of Killers' in Juárez, México." *Chicana/Latina Studies: The Journal of Mujeres Activas en Letras y Cambio Social* 6(2) (Spring): 132–35.
Trujillo, Patricia. 2005, 2007. "Juárez Murders Are the Subject of Powerful Novel." *MySA.comExpress-News.* April, July 17. http://www.mysanantonio.com/entertainment/MYSA041005_5Z_book_juarez_1b4ee5cd0_html.html.
Volk, Steven S., and Marian E. Schlotterbeck. 2007. "Gender, Order, and Femicide: Reading the Popular Culture of Murder in Ciudad Juárez." *Aztlán: A Journal of Chicano Studies* 32(1) (Spring): 53–86.
Wright, Melissa M. 2001. "Feminine Villains, Masculine Heroes, and the Reproduction of Cuidad Juárez." *Social Text* 19(4):93–113. http://muse.jhu.edu/journals/soc/toc/soc19.4.html

Chapter Three

Global Patagonia: Belén Gache's Nomadic Writings

Marta Sierra

Global Encounters: Artistic Imaginations of Place

In 2007 Argentina and Brazil organized the First Biennial of the Ends of the World. Seeking to unite the Arctic and Antarctic poles through art, the biennial focused on themes connected to the global concerns of the twenty-first century: time and its metaphors, ecology, urban topographies, and virtual or possible worlds. More than 100 artists from twenty-five countries exhibited their works in Tierra del Fuego, the Beagle Channel, and Antarctica. Monuments in Tierra del Fuego such as the Old Prison, established in 1896 following Jeremy Bentham's Panopticon model, and the remains of San Juan de Salvamento's lighthouse, built in 1884 on the inhospitable Isla de los Estados, were two central sites of several projects. Although located on the grounds of southern Argentina, the biennial promoted a transnational communication; a complex technological network connected, for instance, Ushuaia, the north of Canada, and the Finnish Lapland and, in different participating cities around the world, screens were installed for the passersby to watch some of its main developments. As one of the main goals was to promote a deeper understanding of cultural diversity, descendants of aboriginal cultures from the North and South Poles also partook in the artistic exchanges. By establishing transnational cultural exchanges, the artists involved in the project explored what Néstor García Canclini describes as the metaphors and narratives of a new "intercultural imaginary" present in global societies (2008, 62). In particular, this event examined how the cultures of globalization reflect transformations in time and spatial relations, and the importance electronic media bears in the construction of "imagined global communities" (65).

In this context this essay addresses the works of Argentinean artist and writer Belén Gache. Here I will review first *Escrituras Nómadas. Del libro perdido al hipertexto* [*Nomadic Writings. From the Lost Book to the Hypertext*] and *El libro del fin del mundo* [*The Book of the Ends of the World*], in which the author defines "nomadic writing" and focuses on how literary transnational networks are built through nonlinear forms of writing, or "rhizome-like" textual structures such as hypertexts. Her literary and artistic projects are influenced both by avant-garde traditions of collage and spatial simultaneity and the ubiquitous presence of electronic media in the global society. For instance, Gache emphasizes how the notion of linear writing has been challenged by electronic formats that encourage, for instance, different levels of interaction between reader and text, such as those present in a computer screen.[1] Written at the turn of the twenty-first century, when the market deregulation and privatization impacted every cultural field in Argentina, Gache's works reflect the weakening of a previously robust print culture in the new primacy of image-centered products (Hortiguera and Rocha 2007, 25).[2] They also evidence the influence of global imaginations of place in the literature of Argentina, a common trend in literary and artistic productions of the period.[3] Thus, her definition of nomadism as a tool that destabilizes literary systems is linked to the technological transformations of globalization and foregrounds contemporary spatial displacements and rearrangements as literary geographies are being reorganized by transnational encounters. As Walter Mignolo states in "Linguistic Maps, Literary Geographies, and Cultural Landscapes: Languages, Languaging, and (Trans)nationalism," the attachment of languages and territories is placed into question in the changing linguistic and literary cartographies of the turn of the twenty-first century (1999, 65). Along these lines, "nomadic writing" expresses how constructions of territoriality are destabilized under the influence of transnational dialogues and the disruption of global designs that pertain to the formations of writing and territory.

The second half of this essay will analyze the installation Gache presented at the biennial, *Diario de la Luna Caníbal* [*Diary of the Cannibal Moon*]. Located in the Old Prison of Tierra del Fuego, this work exhibits a critical revision of the construction of the southern frontier of Argentina. Gache planned the installation so that the spectator could walk through different cells and corridors of the prison as she or he listened to a recording of a diary by a fictional inmate, a Spanish immigrant from Gibraltar stranded in Argentina and imprisoned for political reasons (see figure 3.1). Located at the "ends of the

Figure 3.1 Usuhaia Prison (hallways) where the installation took place

world," at the last continental frontier, *Diary of the Cannibal Moon* questions the creation of national borderlands, as well as the building of a territorial identity for Argentina.

In her works, Gache describes spaces and territories as textual and artistic constructions; she examines how they are crafted as arbitrary representations and how, as cultural constructions, they determine narratives of identity as well as literary patterns that are based upon the identification of language, literature, and nation. Her overall artistic project is mainly an aesthetic examination of how literary and artistic systems build spatial relations. However, the installation in Tierra del Fuego deals with political implications of space and, in the context of the global changes analyzed by the biennial, *Diary of the Cannibal Moon* constitutes a critique of asymmetrical relations of power that are embedded in local and global spatialities.[4] Thus, this essay utilizes a methodology that borrows from transnational feminisms notions of how subjectivities are built through spatial relations and how narratives, in this case those that pertain to the formation of both a national and global identity, are "meaning-making practices with their own logic and cultural specificity." Moreover, spatial relations bring to fore the construction of stories that are "social practices...regulated by the institutions that produce, legitimate, and distribute knowledge" (Stone-Mediatore 2003, 132). Transnational feminisms interrogate the ways in which transnational structures determine cultural exchanges and how gender, class, or race are determined by spatial networks that, in our contemporary world, are scattered, thus rendering insufficient the notions of center and periphery to explain how transnational power relationships are established. In Inderpal Grewal and Karen Caplan's words, "hegemonies are scattered" at a time when we can think of "multiple peripheries" built around transnational networks (1994, 20). In particular, transnational feminisms' analyses have been sensitive to the processes of nation-state building and how they reveal intersections of modernity and coloniality (Grewal and Kaplan 1994, 22). Therefore, several issues brought up by transnational feminisms are relevant to the analysis conducted here. First, the determination of fluid relationships of power within transnational networks; the formation of the nation as a territorial process that brings to fore the complexities of modernity; and finally, the construction of space as a narration of histories of national and global communities. I will focus here on how the notion of "nomadic writing" is instrumental in understanding all of these and, in particular, how the building of Patagonia as a symbolic space in the history of Argentina offers a productive example about spatial formations or spatiality as a territorial and textual identity.

Hypertexts and Transnational Networks: Intersections of Media and Literature

In Gache's works, the notion of nomadism refers first to a textual format that, following the influence of electronic media, invites interactive, fluid, and decentering ways of reading. Her interest in the intersections of media and literature is evident in her writing of digital and video poetry, as well as in the blogs and essays she maintains in her website "The Ends of the World" (www.findelmundo.com.ar/belengache). For instance, the format of "Word Toys," one of the works that can be accessed through this website, resembles that of a book that can be read by clicking on different screens, as if the reader were moving through the actual book pages. "Word Toys" destabilizes the notion of linear reading as evidenced by the chapter entitled "Mariposas-libro." Resembling an insect inventory, "Butterflies-book" displays a digital collection of "dissected words," or literary quotations that are visualized as butterflies that need to be clicked in order to access different texts. As in Cortazar's *Hopscotch*, the reader builds a network of virtual connections in the text, this time aided by the visual supports of the Internet. In "Word Toys," Gache explores the notion of reading as an unpredictable, discontinuous, or nomadic operation led by the reader, and in "Butterflies-book" she defines linear writing as an operation of collecting frozen interpretations: "Writing stops, crystallizes, and in a way it kills writing in order to keep its corpse. An ethereal corpse such as a butterfly's that has been dissected" (www.findelmundo.com.ar/wordtoys/index.htm, 2008).

In *Nomadic Writings. From the Lost Book to the Hypertext*, Gache further defines the impact that electronic supports and formats such as hypertexts have in writing. Hypertexts have been linked to critical theories on reading and writing, such as the decentering proposed by deconstructionism or Deleuze and Guattari's rhizomes. According to George Landow, "all hypertext systems permit the individual reader to choose his or her own center of investigation and experience...[which means] that the reader is not locked into any kind of particular organization or hierarchy" (2006, 58). In the history of hypertexts included in *Nomadic Writings*, Gache establishes its antecedents in the phonic games of futuristic poetry—concrete poetry examples such as the "poesia letrista" by Isou in the 1940s, or the cultivation of the "nonsense" of English writers such as Lewis Carroll in the nineteenth century. Her analysis focuses on how those aesthetic trends deconstructed logical supports of linguistic expression. An important section of *Nomadic Writings* is devoted to the analysis of space as a key component in nonlinear forms of writing: "opposed to the linear traditional literary model, we can track a nomadic model that deconstructs the notion of single plot, and allows for perspectives of multiple readings. The different possible paths (of interpretation), the junctions, the enclosures, and the textual labyrinths of this model appear as the metaphor of the possible ways of walking through a city that are associated with the (informal) stroll and the wandering" (77). Such nomadic models became more systematic, beginning in 1897 with Mallarmé's *Coup de dés*, and the avant-gardes of the early twentieth century fully place them at the center of the literary scene. Different spatial structures support the characteristics of interactivity, randomness, synchronization, and spatiality that are central to nomadic texts. In *Nomadic Writings*, Gache analyzes different genres and textual examples where spatial nomadic representations are central. Maps used in fictional accounts, travel narratives, encyclopedias, or collages are all examples of a nomadic format employed in literature or art.

In her preface, Gache states that electronic media transforms literary culture by uniting different semiotic systems such as the linguistic, the visual, and the phonic, and by challenging the principles of linearity and spatial order that characterize writing. By subverting conventional writing formats, this nonlinear or "nomadic writing" also questions sacred notions such as truth or authority coined by certain dominant cultures (19). *The Book of the Ends of the World* constitutes a good example: a text that can be downloaded as a PDF and that includes a direct link to a CD and a website where many visual texts can be accessed, it further explores the format of hypertexts or nomadic writings. *The Book of the Ends of the World* possesses the traits of an electronic encyclopedia. According to Gache, encyclopedias are excellent examples of nomadic writing because they are based on a "collage of citations that remit to one another without following a logic and linear model; they do not possess a precise beginning nor an end, and they allow for multiple reading entries, determined by the reader's intentions. Further, an encyclopedia is a map that traces symbolic cartographies" (99). A text characterized by the heterogeneity of "object books,"[5] *The Book of the Ends of the*

World continues the tradition that Gache associates with texts such as *La vuelta al día en ochenta mundos* [*Around the Day in Eighty Worlds*] and *Último round* [*Last Round*] by Cortázar, texts that combine articles, essays, poems, stories, photographs, and drawings and whose fragmentary structure points to the absurd condition of human existence (Gache, 108).

Gache's nomadic aesthetic has evident connections with the tradition of the avant-gardes of the early twentieth century. However, I would like to focus on her discussion of how hypertexts reorganize the creative space of the page, since I believe nomadism and hypertexts are linked to the cultural decentering project proposed in Gache's works. As in her installation, *Diary of the Cannibal Moon*, her multimedia works deconstruct spatial organizations by working with the idea of simultaneity, by challenging spatial perspectives, or by exploring what Deleuze and Guattari have described as "rhizome-like structures."[6] As Deleuze and Guattari had argued, rhizomelike structures involve the notion of nomadic thought, which rejects "the word and the world fully mapped as logos" (Michael Joyce, 207, quoted in Landow 2006, 61). The spatial structure of the rhizome is central in hypertexts where "there is no linear configuration, nor an ending or a beginning, but contingent paths of reading...Different screens can be traveled through, from one point of the text to another, or to other texts, in an infinite displacement" (*Nomadic Writings*, 78). As the nomad, the reader of hypertexts is invited to explore surfaces and spatial configurations that challenge notions of fixed spatialities and systems of thought linked to them.

Nomadic writings that establish intertextual connections as described by Gache are linked to a certain kind of spatiality that Gache describes as "free and swarming with possibilities, [a space that] is traversed by deviations and intersections. Spatial formations function as structural models from which narration forms. Maps (of a city, a house, a railroad system, etcetera) give form to textual constellations and make possible a topographic reading of the texts" (78). Flexible or hypertextual spaces contest the fixity and the hierarchical disposition of space embedded in the notion of territory. As in Cortázar's short story, "La continuidad de los parques," where the "real" and the "fictional" parks are interconnected by the exercise of reading, the pieces in *The Book of the Ends of the World* point to a similar spatial volatility. For instance, the story that gives the title to the collection, "El libro del fin del mundo," narrates the creation of imaginary empires. "El libro del fin del mundo" tells the story of an emperor called Roberto "the Inopportune," who creates a new language and imposes it on his entire empire composed of "hundreds of provinces, principalities, and kingdoms" where 200 languages were spoken and 100 different alphabets existed (11). Along with the new linguistic identity, Roberto creates territorial demarcations by building a wall that surrounds its empire and defines its limits. He burns all existing books and creates a unique book, the "book of the truth," that contains the "true name of all things" (11). The story goes on by telling how later emperors, such as Ulrico "the Consistent," undid Roberto's changes and built a "Book of the ends of the world," which they composed by assembling the fragments of the books burnt by Roberto that were found after traveling through "monotonous plains and steep mountains, desolated beaches and inhospitable deserts" (11). "El libro del fin del mundo" thus represents a hypertext and an unbounded territory, a post-imperial geography where utopian worlds could exist. This story also makes evident how the interrogation of territoriality is embedded into a questioning of the culture of books. And Gache deconstructs space in order to alter conceptions of literary authorship and readership, as well as the role of writing within literary culture. Roberto and Ulrico are two examples of authorship; the despotic Roberto functions as the author who, unsuccessfully, seeks to condense all possible meanings into one, the "true," while Ulrico builds a book of infinite possibilities, a collage made of the little fragments of Roberto's authoritarian endeavors. Just like the story "The Book of the Ends of the World," *Diary of the Cannibal Moon* further describes the construction of power relationships in writing. Located in Tierra del Fuego, at the "ends of the world," and in the context of the biennial described earlier, this installation interrogates how spatialities are built as textual and territorial constructions. Moreover, it establishes a rich dialogue with the history of Patagonia and the construction of the Argentinean southern frontier, as examined in the following section.

The Shapes of Territories: Writing the National Borders

In *An Expedition to the Ranquel Indians*, Lucio V. Mansilla recounts with fascination the experience of living in the southern Argentinean frontier in the 1870s while commissioned to complete a topographical description of the region and the study of the customs and traditions of its inhabitants. His labors paved the way for civilizing missions to come, with a precise geographical characterization that ultimately prepared the Argentinean government for the military expedition that, a decade later, would complete the extermination of the indigenous population of Argentina under the tenet of "Gobernar es poblar," proposed by Juan Bautista Alberdi, the political theorist and a writer of the Generation of 1837 whose essay "Bases and Starting Points for the Political Organization of the Argentine Republic" influenced the drafting of the Argentine Constitution of 1853. The creation of the modern state required a demographic cleansing of massive proportions that eventually would favor the colonization of the south by the hundreds of thousands of European immigrants arriving at the Port of Buenos Aires. In 1879 the territorial landscape that Mansilla had documented a decade earlier was completed with the creation of the government of Patagonia. Mansilla's book clearly draws a nation in the making: "I have completed the draft of a topographic sketch of this vast and deserted territory that invites labor, and I shall publish it very soon, along with a memory that will be offered to the rural industry" (1964, 14).[7] Along with a detailed description of what constitutes the last frontier of Argentina, Mansilla composed a model for government based on the dramatic transformation of an infertile landscape converted into agricultural land and the population of the vast regions located to the south of the country.

Concerned with the creation of a modern nation-state, Mansilla's work reflects much of Argentinean concerns with territoriality in the period from 1870 to 1910. In particular, the region of Patagonia offered a peculiar set of challenges to the literary and political elites of the country during the nineteenth century in their aims of configuring a territorial identity for Argentina. Since its earliest representations in the global imagination, Patagonia has been depicted as the outer limit of a global order and, as Gabriela Nouzeilles reminds us, this perception of Patagonia as a deserted land challenged the "spatial production of the State as a territorial entity" (1999, 36). The nation-state sought to "re-invent" Patagonia with two central images: as an untapped resource yet to be fully exploited, the promised land described by Mansilla, and as an unbridled terrain well suited to the embodiment of an incipient nationalism (37). A vast body of scientific and literary works witnesses the different historic moments of appropriation and renegotiation of this complex body of representations, such as those by Estanislao Zeballos or Francisco Moreno. Beginning in the 1930s, the opening of Patagonia to national and international tourism transformed its landscape into an object of mass consumption (Nouzeilles 1999, 43).

During the twentieth century both images of Patagonia remained as powerful representations in the national consciousness. In *Final de Novela en Patagonia* [*Ending of a Novel in Patagonia*] (2001), Mempo Giardinelli depicts Patagonia as a place that shapes the novelistic imagination, thus providing at the beginning of the twenty-first century the ultimate challenge to geographic and literary cartographies. In truth, textual Patagonia has historically been an inspiration to many: Darwin's references in *The Voyage of the Beagle*, Herman Melville's images of Cape Horn in works such as "Benito Cereno," Bruce Chatwin's *In Patagonia* (1975), Roberto Arlt's journal chronicles of the 1930s published in *El mundo*, and films such as *El viaje* [*The Journey*] by Pino Solanas (1990) or *Mundo grúa* [*Crane World*] by Pablo Trapero (1999). Thus, cultural representations of Patagonia develop from complex sets of rhetorical images that Ernesto Livron-Grosman calls "bricolages," as they take the form of narrative collages (2003, 11). As a mythical land, a territorial frontier, a global borderland, or a natural refuge in the light of global collapse, Patagonia's territorial images make evident the conflation of writing and geographic space or, in other words, the construction of territories as textual and cultural productions. At the turn of the twenty-first century and under the influences of neoliberalism and globalization, the depiction of Patagonia as a borderland connecting national and global imaginations of place is particularly relevant as the First Biennial of the Ends of the World demonstrates.

The location of *Diary of the Cannibal Moon* in the Old Prison of Tierra del Fuego is highly relevant. The installation connects two spatial narratives of Patagonia. In the context of the biennial, it brings to fore the image of Patagonia as a media-produced geography exhibited for the consumption of an "imagined global community." As such, the installation foregrounds a questionable relationship with the twenty-first-century global tourist that signals the determining influence of neoliberalism and globalization in Argentinean national identity and, as Hortiguera and Rocha have studied, the impact those forces had in literary culture. In the context of the Argentinean, we could also state *Diary of the Cannibal Moon* establishes a restructuring of what Roger Bartra calls the "cultural territory" that depicts power relations among different cultural classes (2003, 116) as well as dialogues with the rich corpus of literature that used Patagonia as a source of inspiration. As Bartra demonstrates, territorial configurations are directly linked to cultural maps that regulate literary production (116). As evident in the example of Patagonia and its role in the national imagination of Argentina, territorial fluctuations and changes frequently overlap with reconfigurations of literary and artistic notions and the power cultural elites have in shaping a national identity that is both spatial and linguistic.[8]

Diary of the Cannibal Moon explores, however, a second narrative of how Patagonia has been key in configuring territorial identities. This second narrative contests the image of Patagonia as a natural refuge or a promised land and proposes a darker depiction of the area that refers to state repression, such as ethnic cleansing campaigns, led by President Roca in the 1870s.[9] The video that accompanies the installation makes clear this sharp contrast: the colossal beauty of Tierra del Fuego, its open bays and its coasts, the clean presence of its blue skies, set against the oppressive interiors of the penitentiary. The video focuses mainly on the prison's installations; walls, corridors, and windows are transformed artistically by shots that place the spectator in the position of the protagonist's isolation and let us contemplate a sky and a promise of freedom that will never be reached (see figure 3.2).

Figure 3.2 *Diary of the Cannibal Moon* (video still). Usuhaia Prison (exterior). Behind, the Cinco Hermanos mountains

The exterior and interior views are dissected by complex structures of grids and other geometric forms, such as doors, windows, and columns, and aesthetically represent the prisoner's confinement (see figure 3.3). Opposed to what critics of globalization have referred to as the "metaphor of unidirectional flux" (García Canclini 2008, 54) and the fantasies of an unrestricted mobility of first-class global citizens, the suffocation of the prison's interiors renders visible the hidden constraints of spatial practices in the age of globalization. Moreover, the prison functions as a metaphor of the national frontier as a repressive spatiality. As one of the curators for the biennial, Ibis Hernandez reminds us that installations such as Gache's that took place in the prison "send us to experience the psychological time where the present exists only as a memory of the past or as a transit toward a future freedom. Some works staged there refer not so much to physical confinement, but to the temporal experience of being entrapped by invisible walls such as [the ones represented by] the obsession with fashion, the consumerist attitude, the hounding of the media, the restrictions imposed by false beliefs..." (http://bienalfindelmundo.org.ar/site/edicion_07, 2008).

Figure 3.3 *Diary of the Cannibal Moon* (video still). Photograph taken from inside a prison's cell

In *Diary of the Cannibal Moon*, Gache explores such notions of temporal and physical confinement by depicting the prison's interior space as Patagonia's dark side. Thus, Gache's interior and exterior landscapes stress processes of cultural exchange and visual appropriation, as they implicate previous representations of the area. As such, the landscapes depicted in *Diary of the Cannibal Moon* are a "dynamic medium" that interweaves a "vast network of cultural codes" (Mitchell 1994, 9). As spectators, we can appreciate the visual construction of Ushuaia as a site where different cultural codes crash, as repressive perceptions of space supersede the exterior "openness" of the natural world. Such interpretation is further sustained by the journal that accompanies the video, which tells a compelling narrative of the ways in which Patagonia, as the last frontier, has been a violent site of repression. In Gache's previous works, the moon was an icon of futurist imagery (*Electric Moons for Moonless Nights*) or a reference of textual and visual compositions that follow a collagelike structure (*Indian Moon*). Here, the moon is a narrative agent and a cultural reference that points to social and cultural constraints embedded in spatial structures.

The title of the installation comes from a Selk'nam myth that describes a lunar eclipse when the cannibal moon will turn red "with the blood of men who will be doomed in a coming battle" (www.findelmundo.com.ar/lunacanibal, 2008). The text for the installation, organized around twenty-one journal entries that correspond to different moon cycles, reflects the progressive deterioration of the protagonist. The reference to the myth comes from a text by Anne Chapman that describes the importance of matriarchy in the mythical ceremony of initiation: the Hain, in Selk'nam society. According to the myth, women, led by Moon (Kreeh), held the Hain ceremony and guaranteed the ruling of women, or the matriarchal system, for centuries. Men feared women because of the supernatural powers they supposedly displayed while the Hain was taking place and were forced to all sorts of servile tasks, assuring the subsistence of women and other members of the group. According to different accounts by Chapman and Martin Gusinde, men eventually found out women's lies and murdered the moon and the rest of the women. A patriarchal system, where men conducted the Hain, was established and women were forbidden from participating in the ceremony (Chapman 1982, 66–77).

The journal reenacts this myth and its references to women as cannibals. Gache employs a series of aesthetic images to represent the matriarchal order of the moon as a phantasmal or empty space where the inmate sees his delusional fantasies reflected. White imagery predominates in the descriptions of the moon as a shining mirror, as a snowy presence, or a blinding light that confuses the sense of space and time and that progressively reflects the protagonist losing his mind. Contrasted with the history of Patagonia and the recurrent efforts to delimit and mark the national space, the representation of an ambiguous or empty spatiality, described in the journal as feminine, is quite pertinent. Feminist readings about the construction of women as an empty spatiality are relevant here. The image of the mirror has been analyzed, for instance, from a psychoanalytical perspective by Kaja Silverman, who reflects on the impact of the mirror-stage in male and female formations of subjectivity. In her study on psychoanalysis and cinema, Silverman explores how women have been characterized as men's reflections and how "woman has been made the repository not only of lack but specularity" (1988, 26). Along these lines, Gillian Rose has made evident how geography represents women as an empty space where a holistic sense of self can be recreated, a "topophilia," an original place that could be equated with the idea of the mother (1993, 85). In other instances, women have been depicted as the empty nature in landscapes, a passive subject that can be observed, possessed, and represented by men (Rose, 95). Gache employs similar visual constructs when she describes the moon as a phantasmagoric presence that eventually takes over the prison and the consciousness of the inmate. The moon is a mirror that creates fantastic duplications of the prison cell. "In other times, they thought the moon was a mirror. If this were to be true, there would be another prison and, in it, another inmate like myself. Sometimes, I think I am the one who is in the moon and, there on earth, there is an inmate who resembles me," (www.findelmundo.com.ar/lunacanibal, 2008). The moon dematerializes space; its shiny light invades the cell to the point that the constraining interior becomes a site of delusion and madness. The presence of the moon is also compared to the empty space of the page that the inmate seeks to cover with "black ink": "During my sleepless nights, I write hiding from the moon. She should not find out (about my writing). She wants white, silver, brilliant papers. The moon always writes using white ink. I cover the paper with the shadow of my black letters." At the end, his precarious writing is interrupted by intense migraines and the demonic presence of the moon: "At night, when everybody else is asleep, I write on the walls of my cell in the dark. I write truths and I denounce injustices; I accuse traitors and reveal secrets. In the morning, when I try to read my texts, I find the wall covered with senseless scratching." (www.findelmundo.com.ar/lunacanibal, 2008) (see figure 3.4).

Global Patagonia 91

Figure 3.4 *Diary of the Cannibal Moon*. Promotional image for the installation

The fragility of the prisoner's writing as described here invites several reflections. Gache establishes a dialogue with the Patagonian imagery of travel journals or navigation diaries that proposed writing in the borders of empires or national frontiers as transitional passages of self-definition, although the diary represents a progressive dissolution of the exile's subjectivity, as the fantastic ending makes evident. Located at the "ends of the world," this fantastic drive can be interpreted as a consequence of the cultural contrasts and perceptions the protagonist experiences, but read from the feminist frame proposed by Silverman and Rose, the "failing" to write and the progressive loss of reason can be directly linked to the impossibility of symbolization. In other words, the moon is the empty space that needs to be demarcated and symbolized in the process of identity creation; however, such attempt fails along with the protagonist's disappearance. The maddening effects of the moon are, therefore, consequences of the life on the border and, in this way, *Diary of the Cannibal Moon* establishes a dialogue with previous narrative accounts that have shaped the imagery of Tierra del Fuego as a site that disrupts cultural and epistemological codes. Thus, Gache's installation plays with a double image of Patagonia that is both spectacular, a touristic construction for the global eyes, and spectral, for it brings to fore the failed narratives of identity and space that historically have tried to accomplish the writing, for instance, of national borders. On another level, the reference to the Selk'nam myth foregrounds the histories of repression and genocide and makes evident the role of memory in the territorial identity of Argentina, for it reworks many of the imperial fantasies that, through the discourses of nation building or tourism, sought to "mercantilize" the experiences of a natural world (Nouzeille 2005, 258). In particular, *Diary of the Cannibal Moon* is a counternarrative that interrupts the historical association between Patagonia and utopian dreams of modernization, for it is memory that allows for the redefinition of such foundational discourses that, as in Mansilla, sought to define a territorial identity for Argentina. Thus, *Diary of the Cannibal Moon* is an example of a process of deterritorialization that questions the building of territories both as spatial and symbolic practices that create narratives of identity used in processes of nation building and modernization. Read against other literary projects embodied by writers such as Diana Bellessi, Sylvia Iparraguirre or Eduardo Belgrano Rawson in Argentina, or Juan Pablo Riveros and Clemente Riedemann in Chile, who also located their literary projects in Patagonia and Tierra del Fuego, Belén Gache's *Diary of the Cannibal Moon* establishes a dialogue with those writers who also questioned the violent history of territorialization of the southern areas of Argentina and Chile.[10] The reference to the original inhabitants such as Selk'nams, Yagans, or Mapuches in all of these accounts is not accidental, for it makes evident how territories are the result of historic power struggles in the borders of national and global orders. Moreover, by stressing the importance of displaced voices in the historical building of the nation-state, a text such as Gache's establishes the need to question the construction of an imagined community and deconstructs the notion of territoriality as a discourse that enables dramatic narratives of place (Andermann 2000, 17).

Conclusion: Critical Nomadism

The history of Patagonia abounds in examples of how the construction of this national and global frontier has placed into question territorial identities. In a similar vein, *Diary of the Cannibal Moon* makes a political gesture that invites the reader/spectator to reflect on the connections between spatiality and power. Global and local narratives of Patagonia as the "Promised Land" or an ideal tourist destination take on a completely different shape in *Diary of the Cannibal Moon*. In the context of the First Biennial of the Ends of the World, this installation renders visible ways in which processes of territorialization that circulate as local and global narratives can be critically revised. As such, it relates to Gache's ideas on nomadic writing as a destabilization of spatial hierarchies and, as evidenced by the moon's final takeover, as the deconstruction of the associations between writing and space. If the history of Argentina entails the building of a national territory that parallels the establishment of local literary traditions, we can link *Diary of the Cannibal Moon* to Gache's project of nomadic writing as a way to revise literary conventions of reading and writing. Thus, in Gache's works, nomadism refers not only to literary configurations, but also to what Gillian Rose denominates the construction of paradoxical spaces that contest the "territorialities of masculinism," that is, a "multidimensional, shifting and contingent" entity that challenges organizational dimensions such as center and margin (140).

Through a creative use of technology and its intersections with literary notions of modern creativity, Gache rewrites spatial narratives of Argentina. *Nomadic Writings. From the Lost Book to the Hypertext*, *The Book of the Ends of the World* and *Diary of the Cannibal Moon* offer examples of the "technological countercultures" that Constance Penley and Andrew Ross define as ways of rereading and reinterpreting the powerful influences and control exerted by what they call "Western technoculture" (xi). As stated by Penley and Ross, "cultural technologies are far from neutral and that they are the result of social processes and power relations" (Penley and Ross, xii). In the examples analyzed here, Gache explores the powerful possibilities of a technological culture that can reinvent notions of space both as a social and literary construct. Within the context of the First Biennial of the Ends of the World, the use of technology in Gache's works is also relevant, as it helps us to rethink about the complex intersections of nature and technology and the role cultural producers bear in this difficult dialogue taking place at the beginning of the twenty-first century.

Transnational feminisms have also questioned the limitations of territoriality and power by establishing what Chandra Mohanty calls "feminism without borders" (2003, 3). Built within and around transnational hegemonies, such transnational feminism challenges colonization and capitalism, and questions "the globalized economic, ideological, and cultural interweaving of masculinities, femininities, and heterosexualities in capital's search for profit, accumulation and domination" (9). Gache's nomadic writing establishes an implicit dialogue with this project, as nomadism can be understood as a feminist interpretative tool that enables a feminist decentering of the negative effects of globalization (Braidotti 1994, 22). In the case of Latin America, for instance, a nomadic memory questions, during the 1990s, the association of body and territory and contests the overarching presence of neoliberalism. Hence, for Ana Forcinito, women writers in Latin America practice a "nomadic memory," an interpretative tool that seeks to deconstruct territorial forms of patriarchy and authoritarianism (2004, 20). Such critical nomadism is key in Gache's literary project as evidenced by *Diary of the Cannibal Moon*.

To conclude, global imaginations of place play a central role in the works of Belén Gache as they reshape nationalist topographies such as the frontier or the national territory. Gache reworks the Patagonian landscape as a place of national and global connections, an opportunity to redefine territoriality, and a liminal space or borderland that includes previously marginalized voices in the shaping of a spatial memory for the country. In the context of her literary and artistic project of nomadism, Gache challenges certain narratives and metaphors of globalization and proposes alternative forms of authority, as they question the concept of territory as a historic legacy of authoritarianism and repression. By connecting the tradition of the avant-garde and linking it to creative uses of media and hypertexts, Gache blends in nomadism and memory and constructs borderland topographies that foreground the relationships space maintains with gender, class, race, and nation. As her new cartographies rewrite traditional supports of writing through the use of hypertexts and electronic media, Gache's works develop strategies for decentering the connections between writing and territorialism, both understood as key strategies in the composition of cultural maps of struggle and domination.

Notes

1. The notion of the hypertext is relevant here, a format that many believe is a direct consequence of the technological inventions of the twentieth century. Theodor Nelson coined the term that refers to nonsequential writing and the fusing of different semiotic systems that include words, images, and sounds. As in his project Xanadu, the hypertext includes a branching of texts and innovative organizations of materials, which allows the

reader to go through interactive screens, as in some of the multimedia works crafted by Gache.
2. According to Hugo Hortiguera and Carolina Rocha, the years between 1989 and 2001 represent the rise and fall of neoliberalism in Argentina. This is the period when President Carlos Menem deregulated the Argentinean economy and privatized the country's major assets and primary services, such as transportation, gas, and telecommunications. In 1995, after Menem's reelection, neoliberalism became consolidated as the predominant economic and social force in the country. Toward 1999, when Fernando de la Rúa was elected to the presidency, the neoliberal model was collapsing when thirteen million Argentineans were living under conditions of poverty. In 2001, the signs of the crisis became acute and the socioeconomic situation of the country deteriorated. Because of the social and financial meltdown, de la Rúa was forced to resign and the country sank into an institutional crisis; five interim presidents were named in a short time span of only a couple of months. The social legacies of this turbulent period in Argentina were the disintegration of social relations as well as the deregulation and privatization of culture (Hortiguera and Rocha 8). The market became a central force in regulating cultural productions. As Hortiguera and Rocha explain, "every cultural field—narrative, music, film—was influenced by the prioritization of market forces and rules" (9).
3. As studied by Francine Masiello, an important oriental trend in the literature of the period reflects global exchanges in Argentina as evidenced by novels such as *El Cangrejo* (1995) by Graciela Safranchik or *La perla del Emperador* (1990) by Daniel Guebel. See, in particular, the chapter "Bodies in Transit: On Travel, Translation, and Sexuality," *The Art of Transition*, 141–73.
4. I employ here the term "spatialities" instead of "space" intentionally. In Edward Soja's words, it is necessary to make a "space per se, space as a contextual given, and socially based spatiality, the created space of social organization and production" (2003, 79). As analyzed here, Gache's works explore the construction of such spatialities as territorial and textual entities.
5. The "object book" has acquired a tremendous importance in Spain and Latin America in recent years. Chilean writer Pia Barros is a strong believer in the format. She states that object books remove the notion of "sacred" text and reject massive commercialization since they are published in small numbers; they resemble a craft and establish a more personal and intimate relationship with the reader. Pia Barros preferred the format as it sheltered her literary creations during the dark years of the Pinochet regime (personal interview, June 3, 2007).
6. An additional element of the rhizome has to do with the notion of deterritorialization: "The rhizome is made only of lines: lines of segmentarity and stratification as its dimensions, and the line of flight or deterritorialization...The rhizome is an antigenealogy. It is a short-term memory, or antimemory" (Deleuze and Guattari 1998, 21).

7. All translations, unless otherwise noted, are mine.
8. In his study on "mapping" and "literary culture" in Argentina, Jens Andermann explains how the territorial configuration of Argentina is directly linked to a literary project. He states the need to conduct a "literary archaeology" that uncovers the "maps of power" that have shaped the literary and territorial imagination of Argentina. See his introductory chapter to *Mapas de poder. Una arqueología literaria del espacio argentino.*
9. Julio Argentino Roca directed the military campaign "Conquest of the Desert," beginning in 1873. The campaign was a genocide by which the Argentinean government exterminated indigenous tribes and established the southern frontier. It was completed around 1884.
10. I am referring here to the texts by Diana Bellessi, *Sur* (1998); Eduardo Belgrano Rawson, *Fuegia* (1991); Sylvia Iparraguirre, *La tierra del fuego* (1998); Clemente Riedemann, *Karra Maw'n* (1984); and Juan Pablo Riveros, *De la tierra sin fuegos* (1996), which all address the process of colonization of the southern areas of Argentina and Chile. From the perspective of the narrative or poetic discourse, these authors address how original populations such as the Selk'nam, Yagans, or Mapuche were exterminated at the turn of the nineteenth century. They address the issue of colonization as both a process of territorial displacement as well as a violent cultural and linguistic conflict.

Works Cited

Andermann, Jens. 2000. *Mapas de poder. Una arqueología literaria del espacio argentino.* Rosario, Argentina: Beatriz Viterbo Editora.
Barros, Pia. 2007. Personal interview, June 3.
Bartra, Roger. 2003. "Allegories of Creativity and Territory." Trans. Dierdra Reber. *PMLA* 118(1):114–19.
Braidotti, Rosi. 1994. "Introduction: By Way of Nomadism." *Nomadic Subjects. Embodiment and Sexual Difference in Contemporary Feminist Theory.* New York: Columbia University Press. 1–39.
Chapman, Anne. 1982. *Drama and Power in a Hunting Society: The Selk'nam of Tierra del Fuego.* Cambridge, MA: Cambridge University Press.
Deleuze, Giles and Guattari, Felix. 1998. "Introduction: Rhizome." *A Thousand Plateaus. Capitalism and Schizophrenia.* Trans. and foreword by Brian Massumi. 7th ed. Minneapolis: University of Minnesota Press.
Forcinito, Ana. 2004. *Memorias y Nomadías: géneros y cuerpos en los márgenes del posfeminismo.* Chile: Editorial Cuarto Propio.
Gache, Belén. *Diario de la luna caníbal.* www.findelmundo.com.ar/lunacanibal/index.html. Last accessed Sept. 2008
———. *El libro del fin del mundo.* Last accessed Sept. 2008
———. *Word Toys.* http://www.findelmundo.com.ar/belengache/index.html#ficcion. Last accessed Sept. 2008

———. 1994. *Luna india.* Buenos Aires: Planeta.
———. 2004. *Noches eléctricas para una noche sin luna.* Buenos Aires: Editorial Sudamericana.
———. 2006. *Escrituras nómadas. Del libro perdido al hipertexto.* Gijón, España: Ediciones Trea.
García Canclini, Néstor. 2008. "La globalización: objeto cultural no identificado." *La globalizacion imaginada.* Buenos Aires: Paidos. 4th ed. 45–65.
Giardinelli, Mempo. 2001. *Final de novela en Patagonia.* Barcelona: Biblioteca Grandes Viajeros.
Grewal, Inderpal and Caren Kaplan. 1994. *Scattered Hegemonies Postmodernity and Transnational Feminist Practices.* Minneapolis: University of Minnesota Press.
Hernandez, Ibis. 2008. www.finaldelmundo.org. BienalFindelMundo.
Hortiguera, Hugo and Carolina Rocha. 2007. "Introduction." *Argentinean Cultural Production during the Neoliberal Years (1989–2001).* Lewiston, Australia: Edwin Mellen Press. 1–20.
Landow, George P. 2006, "Hypertext and Critical Theory." *Hypertext 3.0. Critical Theory and New Media in an Era of Globalization.* Baltimore: Johns Hopkins University Press. 53–68.
Livron-Grossman, Ernesto. 2003. "La literatura de viaje: género, naturaleza y nación." *Geografías imaginarias. El relato de viaje y la construcción del espacio patagónico.* Rosario, Argentina: Beatriz Viterbo editora.
Mansilla, Lucio V. 1964. *Una excursión a los indios ranqueles.* Buenos Aires: Peuser.
Mignolo, Walter. 1999. "Linguistic Maps, Literary Geographies, and Cultural Landscapes." *The Places of History. Regionalism Revisited in Latin America.* Durham, NC: Duke University Press. 49–65.
Mitchell, W. J. T. 1994. *Landscape and Power.* Chicago: University of Chicago Press.
Mohanty, Chandra Talpade. 2003. *Feminism without Borders. Decolonizing Theory, Practicing Solidarity.* Durham, NC: Duke University Press.
Nouzeilles, Gabriela.1999. "Patagonia as Borderland: Nature, Culture, and the Idea of the State." *Journal of Latin American Cultural Studies* 8(1): 35–48.
Penley, Constance, and Andrew Ross. 1991. "Introduction." *Technoculture.* Cultural Politics, vol. 3. Minneapolis: University of Minnesota Press. viii–xvii.
Rose, Gillian. 1993. *Feminism and Geography. The Limits of Geographical Knowledge.* Minneapolis: University of Minnesota Press.
Silverman, Kaja. 1988. *The Acoustic Mirror. The Female Voice in Psychoanalysis and Cinema.* Bloomington and Indianapolis: Indiana University Press.
Soja, Edward W. 2003. *Postmodern Geographies. The Reassertion of Space in Critical Social Theory.* 8th ed. London: Verso.
Stone-Mediatore, Shari. 2003. "Storytelling and Global Politics." *Reading across Borders. Storytelling and Knowledges of Resistance.* New York: Palgrave Macmillan. 125–59.

Chapter Four

Family Imaginaries and Postmemory in Chilean Narrative: Andrea Jeftanovic's Escenario de guerra *and Lina Meruane's* Cercada

Bernardita Llanos

The need to give meaning to a traumatic historical and personal experience has been an ongoing theme in the literature produced in Chile in the past thirty years. The brutal force and stark violence experienced by Chileans during the Pinochet dictatorship (1973–89) has left an intractable trauma in Chilean society and its imaginary that is expressed in literature, theater, and the visual arts with acute persistence and with different aesthetics paradigms. Contemporary narrative also shows a need to reexamine this traumatic past and the different and disputed memories it has engendered through experimental approaches that depict family relations and subjectivity. The reexamination of recent history is most often textually located in the years of the Pinochet dictatorship and the ways persecution, imprisonment, and repression by the state shaped new subjectivities and understandings of the nation and the citizen. Women's writing and feminism in the dictatorial period developed a narrative that linked gender to political and social oppression, anticipating the core themes in the collective opposition to the Pinochet regime. Feminists have been united by the common past struggle against the dictatorship and their shared memory. This memory serves as an identity marker that contrasts and highlights the progressive fragmentation of the women's movement in the present. Furthermore, the historical narrative of the struggle against gender oppression and authoritarianism provides a gender identity that resists present-day politics and the neoliberal culture of Chilean society today. The scattering of women's collective power has given way to a wide range of individual voices located in diverse cultural positions, among them literature, in which gender is shown to be a resistant position to the official consensus to forget the past. As the novels analyzed in this essay show, gender-based stands politicize the past and dispute memory from a personal and gendered experience of a traumatic past and its legacy. Many parallels may be found with a transnational context in which women's cultural resistance to global processes of political and economic transformations posits intersectionality of gender, class, sexuality, and ethnicity as sites that shape identity, reconfiguring a new subjectivity in which place and location are defined by a challenge to hegemonic narratives. Women's writing in this context is a contestatory practice that shows not only the shortcomings of globalization but also its oppressive streak and how to subvert it by creating new alternatives to thinking and imagining the world. This essay reveals those hidden or perhaps less noticeable places women occupy in their localities and transnational contexts. It analyzes how contemporary literature written by women writers in Chile shows local histories intertwined with transnational events that today are part of the fabric of contemporary citizenship and subjectivity in a global world.

This essay develops two lines of discussion: one that addresses international militarism and the impact of globalization, and a second that focuses on the local/national dimension of these transnational policies in the context of Chile during the post-dictatorship through the examination of memory and identity. The literary work of the writers I discuss questions the impact of neoliberal culture and the legacy of the military state in contemporary Chile through the representation of a conflicting memory and postmemory. I define *postmemory* here as memories about a historical event that has not been necessarily experienced by the enunciating subject.

Andreas Huyssen has argued that memory in countries such as Argentina, Chile, and South Africa is not found in the media or cyberspace and their model for a global future, but rather in the embodiment and the lived experience of subjects, families, groups, nations, and regions. These are the necessary memories to build the different local futures in a global world (2000, 39). Memory in this context is understood as a search among the remainders and fragments of the past.

The perspectives of the younger generation of writers whose parents lived during the most repressive years of Pinochet's authoritarianism sheds light on the past as well as the present by creating a new imaginary in which the family and subjectivity are central to the development of a cultural and political awareness, which provides a new way to look at the past without the inherited binary oppositions and the dictatorial order. These writings address a silenced memory through a family imaginary, as Claudia Martínez Echeverría argues, where young narrators do not accept the official story of silence or forgetfulness. On the contrary, they search in the past (their families' and their own) in order to reconstruct their identities and thus inquire about the secrets, gaps, and denials that their parents and relatives have kept (Echeverria 2005, 68–72).

Many writings published in Santiago, Chile, from the year 2000 onward show a particular interest in the early stages of psychic and physical development in which identity formation, as well as understanding, is not only in process but oftentimes in flux. These young female narrators share feelings of being totally vulnerable and out of control in a world determined by adults. The world is often depicted as a stage where each individual (especially adults) acts and performs a role that is at odds with how he or she thinks or feels. This contradiction is central to the narrator's realization that social life is like a theater, and identities are roles mostly determined by the contractual nature of relationships in an unpredictable and sometimes uncanny reality that lends itself to multiple stories and secrets.

More important, perhaps, is that the myth of childhood as a sacred stage, a period of stability, protection, and love, is shattered and depicted instead as an age of fear and extreme uncertainty as the novel, *Escenario de guerra* (2000) [*War Stage*], by Andrea Jeftanovic reveals through her girl narrator, Tamara. In the case of *Cercada* (2000) [*Besieged*], by Lina Meruane, adolescence and young adulthood are revised in a love plot where familial and sexual relationships are inextricably linked through a personal as well as a national story of secrecy, exile, and treason.[1] Both novels examine the ways a state of war creates an uncertain and arbitrary world resembling a stage or film script that shapes relations and identity while disallowing trust and social bonds. The impact of the world experienced as unpredictable and dangerous may be seen in the formative years and the process of coming to terms with the trauma that the Second World War and the dictatorship have for the next generation, as Jeftanovic's novel shows. Both Meruane's and Jeftanovic's narratives may be placed within a female narrative tradition in Chile, particularly the one that addresses issues of subjectivity and authoritarianism, that is concerned with the relationship between a gendered subject and culture. The literary works written by Diamela Eltit, Pia Barros, Guadulupe Santa Cruz, Ana María del Río, Andrea Maturana, and Nona Fernández also belong to this contestatory writing tradition in Chile.[2] Moreover, family imaginaries are also present in their texts, showing the impact of historical and personal trauma as well as oppressive political and cultural structures over female bodies and psyches.

Experimentation in the novels analyzed here serves as a way to represent postmemory as well as a feminine subjectivity torn by omissions, lies, and fragmented stories. Family relations, as well as family imaginaries, are central to the ways this young and vulnerable subjectivity develops in a world divided by the past. For this reason, the *bildungsroman* structure is used to represent the development of a female character who struggles with contradictory and violent memories. Both national and transnational memories have an impact in shaping a contemporary feminine subjectivity that has to come to terms with family and state violence.

As Steve Stern highlights, the memory question for Chileans revolves around "how to remember the origins, violence and legacy of Pinochet's rule" (2004, 1). The relevance of memory, as he adeptly explains, is linked to providing meaning to "formative life experience or rupture" and the "drama of living with a divided memory of violent state-sponsored atrocity, a condition of life all too familiar in the world of the late twentieth- and early twenty-first centuries" (2). Jeftanovic's and Meruane's novels wrestle with these questions as they are experienced subjectively and intersubjectively within familial and intimate relations. Both novels address the ways militarization, globalization, and whitewashing the past affect politically and culturally a female subject. Faced with the weariness of national discourse, the novels claim the reconstitution of identity in the act of writing about a self that searches for meaning in a fragmented and obliterated memory of the past.

Both Chilean authors address what a silenced and effaced history and its stories mean in terms of a sense of national identity, as many other artists and writers at the beginning of the twenty-first century have done in an attempt to break with the nationalist discourse of power inherited from the dictatorship while "demythifing" the sacredness of the nation and the family. Furthermore, *Escenario de guerra* and *Cercada* show an interest in the voices that have been ignored or erased because their protagonists are not male heroes of the fatherland and tell what may be considered a private or personal story.

In her essay "El rol de la cultura en Chile de la transición," [The Role of Culture in the Chile of the Transition], Jeftanovic writes of the absence of male heroes in the narratives produced in the transitional political period of the 1990s and early 2000, highlighting the turn to these unauthorized voices embodied in young or childlike narrators (2000, 3). Another writer that also presents this new voice is Diamela Eltit, particularly in her novel *Los vigilantes* (1994), published in English as *Custody of the Eyes* (2005), where the place of the mute and drooling child is essential in the narrative's disruptiveness. Interestingly, the father here is an all-powerful and absent figure who places his wife and the child's mother under surveillance and controls every one of her movements.[3] His omnipotent power is closer to a Panopticon in that it manifests in every corner of the city and the woman's consciousness. The underlying question in this post-dictatorship novel, as in *Escenario de guerra* and *Cercada*, is how to forge a real and fair recognition, not only of the crimes, but of the standing debts after the traumatic and terrifying experience of the dictatorship.

In this way the years of the political transition to democracy (1990–2000) in which the novels were published are the background of the personal and political dispute about remembrance and what stories to remember or forget. As Stern notes, memory is "the meaning we attach to experience, not simply recall of the events and emotions of that experience" (105). Thus, what is important is the framework used to provide meaning to the specific events and contents that took place in Chile's recent past and manifest in what Stern calls "memory camps." These myriad memories cut across generational, political, social, and personal experiences, forming a web of narratives that have not crystallized into a hegemonic memory of the past (Stern 102–03). In addition to the cultural and political disputes of political opposing views, the role of the Concertación[4] in the transitional years was, as Tomás Moulian has argued in *Chile Actual. Anatomía de un mito* (1997) [*Present Chile. Anatomy of a myth*] mostly to whitewash the past and create a politics of consensus where no real changes would take place. The free-market economy remained untouched and unquestioned with the coming of democracy that provided political rights to Chilean citizens and a series of political mechanisms in order to reconcile the country.[5] The notion of the capitalist model as the only foreseeable road became an unquestioned truth in a neoliberal culture in which consumption and money were the only defining identity values.

Fragmentary Memories and the Arbitrariness of the Dictatorial State

What is interesting in the literary production of the political transition is the obliqueness of the perspective in which historical and social issues are kept in the background, oftentimes indirectly alluded to.

This experimental writing opts for individual narratives and actions resembling performance acts or fragments of memories. Rather than a realist storyline or testimony, these two novels deploy theatrical strategies in which identity and memory become tied to parody and a self-reflective writing in a coming-of-age narrative. The evident disconnect between truth and justice cuts across stories in which trauma and living under dictatorial conditions leave a sense of intractable meaningless and arbitrariness. As Hernán Vidal claims, the transition, as well as the different official commissions on human rights violations, was crafted upon the separation between truth and justice, circumscribing the debate of the cultural and political implications to the delay and abandonment of justice to the symbolic realm. In this way, the implementation of justice, as Vidal argues, was substituted by the reparation to the victims and their relatives, disallowing any legal responsibility to the parties involved or responsible for the crimes committed (1997, 14–15).

In *Escenario de guerra* the narrator provides us with a story pieced together through the fragmentary memories, images, and sensations related to her body, her first menses, to watching her mother's affair. However, Tamara, the narrator, oscillates between the voice of childhood and the distance provided by time, speaking from a place determined by lived experiences as well as postmemory through the photos in family albums and the legacy of the stories heard. The novel presents a diasporic family of Jewish European (Bulgarian and Serbian) background who comes to Chile, fleeing the war in Europe, to build a new home. The story is told by the youngest daughter of the marriage, who grows up in Chile feeling split between her family's background and her own country of origin. Despite feeling Chilean, she feels this national identity betrayed by her parents' origins. They are obviously foreigners and live by other cultural parameters in their home. In many ways, Tamara's narration resembles Marianne Hirsch's description of her "displaced girlhood," as she writes in her book *Family Frames. Photography, Narrative and Postmemory*. Here she notes that

> the legendary place of origin I invest with nostalgia is not, like Hoffman's, a place I remember or have even ever seen. My parent's Czernowitz, my cultural home, is the space of my postmemory. Throughout my childhood, my parents and all their friends spoke of this city, where they continued to speak German through years of Rumanian rule, where they studied French and poetry, went to concerts, swan in the Prut River [...] These scenes and objects are in many ways more real to me than the scenes of my own childhood, especially when it comes to the narrative of my parents' survival during the war... (1997, 226)

This feeling of nostalgia for the origins and the unimaginable story of suffering and survival from the war is what daughters of immigrants' parents share. This is also what we find throughout *Escenario de guerra* where Tamara is faced with the task of reinventing her own story while putting together the remnants of her parents' survival. The process of writing and filling in the gaps and silences left by her parents and the world Tamara grows up in also traces her own awakening to a contradictory reality and the trauma that ensues in the wake of war in her own family as well as herself.

Tamara's sense of displacement is further heightened by restricting and constantly changing economic circumstances that determine where and how the family lives in Chile. She often changes schools; they move in and out of neighborhoods and houses while Tamara and her siblings are instructed by their mother to look for old furniture in the neighbors' trash. These experiences develop in Tamara a desire to invent stories about herself while locking herself in, reading for hours and writing her own biography in her blue notebook.

The flux of memories and past scenes are triggered when Tamara looks at an old photograph of her parents hugging each other during "a stable period" in what she calls their "circular migrations" that later looked more like a "spiral" (48), separating the family members and forcing them to live with relatives or friends to later reunite in an old house they could afford to rent (48–49). In this instance we clearly see how the state of warfare in Europe and later in Chile penetrates the family and the private sphere. As Andreas Huyssen has shown, the discourses on memory arise in the West in the 1960s as a consequence of decolonization and the new social movements that searched for alternative and revisionist historiographies. The narratives of the Holocaust were part of the debate in the 1980s in Europe and the United States and received great attention from historians, particularly after the fall of the Berlin Wall in 1989 (Huyssen 2000, 14–15). In the Chilean context, Jeftanovic, along with a few other women writers, has incorporated these narratives of the Holocaust and migration.[6]

The state violence in Europe and the impact of Nazism follows this Jewish family to Chile only to be relived in the dictatorship and its impact over subjectivities, particularly in the younger generation. Thus, in Jeftanovic's novel international violence becomes national violence and domestic violence in a century in which warfare rules. Rubí Carreño (2000) has pointed out that *Escenario de guerra* is one of the few novels in Chile that provides a historical interpretation of family violence and how its own dynamic and crisis is intertwined with war in present times. In this writing, violence and memory meet to represent a world in which ideologies have collapsed to the rule of force. The virtual disappearance of the rule of law turns the world into a stage in which memory and identity are intertwined within the narrative structures inherited from the past and the desire to create new ones. Jeftanovic, in contrast to other contemporary writers, makes fiction the only way out of the state of violence and the only possible country for humanity.[7]

Jeftanovic chooses theater and virtual technologies, as in her latest novel *Geografía de la lengua* (2007) [*The Geography of the Tongue*] to reveal that the communications and technology revolution may also contest globalization and its neoliberal culture by putting social bonds and effects at the center of subjectivity. The development of urban tribes and a wide range of communities around blogs, Facebook, and the Internet in Latin America today shows that these technologies might shape a new form of democracy that promotes access across classes, gender, and ethnicities in the post-dictatorial generation.

Another salient trait in this narrative is that globalization as a universal cultural and economic model is not viewed as the utopia of internationalization but rather as a worldwide nightmare that illuminates the devastating and destructive power of warring national states. The cost of resolving conflict with violence is the death and displacement of millions of citizens. Jeftanovic's novel highlights the impact of the Second World War on Tamara's father as his traumatic childhood memories haunt and entrap him in recurring scenes where military occupation, vigilance, Nazi soldiers, and imprisonment repeat (18–19).

The revision of the past and the ways memories travel across continents and generations is fundamental to Jeftanovic's representation of the family of émigrés and the Chilean protagonist's displaced childhood. The transnationalism imbedded in the narrative may be viewed not only as a narrative strategy but also as a cultural and social position toward globalization and militarism and their negative effects. The way that childhood memory shapes subjectivity is poignantly recognized by Tamara as a young adult during one of her therapy sessions when she admits:

> Mi infancia comienza a poblarme, a invadirme de ausencias, me deja tan poco espacio para vivir el presente. Constantemente aparecen escenas omitidas. Cito las frases que mamá pronunciaba mientras se maquillaba frente al espejo, o barría la cocina, o cuando danzábamos en el salón. (77–78)

[My childhood is beginning to populate me, to invade me with absences, it leaves me so little space for the present. Constantly omitted scenes show up. I cite the phrases my mother pronounced while putting on makeup in front of the mirror or while sweeping the kitchen or when we were dancing in the living room.][8]

Their different religious celebrations, foods, and languages, and having parents who speak Spanish with an accent, make Tamara even more aware of their difference, and therefore her own sense of estrangement intensifies. She succinctly expresses this feeling of otherness while describing her parents' origins and their different cultural practices:

> Papá y mamá vienen de tan lejos, se nota en la distancia que establecen con otras personas. Sus ciudades remotas se hacen presentes en discos en otro idioma, en particulares expresiones que acuñan en casa. En casa rezamos a otro Dios, celebramos otras fiestas, se habla una lengua que me es familiar y no entiendo. Nuestra casa huele distinto, la cocina tiene aromas más dulces, el horno siempre está tibio. En el salón hay otros adornos, objetos que no encuentro en la casa de mis vecinos. [...] Mi apellido es difícil de pronunciar, debo deletrearlo. La gente me aborda con preguntas. (31)
>
> [Father and mother come from far away; you can tell by the distance they have with other people. Their remote cities become present in long-plays in another language. In our home we pray to another God, we celebrate other holidays, they speak a language that is familiar to me and that I do not understand. Our house smells different, the kitchen has sweeter smells, the oven is always warm. In the living room there are other ornaments, objects I don't see in my neighbors' homes [...] My last name is hard to pronounce, I have to spell it out. People come to me with questions.]

This sense of being different from others (neighbors, classmates, friends) and feeling separated from a national community or a community of peers becomes even greater as the family suffers the consequences of the parents' deteriorating marriage. On the one hand, Tamara is unable to change the past and the wounds that the war has inflicted on her parents and, on the other, she cannot prevent her parents' marriage from ending, despite her childlike desire to keep them together at all cost. Her father's depression and unemployment, the ongoing fights between the couple, the mother's affair and mental instability erode the family's bonds and finally separate it. However, the father's presence and pain are felt through his memories of the wars in Europe, particularly the Second World War and later, the more contemporary war in Kosovo where he grew up. Tamara and he watch his childhood house being bombed in front of their eyes on the TV news in a war in which the North Atlantic Treaty Organization (NATO) and the United States allegedly ally to end ethnic cleaning. NATO's controversial bombing of bridges, industrial facilities, and factories in Belgrade and later in Kosovo made this war a devastating testimony of atrocities. First it showed the volatile conflict among age-long enemies for whom Kosovo was the sacred place of their ancestors.[9] The war also showed to the world the impact of international military intervention in the Balkans. American economic interests in the region would have a devastating effect on national politics and the rights of citizens, as the Chilean dictatorship also proved, lasting seventeen years through one of the most brutal dictatorships in the continent. The legacy of U.S. intervention in regional and national conflicts intertwines in Tamara's formative years in a childhood shaped by her parents' memories from Europe, as well as her own experience of a world of loss and death wrought by warfare. In this way the reader becomes aware of how international militarism and the global context are inextricably connected with the local through memories, trauma, and loss.

In the novel the war becomes a constant historical reminder of migration, otherness, and exile through the memory of the parents and postmemory of the daughter in a family imaginary across generations. Consequently, the daughter inherits this diasporic or displaced memory through a generation's displacement, as well as the aftermath of the Chilean dictatorship, creating her own postmemory of the events. We can link this diasporic memory to the effects brought about by international militarism, as well as globalization, displacing massive numbers of citizens in search of freedom, livelihood, or mere survival across countries and continents. Their stories of exile and migration are kept through fragmented memories passed on through generations in transnational settings. This notion of diasporic memory also may be linked to a nomadic memory and identity found in feminist discussions among Argentinean and Chilean scholars regarding the transition to democracy and the dictatorial past. Ana Forcinito (2004) has discussed this nomadic memory, paying attention to the political discourse of women (as mothers and grandmothers of the disappeared) and memories of violence during the dictatorship in Argentina and Chile. Feminist social scientists in Chile claim that the feminist silence and fragmentation of the women's social movement during the post-dictatorship reveal a disillusionment with the democratic governments and their politics as usual.[10] The book ¿*Un nuevo silencio feminista? La transformación de un movimiento social en el Chile posdictadura* (2003) [*A New Feminist Silent? The Transformation of the Social Movement in the Chile of the Postdictatorship*] provides a valuable historical account of Chilean post-feminism of the 1990s and the frustration that cuts across feminists (who have not joined the political parties) from 1990 onwards after having worked within the women's social movement of the 1970s and 1980s to end the dictatorship. The common narrative that feminists share is a "homogeneous traumatic memory" of the dictatorial past, which was provided in large part by the work of the feminist sociologist Julieta Kirkwood. However, today many feminists are discontent with what women have actually gained, or better said, have not gained with the advent of democracy. In the context of the transition to democracy, feminists who participated in the Concertation's political alliance by joining political parties were able to incorporate gender demands into the political agenda through what has been called a state feminism. In response to these demands the Servicio Nacional de la Mujer (SERNAM) [National Service of Women] was created in 1991 to introduce a gender perspective to state policies, protect women's rights, and the family. In addition, legal reforms against gender discrimination have been incorporated into the civil, penal, and labor codes. Centros de Información de los Derechos de la Mujer (CIDEM) [Centers of Information for Women's Rights] have also been created to implement campaigns and provide information against women's discrimination and abuse. Nevertheless, it has been not been easy to accomplish all of the goals because of the need to achieve consensus among the different political parties and women's organizations. Ana María Carrasco states, furthermore, there is outright rejection to implement an effective and efficient gender politics within a coordinated plan of action among the different ministries and their organisms (2008, 148–50). As a result, many feminists have ceased believing that it is possible to work within the government's structure because of censual politics.

In Jetanovic's novel the devastating effects of contemporary wars and antidemocratic states highlight the connection between subjectivity and exile through memory. It is precisely in photo albums (of different cities and houses, of relatives lost, and neighborhoods bombed), newspaper clips, and TV newslines where we find the instances that shape the problematic identity of the protagonist who feels uprooted, and thus, decides to go in search of her past and invent a present for herself. In this way, she becomes the narrator of a memory of origins, as Carolina Andrea Navarette asserts, providing a circular and at times dramatic account of the family and their experience. Her own identity, however, is constituted through her written account recorded in the blue notebook. Writing and memory intertwine in the blue notebook where Tamara is able to re-create a different world, a world where national origins are not what define identity and where violence may be kept at bay. Memory in this writing becomes a site of new meanings in which selected events and family scenes are reinterpreted and filtered through Tamara's anxieties and desire.

The novel *Cercada* by Meruane is also a fragmentary family story that more directly invokes the recent political past of Chilean society. The characters' experiences are here inextricably connected to a national history of abuse and the violation of human and civil rights during the dictatorial years. Meruane's novel disrupts the narrative structure and introduces a narrator that resembles a film director or play director who voices the need to make cuts, change roles, and emphasize tones or acting, breaking away from any sense of narrative verisimilitude. The narrator's directions instruct the characters on what to do in the script, erasing from the start the idea of neutrality or objectivity, while also emphasizing the notion of the artificiality and constructiveness of reality and identity.

In *Cercada* the narration is located in the margins of different media and genres, likening it to the short story, the novel, the film script, and the play, opening with the mise-en-scène of the love triangle of Lucía, Ramiro, and Manuel. The memories of loss and persecution they inherit from their parents form a turning point in the plot and the ways justice is understood by the younger generation. Manuel and Ramiro, who are brothers but have lived apart due to their father's political affiliation, unexpectedly meet Lucía (whom they both are in love with) only to find out that her father was the military officer who murdered their father, a socialist activist. Colonel Camus arrives in Ramiro's apartment searching for his daughter, Lucía. He then threatens Manuel at gunpoint. The brothers have plotted their revenge by bringing the colonel to the apartment to witness Ramiro holding a gun to Lucía's head. The rest of the story line goes forward and backwards through its founding family plot, in which individual personalities, treasons, and unexpected turns of events mirror recent Chilean history (Edwards online). This same history may be found in the wide range of memories that are still today at odds and struggling with one another. One emblematic memory tells of the military as heroes in an epic of national salvation, while its countermemory posits them as traitors of what used to be a democratic nation until the coup d'état in 1973. These emblematic memories, as Stern shows, have not reached a cultural and political memory consensus in which all Chileans come to accept a common ground and their historical legacy. On the contrary, what we see in Chile still today is a divide across political camps that tell completely different versions of what took place and why. The fact that the legal system has been extremely slow and ineffective in bringing to trial the persecutors, leaving Pinochet untried for his crimes against humanity, has left an insurmountable obstacle, in my view, that hinders the development of an inclusive and shared history of the past across ideological lines.

Lucía Camus was still in high school when she fell in love with Manuel Merino, a bookseller with whom she shared her love of books. Now the grown-up Lucía is a young journalist who has remained uninformed of the political repression in the country, revealing the extent of censorship and self-censorship. As the narrator asks fundamental questions about the political and social situation of the narrative present, Lucía's unawareness is evident. She says she never heard anything at the university, not even rumors about the secret police services (the Directorate for National Intelligence (DINA) and later the National Center for Information (CNI)), their illegal actions and murders. She grew up sheltered from the regime's violence, spending her days playing chess with her father and living secluded in an army neighborhood under a military code that valued discipline, order, security, hierarchy, and family (35). As Nelly Richard has shown, the military state in Chile propagated an ideology where females served their nation while upholding the most traditional gender values and behaviors, following to the letter dictatorial ideals that equated females to mothers and housewives (1998, 200–1). During the dictatorship, staying at home and taking care of the domestic sphere and the family were seen as female duties that supported the national ideals of the fatherland and its Catholic morality.

This is why in the novel *Cercada* Lucía lives such a limited and confined existence, dictated by her military father. Only during the weekends is she free to do what she wants and reads, even those books that her father had forbidden, acting as her personal censor and custodian. At age twenty-five Lucía finally leaves her father's house to rent a room somewhere else in the city. It seems that the motivation to move out is her relationship with a screenwriter she met in 1987 when she was doing her professional practice in the south (36). Surprisingly, she keeps the relationship a secret because she fears her father's disapproval. Thus, despite the fact that she is living on her own and has claimed a certain degree of independence from her father, his influence is still strong, as was Pinochet's in the Chilean landscape in 2000 when the novel was published. In this sense, the novel makes a correlation between Lucía's coming-of-age independence and Chile's road to democracy and the struggles against the influence of the dictatorial patriarch. Sociologist Tomás Moulian has studied how, through the seventeen years of the dictatorship, the figure of Pinochet changed from that of the dictator to the old patriarch who oversaw the transition to democracy in the new consensual political system in which all parties, except the communist party, accepted neoliberalism as the only viable utopia in a global market. Furthermore, Moulian states that contemporary Chile was forged in the matrix of a terrorist dictatorship that became a constitutional dictatorship obsessed with forgetting its origins (1997, 18, 33, 58). Thus, the blocking of memory, which also may be found in other societies that lived extreme experiences, is expressed in the loss of discourse and the obstacles of speech. Moulian's analysis shows that in Chile there is a lack of words to name the experiences lived in the past, which became a victory for some and a trauma for others (31). Lucía's ongoing fights with her lover, Ramiro, about Chile's political climate and her father's military affiliation make her want to forget who she is and invent for herself a different background, one where she can omit her father's job, what he did or did not do, or at least invent new work for him (38). This desire to forget her origins and discount her father's collaboration with the dictatorship haunts Lucía until the end of the narrative, highlighting that forgetting in order to come to grips with the past and its legacy is not possible. The impossibility of resolving this dilemma is proper to the narratives of memory during the age of globalization, as Huyssen asserts. The desire to forget, on the one hand, and an obsessive reconstruction, on the other, are two phenomena that determine the unsatisfactory or unresolved ending of a post-traumatic memory narrative (10).

A similar national narrative is still haunting Chileans today, dividing them along two opposing views of the past: forgetting and moving on or remembering the trauma that the dictatorship meant for many. This is precisely what Lucía seems to have trouble confronting and assuming as part of her own history and identity.

In one of Ramiro's jobs filming in another city, Lucía meets by chance Manuel, the bookseller, and begins an affair with him. All the time, though, she feels she is being watched by a man in a blue Dodge, just like Ramiro has told her many times to her disbelief (42).

In a monologue the narrative voice states:

> Lucía tu padre te controla. Lo sabes perfectamente. Pero si te dieran a elegir preferirías el agobio de ese cerco a la certeza de que nadie te protege.

El no tener padre porque tu padre ha desaparecido. Y que tu hermano vive en el exilio. Que tu nombre sólo suena para el enemigo. (49)

[Lucía, your father controls you. You know it perfectly well. But if you had to choose you would prefer the overwhelming sensation of that siege than to have the certainty that nobody protects you. Or not having a father because he has disappeared. And that your brother lives in exile. That your name only sounds for the enemy...]

A feeling of orphanhood besieges Lucía and faces her with her greatest fear: that of being alone in a world where she can become bait among enemies (50). It is precisely this fear of becoming the victim in an all-encompassing and panoptic power that Lucía has grown up with in her house as well as the nation. Through fear she has accepted her father's rule and hidden from him what he would condemn about her. Her choice to remain ignorant and unaware of the political and social problems plaguing the country is another aspect of her submissiveness and apathy toward others during the dictatorship. She prefers not to know and not to ask questions about what everyone suspects or knows. As Juan Armando Epple has pointed out, this novel is an example of the "broken memory" and the attempts of identity reconstruction that have developed as an answer to the dissolution of the family contract and the virtual absence of a national narrative of collective cohesion (2006, 108–9, 118).

Toward the end Lucía has to face the violent mise-en-scène at gunpoint that opened the novel, repeating again among the four characters (Ramiro, Manuel, Lucía, and her father). In the previous scene Lucía and Ramiro argue about her father's murder of Ramiro's dad. Lucía, however, forgives her father's deed by claiming her blood tie, as well as his own fears and sense of duty: "Es mi padre...Tenía miedo, tal vez creía que era su misión (86) ["He is my father....He was afraid, perhaps he believed that it was his mission."] This same sense of mission and national duty was used by the military to justify the brutality and violation of the state of law in order to save the nation from the illness brought about by the left. Lucía's acceptance of this tenet places her on the side of those who won and benefited from the dictatorship. In the political and cultural context, Lucía's defense of her father is by default a defense of the dictatorship in a world where one has to take sides and assert a position.

On the other end of the political spectrum is the position of Ramiro, who condemns the military who unmercifully killed his father for his political views. He represents the voices of many of the relatives of the disappeared and the claim of those who demand justice for the loss of their loved ones to the military rule. Their discourse is also one that enfolds the paradox of memory in that in its very constitution, as Paul Ricoeur shows, presence and absence intertwine, making its *escenification* of the past an imaginary yet real claim (2002, 26–27). This vindication proper to memory shows its fundamental relation to truth, to what is not now but was in the past. Ricoeur asserts that testimony is closer to memory because it is a sort of conversation we have with someone who is telling us his or her story, that he or she was there and lived through it and that what he or she says is true. This is precisely what is taking place between Ramiro and Lucía's conversation where he is claiming his experience of the dictatorship through his father's murder and his brother's exile. His testimony is the best evidence then of the need to incorporate memory into discourse since it can move things that were seen or said to the place of things that can be trusted, due to our capacity to believe in the other's word (Ricoeur, 26–27). Thus, in Ramiro's words we find the testimony of those who are still suffering for unspeakable losses and who "refuse to bury traumatic memories and struggle daily, despite obstacles to advance the cause of human rights," as Michael Lazzara underlines (2006, 1).

A clear evidence of the inherent aggression of the dictatorial world and its premises is shown through gunpointing in scene 3 and at the end when Ramiro is holding a gun to Lucía's head while her father is doing the same to Manuel in an enactment of violence. The colonel has come to Ramiro's apartment to rescue his daughter as a result of the brothers' plot to seek revenge.

In the section "Voces en off," we read what presumably are Lucía's words to Manuel and Ramiro: "Yo debería matarlos, sería la manera de acabar" (87) ["I should kill you, it would be the way to end"] and finally "No soy la víctima. (Ahora. ¡Cámara!). No soy." ["I am not the victim. (Now. ¡Camera!) I am not.]" With this interrupted sequence of cuts and scriptlike lines, we see Lucía's personal dilemma in which words cannot be uttered without the voice of the director and the law at large amidst Ramiro's accusations. This sort of structural limit is also applicable to her memory and how the "belated stories," as Hirsch calls them, from opposing and warring ideological sectors intertwine with her own individual and imaginative narrative (1997, 22).

In this way the novel ends with Lucía's realization that her father actually killed the brothers' father for his political views as part of his military duty, coinciding with the testimonies of other military officials. She also has to face the ways memory determines her relationships to both brothers and to her own father. However, in this realization she refuses to become another victim in a system of arbitrary and abusive power. In fact, she asserts her own will to defend herself in the triangle she constitutes with the two brothers and refuses to take responsibility for her father's murder. The novel leaves unanswered the question of justice once the truth is known (something that certainly alludes to the ways authorities and the political elite have dealt with it in Chile). Despite the fact that Lucía's self-assertion and distance from her father's power and legacy here may be read as a positive step in female empowerment, the issue of justice is sidetracked and its impact on memory is left unresolved. Perhaps in the title we find the impossibility of claiming a position that determines Lucía's subjectivity as besieged by the historical past and how it is remembered by those close to her. Here the affective web, rather than liberating, confuses and entangles the character, making it virtually impossible to act and speak outside the box; that is, the script provided by the director, as well as the conflicting memories of the past.

Both Jeftanovic and Meruane represent the nuisances of a traumatic memory and the ways it haunts young subjectivities. Both novels address through different perspectives, both local and transnational, the difficulties in reconstructing the past, as well as the force of family and personal memory in national and transnational contexts. From another angle, both *Escenario de guerra* and *Cercada* are shaped by a sense of mourning and loss that cuts across the perspective as well as their postmemory. The writers themselves were born in 1970 during the Allende government and were only three years old when the coup occurred. Thus, their parents were the ones directly involved or affected by the violence of the dictatorship and its traumatic and epic memory. The younger generation did not share the sense of a fractured national identity, but instead, as we have seen in these two novels, creates a memory field that is constituted by familial and personal imaginaries and post-narrative memory in what is a *bildungsroman*. In many ways this emphasis on the self is a new form of articulation that reflects "an exhaustion of the cultural resources of national identity and a restructuring of society," as Julia A. Kushigian asserts in her cultural and gender reading of childhood in contemporary Spanish American *bildungsroman* (2008).

The incorporation of international militarism and globalization as part of Chile's recent history and its legacy of disputed memories in a neoliberal present today shows the link between transnational and local realities and the manners in which literature contests and critiques the dissolution of national sovereignty, the violation of civil and human rights to the military state, and its use of systematic force in the international and national arena. These two writers contest neoliberalism in Chile as a form of global neocolonialism, denouncing state terrorism and capitalism as projects that dismantle the rule of law and promote unedited forms of inequities and forgetfulness across the globe.

Notes

1. For further bibliographical references on Meruane, see my article "Lina Meruane" in *Latin American Women Writers. An Encyclopedia*. Eds. Maria Claudia André and Eva Pauline Bueno (New York, London: Routledge, 2008). 329–30.
2. For a more in-depth analysis, see my book *Passionate Subjects/Split Subjects in Twentieth-Century Literature in Chile (Brunet, Bombal, and Eltit)*.
3. For further discussion, see my article "Pasiones maternales y carnales en la narrative de Diamela Eltit" in *Letras y Proclamas. La estética literaria de Diamela Eltit* (Santiago: Cuarto Propio, 2006) 103–41. Also see chapter 6 in my book *Passionate Subjects/Split Subjects*.
4. The Concertación is the political coalition established between the Christian Democrat Party (PDC), the Socialist party (PS), the Party for Democracy (PPD), and the Social Democrat Radical Party (PRSD), which was in power until 2010 and since Christian Democrat Patricio Alwyn won in 1990.
5. Here I am referring to the Truth and Reconciliation Commission during Patricio Alwyn's presidency, which was charged with collecting testimonies related to human rights violations during the military regime. The testimonies came from victims and perpetrators who voluntarily told their experiences. The condition to make these declarations was that there would be no legal prosecution but only a register of the truth in order to achieve a political reconciliation in the country. With this initiative, truth and justice were forever dissociated in Chile, as Hernán Vidal argues (1997, 11–64).
6. Marjorie Agosín has also addressed this cultural experience as a family memory in Chile in her book *Sagrada memoria* (1994). Writer Sonia Guralnik has also written narratives in which a diasporic memory cuts across generations in her *El samovar* (1987), *Retratos en sepia* (1987), and *Sonata de carne y hueso* (2000).
7. Writers like Alberto Fuguet and Mauricio Electorat resort to media culture and filmic images as literary materials rather than making history the defining matrix of fiction.
8. All translations are mine unless noted.
9. NATO's participation as a multilateral military force that supported the American mission in Europe, through its direct intervention in the Balkans, gave NATO a new military role in the geopolitical map of the

twenty-first century designed by the United States. As some have said, among them Senator Bob Dole, the Kosovo war was the first casualty of the Monica Lewinsky affair during the Clinton administration. Secretary of State Margaret Albright forcibly stated that the United States would not be a bystander and would not stand up to Milosovic's aggression and massacre of Albanians and the members of the Kosovo Liberation Army. Kosovo's geographic location inside the Yugoslav national boundary made it a volatile territory the moment it wanted independence. TV images of massacres involving Serbs and Albanians could be seen throughout the world, making this a transnational warfare viewed by millions.

10. See Marcela Ríos, Godoy, and Guerrero, especially chapter 4. See also Ana Forcinito, *Memorias y nomadías: Géneros y cuerpos en los márgenes del posfemenismo* (Santiago: Cuarto propio, 2004).

Works Cited

Agosín, Marjorie. 1994. *Sagrada memoria*. Santiago: Cuarto Propio.
Carrasco, Ana María. 2008. "Espacios conquistados. Un panorama de las organizaciones de las mujeres chilenas." *Mujeres chilenas. Fragmentos de una historia*. Sonia Montecino, ed. Santiago: Editorial Catalonia. 139–53.
Carreño, Rubí. "De niños de septiembre a pasajeros de tránsito: memorias del 2000 en Electorat y Fuguet." www.mundodepapel.cl/datos/ftp/rubielectoratyfuguet.htm. Last accessed Feb. 9, 2011.
Echeverría, Claudia Martínez. 2005. "La memoria silenciada. La historia familiar en los relatos de tres escritoras chilenas: Costamagna, Maturana y Fernández," *Taller de Letras* Vol. 37:67–76.
Edwards, Javier. "Lina Meruane: *Cercada* [Novela]." www.letras.s5.com/meruane200103.htm. Last accessed Feb. 9, 2011.
Eltit, Diamela. 1994. *Los vigilantes*. Santiago, Buenos Aires: Editorial Sudamericana.
Epple, Juan Armando. 2006. "La nación en la nueva narrativa femenina chilena." *Ideologías y Literatura. Homenaje a Hernán Vidal*. Mabel Moraña and Javier Campos, eds. Pittsburgh: University of Pittsburgh. 107–24.
Forcinito, Ana. 2004. *Memorias y nomadías: Géneros y cuerpos en los márgenes del posfemenismo*. Santiago: Cuarto propio.
Guralnik, Sonia. 1987. *El samovar*. Santiago: Editorial Sudamericana.
———. 1987. *Retratos en sepia*. Santiago: Editorial Sudamericana.
———. 2000. *Sonata de carne y hueso*. Santiago: LOM.
Hirsh, Marianne. 1997. *Family Frames. Photography, Narrative and Postmemory*. Cambridge, London: Harvard University Press.
Huyssen, Andreas. 2000. "Pretéritos presentes: Medios, política, amnesia."*En busca del futuro perdido. Cultura y memoria en tiempos de globalización.* Trans. Silvia Fehrmann. México: Fondo de Cultura Económica. 13–40.

Jeftanovic, Andrea. 2000. *Escenario de guerra*. Santiago: Alfaguara.

———. "El rol de la cultura de Chile de la transición: Chile=Pinochet, y otras sinopsis de los años 90." www.letras.s5.com/aj300608.html. Last accessed Feb. 9, 2011.

Kushigian, Julia A. 2008. *Reconstructing Childhood. Strategies of Reading for Culture and Gender in the Spanish American Bildungsroman*. Lewisburg: Bucknell University Press.

Lazzara, Michael. 2006. *Chile in Transition. The Poetics and Politics of Memory*. Gainsville, FL: University of Florida.

Llanos, M., Bernardita, ed. 2006. "Pasiones maternales y carnales en la narrative de Diamela Eltit." *Letras y Proclamas. La estética literaria de Diamela Eltit*. Santiago: Cuarto Propio.103–41.

———.2008. "Lina Meruane." *Latin American Women Writers. An Encyclopedia*. Maria Claudia André and Eva Pauline Bueno, eds. New York, London: Routledge. 329–30.

———.2009. *Passionate Subjects/Split Subjects in Twentieth-Century Literature in Chile (Brunet, Bombal and Eltit)*. Lewisburg: Bucknell University Press.

Meruane, Lina. 2000. *Cercada*. Santiago: Cuarto Propio.

Moulian, Tomás. 1997. *Chile Actual. Anatomía de un mito*. Santiago: ARCIS.

Navarrete. Carolina Andrea. "Escenario de guerra de Andrea Jeftanovic: Entre el flujo femenino y el desarriago familiar y personal." www.critica.cl/html/navarrete_00.htm. Last accessed Feb. 9, 2011.

Richard, Nelly. 1998. *Residuos y metáforas. Ensayos de crítica cultural sobre el Chile de la Transición*. Santiago: Cuarto Propio.

Ricoeur, Paul. 2002. "Definición de la memoria desde un punto de vista filosófico." *¿Por qué recordar?* Françoise Barret-Ducrocq, ed. Buenos Aires, Barcelona, México, Santiago, Montevideo: Granica. 24–28.

Ríos, Marcela et al. 2003. *¿Un nuevo silencio feminista? La transformación de un movimiento social en el Chile posdictadura*. Santiago: Centro de Estudios de la mujer/Cuarto propio.

Stern, Steve. 2004. *Remembering Pinochet's Chile. On the Eve of London 1998*. Durham and London: Durham University Press.

Vidal, Hernán, ed. 1997. "Introducción." *Política cultural de la memoria histórica. Derechos Humanos y discursos culturales en Chile*. Santiago, Chile: Mosquito Comunicaciones. 11–64.

Chapter Five

Iraqi Women, Jewish Men, and Global Noises in Two Texts by Ya'qub Balbul

Orit Bashkin

This essay examines the representations of minority women in colonial and postcolonial contexts. Although in national discourses women were often represented as both symbols of national authenticity and as objects of modernization reform efforts, the representations of their bodies and daily practices were also constructed within narratives relating to ethnic and religious differences (Bhabha 1994, 157; Bhabha 1997, 431–59; Spivak 1988, 271–313). To investigate what happens when the category of nation intersects with the categories of religion *and* gender, I look at two short stories written by Iraqi Jewish intellectual Ya'qub Balbul (1919–2003).

Like many of his upper- and middle-class Jewish peers, Balbul graduated from the Baghdadi Alliance Israélite Universelle school (established in 1864), which offered a French education. His knowledge of French and other Western languages later enabled him to find employment in the French embassy as a translator. Concurrently, he published works of poetry and prose in the Iraqi and Egyptian press. In 1938, his collection of short stories, *al-Jamra al-ula* [*The First Ember*] was published. Balbul was very young at the time of the publication of his collection (less than twenty years old), and his youth might have motivated him to challenge traditional conventions and norms. Indeed, his writings, often combining notions of spiritualism and secularism, angered conservatives and high-ranking officials. Nonetheless, Balbul's literary talents were recognized by his fellow Iraqi intellectuals—Jewish, Muslim, and Christian alike—and his works were printed in the Arab press published outside of Iraq. Whereas his texts did not generate any meaningful changes in the Iraqi public sphere, they nonetheless reflect a context in which Iraq was changing from a traditional and religious society to a secular, Westernized nation-state.[1] Balbul, as I will try to illustrate, both challenged and appropriated certain elements of the Iraqi-Arab national discourse in order to construct his own image as a loyal Iraqi-Arab nationalist.

During the first decade of Iraq's independence (1931–41), Iraqi nationalists and religious reformists increasingly wrote about Iraqi women, their lives, and their desired progress. The gradual entry of elite and middle-class women into schools (both elementary and secondary) and the limited female public sphere of reading salons, cultural journals, and clubs inspired both enthusiasm and a host of cultural and religious anxieties among the Iraqi intelligentsia. Although the feminist movement in Iraq began its activities in the mid-1940s, essays and works of narrative prose on Iraqi women colored the Iraqi print market of the 1930s as well. By stating that Iraqi feminism began in the 1940s, I do not mean to imply that the Iraqi women's struggle for equality subscribed to the same periodization as in Europe or the Americas (where we discuss first and second waves of feminism), but rather that specific political activities of women's organizations calling for suffrage, reform in education and citizenship rights emerged in their fullest form only after World War II, with the expansion of mass education and urban life in Iraq. In the 1930s, in contrast, the activities of women's organizations were more sporadic, and, oftentimes, Iraqi men wrote about the plight of Iraqi women. In other words, to represent themselves as modern, Islamic, nationalist, or anticolonial, Iraqi men needed to define where they stood with respect to such dilemmas as veiling, women's entry into the labor market, women's education, and reform of religious practices.[2]

Debates about gender during the 1930s took place within a global and a transregional context. The local was very much globalized in this period, with British intervention in Iraq's foreign politics, the slow integration of Iraq into the global economy (expedited by the budding oil industry), the sending of Iraqi students to missions abroad by the new Iraqi state, and the acceptance of a Western lifestyle among the ranks of the middle and upper classes. Iraqis, moreover, needed to come to terms with the ways in which the British, who governed Iraq in the 1920s under a mandate from the League of Nations, conceptualized the relationship of Arab-Muslim men to Arab-Muslim women. Transregionally, social and cultural networks linked Iraqis to other Middle Eastern countries, such as Turkey, Egypt, Lebanon, and Iran, and thus Iraqi national elites were highly interested in the secularizing reforms happening in these nations (Bashkin 2008, 52, 78). Peter Wien (2006) has further demonstrated that concepts of Iraqi-Arab nationalism were influenced by German, Turkish, French, and Arab models. These hybrid national models generated new ideas about masculinity and gender.

During the 1930s, Iraqi nationalists contended that their country, although officially independent, was still very much under British control because of Britain's decisive role in molding Iraqi foreign policies, strategic decision making, and economic affairs.[3] To achieve the desired goals of liberation from British control, they believed that women should be guided by Iraqi nationalists in order to make them aware of their importance to the national struggle. Within this context, the Iraqi household became a crucial site of interest to nationalists, women activists, writers, and journalists. Iraqi homes, it was thought, ought to be modernized in a way that would allow women to respond to both the material and spiritual requirements of the Iraqi household. Management of the household itself was seen as being influenced by sciences like biology, chemistry, physics, bacteriology, psychology, and esthetics (*Gharib* 1938, 206–13). Not only the home, however, but also the public domain generated anxieties. Iraqi nationalists protested the leisure practices and cultural habits that shaped the lives of the new urban middle classes. They cautioned the reading public against individuals who spent their time in coffee houses and casinos, thus damaging, in their opinion, the fabric of Iraqi family life. The clientele of such institutions was also responsible for such problems as alcoholism, drug use, and prostitution (*al-Istiqlal* 1939, 1). Intellectuals were likewise concerned with the fact that upper- and middle-class women blindly mimicked Western practices and adopted Westernized clothing and lifestyle. Thus, the debate over the practices of women, namely the way in which they dressed (veiled/unveiled; Westernized clothes/traditional clothes), ate (with men/without men), raised their children, and acted in the household and in the street, turned into a battle signifying the degree to which Iraqi nationalists were willing to adopt certain Westernizing mores while rejecting British colonialism.

In the 1930s, women became central objects of national education plans. Nationalist educator and physician Sami Shawkat (b.1893), who served as a director general of education (1931–33; 1940–42) and minister of education (1940), discussed women in his writings. While his ideas were not particularly original and reflected many of the themes current in the press of the time, being in a position of power, Shawkat was able to influence legislation and educational practices within Iraq. Focusing his efforts on combating the ignorance of Iraqi women for the sake of the Iraqi nation, Shawkat claimed that mothers were incapable of taking proper care of their children and that young girls were oblivious to their national obligation as the future mothers of the soldiers who would fill the void of those who died in battle. Educating mothers and young female students would terminate social diseases, like prostitution, and shield women from the mismanagement of the household's funds, exemplified in their tendencies to acquire frivolous products, such as imported clothes and high-heeled shoes. In order to change women's mentalities, their bodies and souls needed to be guarded through lessons in physical education. Shawkat saw no contradiction between the health of women and their function as a demographic vehicle that provided manpower to the armed forces. He claimed, in fact, that a woman could not reach her mental, psychological, and physical potential unless she married and gave birth. Hence, the goal of providing women with education was significant, because women should understand that matrimony and childbirth were the best means to safeguard them from various illnesses, which could be damaging to their uteruses or their psyches. To facilitate an increase in the number of marriages in Iraq, nationalists, although hostile to the idea of polygamy, offered a number of creative ideas such as levying a special tax on unmarried men and granting tax benefits to families with many children (Shawkat 1939, 80–84).

Iraqi women writers responded to these discourses in several ways. On the one hand, in women's journals and magazines, they advocated for the expansion of women's education, unveiling, and ending of seclusion. On the other hand, they tried to affiliate themselves with the nationalist movement and echoed its desires for independence and sovereignty, as well as its willingness to combat colonialism and Zionism. This was attested to in speeches that Iraqi women delivered in international conferences of Arab and Eastern women and in the Iraqi Pan-Arab club *al-Muthanna* (al-Jawahiri 1984, 83–84; Efrati 2001, 165). Writing about the ways in which women should support their men, 'A'isha al-'Abbasi turned the attention of female readers to the fact that women were warriors in the service of their nation. As such, they were willing to sacrifice their lives, as exemplified in the case of 'A'isha bint Abi Bakr (*al-Istiqlal* 1940, 4).[4]

Iraq was a nation in which the Sunni minority was privileged over the Shi'i majority, as Sunnis hegemonized the state's leading political institutions. The country, however, also included a number of additional minorities, most notably the Kurds, an ethnic group located in the north, and a number of religious communities belonging to various Christian denominations. The Jews, then, were only one minority group among many others. Historians of modern Iraq, however, noted that this community, in comparison to other Jewish communities in the Middle East, integrated effectively into the nation-state and that the community's intellectuals enthusiastically supported Iraqi nationalism. The community was relatively affluent. Many of its members received a Western education, and therefore they were able to find employment in British institutions, companies, and banks in Iraq. However, since Iraqi-Jewish intellectuals considered themselves loyal Iraqi patriots, they opted to construct a Jewish-Arab identity that would reflect the community's desire to become fully integrated into the Arab and Iraqi nation. This desire was manifested economically and socially as Jews became involved in the new institutions of the Iraqi state, ranging from clerks working in different government offices, to traders and merchants. Culturally, Jews abandoned Judeo-Arabic (Arabic written in the Hebrew script), adopting Arabic in its stead. Iraqi-Jewish intellectuals played a seminal role in the new Arab-Iraqi national culture that emerged in the interwar period, and in the experiments in narrative prose and poetry that colored the Iraqi public sphere of the 1930s. Jewish poets, journalists, editors, and writers wrote in Arabic about the virtues of the Iraqi nation and its need for independence and sovereignty, hoping that the new state would provide a nonreligious basis for citizenship that would surmount religious and ethnic categories. Noticeably, despite the Arab-Israeli conflict enfolding in mandatory Palestine, and despite the fact that certain ultranationalist Arab intellectuals in Iraq tended to confuse Zionism and Judaism, other voices were highly open to the integration of Jews within the national culture. The position articulated by many a Jewish intellectual—that in order for Iraq to progress, new modes of Westernization and modernization should take root in Iraqi society—appealed to many Iraqi intellectuals, Christian and Muslim alike (Shiblak, Rejwan, Snir, Shenhav, and Kazzaz.)

The discourses on gender and nationalism were relevant to the context of the Jewish community. Middle- and upper-class Jewish women received a relatively high degree of education. The first Jewish school for girls was opened in 1893, and Jewish women made use of the school to acquire a secondary education. In the 1930s, upper- and middle-class Jewish women began working as teachers, and some published their works in cultural and literary magazines. Western clothes, which were sold in the finest European department stores, were adopted by Jewish middle- and upper-class women, while more Jewish girls attended public schools. The discourse about the practices of Jewish women was conducted both within the boundaries of the religious community and outside of these boundaries. Within the boundaries of Jewish gendered identity, certain customs relating to Jewish women, like the age of marriage, arranged marriages, dowry payments, the expenses involved in wedding ceremonies, and the tendency of certain Jewish women to cover their heads like Muslim women, were all discussed within the community, for example, in Jewish newspapers and magazines.

Nonetheless, in their writings about Jewish women, Jewish intellectuals were also influenced by Muslim reformers and saw the writings of such reformers as relevant to Jewish audiences. The understanding that both Jewish and Muslim women were Eastern women and, as such, subscribed to certain specific cultural norms, was important to them. Thus, although Jewish middle and upper classes pursued Western commodities and more Jewish girls attended public schools, Jewish writers have repeatedly emphasized that their positions on gender benefited the Iraqi community in its entirety. As Arab-Jews, they were interested in concerns shared by their Muslim and Christian peers. As a result, Jewish men and women, as Iraqis, began writing to Muslim and Iraqi audiences. Jewish writers like Anwar Sha'ul (b.1904) and Shalom Darwish (b.1913) addressed the needs of Iraqi women and often wrote about women whose sectarian identity was unmentioned and could have been Jewish, Christian, or Muslim (Shi'i or Sunni). In such stories, they addressed the need to reform certain practices that curtailed the progress of Iraqi and Arab women, like the marriage of young women to older men within all religious communities in Iraq, honor killings[5] (a practice rarely performed in the urban Jewish milieu), women's education, women's poverty, and the lack of a social system that supports such women.[6] The stories of Ya'qub Balbul should, therefore, be read within this context, in which Jewish authors expressed their opinion on matters relating to gender, nationalism, and cultural and religious reform.

A Portrait of a Silent Woman

Balbul's most celebrated story, "An Accurate Portrait (*sura tabq al-asl*)," which was translated into several European languages, tackled the practice of honor killings in Iraq. The story opens with a scene depicting two brothers, 'Aziz and Salih, approaching the house of an elderly midwife, Sa'ida, who is inspecting the merchandise she received as a payment for her hard labor the day before. Intuitively, Sa'ida is fearful of the men's menacing features, yet the brothers convince her to come with them, assuring her that their sister is about to give birth;

'Aziz shouts at the midwife, while Salih endeavors to persuade her calmly that her assistance is badly needed. Although petrified, Salih and 'Aziz's words affect Sa'ida, and she leaves with them. In a narrow alley, 'Aziz suddenly covers her eyes and begins carrying her on his shoulders to an unknown location. "Sa'ida's body quivered, and she screamed: 'I ask the protection of Allah (*aman*)! 'Aziz answered: 'By Allah, don't be afraid, auntie. We just want to bring you to the house without you knowing its address. Don't worry.'"[7] When 'Aziz finally lets Sa'ida off his shoulders and uncovers her eyes, she finds herself in a narrow, dark alley and is then let into an even darker house, where she discovers a young girl, whom 'Aziz identifies as his sister. He then orders the midwife to determine whether the girl is pregnant or not, and threatens that her own life might be in danger if the girl is not with child. "When the girl saw her brothers with this strange woman, she was startled and perplexed as to the interpretation of this unknown occurrence. Out of curiosity, she rose from her seat, but a shout from 'Aziz ordering her to stay put aborted her motion" (Balbul 2006, 38). Pale and breathing heavily, Sa'ida obeys 'Aziz's commands and inspects the girl, as 'Aziz hastens her to inform him of the results of her inspection:

> The girl trembled all this time, her face growing even more yellowish than before, and she breathed heavily. The midwife answered 'Aziz, whilst her compassionate gaze still focused on the poor girl *about to be slaughtered in front of her eyes*:
> Yes, she is pregnant. [...] She...I say...by Allah...is a poor girl...Have mercy on her. *I plead you in the name of Allah and the prophets*. Have mercy on her...*Allah does not agree to such a thing*. (38, emphasis mine)

'Aziz, however, remains unimpressed. Pulling a knife from his pocket, he addresses his sister for the first time: " 'Say your last prayer...Say: There is no God but Allah.' Yet the girl remained frozen" (40). Despite his pleas, she refuses to speak. Upon Sa'ida's verdict, 'Aziz butchers his sister. The girl's blood flows to the gutters for five long, torturous minutes. While 'Aziz never stops watching his sister's last moments, Salih and Sa'ida turn their heads away. 'Aziz then wishes to pay the midwife, but she "resolutely refused to trade in her illegal crime" (*bi-jarimatiha al-ghayr mashru'a*). She is then carried out, blindfolded, by Salih to her home, where she collapses helplessly on the bed and falls asleep.

The theme of honor killings was common in interwar Iraq. Iraqi writers often depicted the murder of a poor woman by a relative in her own home in order to caution against the perils of misguided notions of religiosity and popular religious beliefs, which had been sanctified as holy traditions. Underscoring the suffering inflicted by ignorant men on their wives, sisters, and daughters, and more generally, on their nation, the household in such stories often represented the fragmented nature of the nation, torn by outdated norms and victimizing its innocent women (Bashkin 2008, 71–75). Balbul's story, however, represents a few radical shifts from other texts published in this period. First, while novelists like 'Abd al-Majid Lutfi or Jewish female writer Miriam al-Mulla presented images of innocent women who were either virgins whose repute was tarnished by malicious gossip, or victims of rape,[8] here the question of how the woman became pregnant (or whether she is pregnant at all) becomes irrelevant. It is the discovery of the pregnancy that is the crucial core of the text. Not focusing on questions relating to morality or innocence, Balbul is thus able to underscore the sadism and violence affiliated with the practice. The ways in which the brothers manipulate a fellow woman to betray the secrets of another, the modes in which the brothers humiliate and abuse their sister, and the reactions of the women to these situations are far more important to him than questions relating to virginity.

Second, the text reflects on the themes of passivity, action, and especially voice, by juxtaposing the conduct of Sa'ida and the innocent slain girl. Both women are silent and at the mercy of 'Aziz, a man resembling an all-powerful god whose commanding voice generates the actions of all the other human beings in the text. Nonetheless, significant differences arise between the two women. Sa'ida is able to act, move, and speak only upon the orders of men. She is both passive and active; she does perform a medical examination and she speaks to the brothers in an attempt to save the girl's life, yet her actions are always performed as a response to a situation that she cannot control. Represented as a passive collaborator whose obedience is motivated by a desire to survive, Sa'ida's attempts to protect the girl and her rejection of the payment offered by the brothers, as she acknowledges the criminality of her actions, are contrasted with the fact that her medical diagnosis enabled the brothers to carry out the murder. Sa'ida's passivity, moreover, is demonstrated by her lack of movement: she is carried by the brothers to and from the household-turned-slaughterhouse, she is blinded, and her final reaction to the tragedy is to fall asleep. Although older than the brothers, her voice in this fatherless and motherless household is ignored.

Sa'ida's conduct, however, is contrasted with that of the nameless girl who initially obeys 'Aziz's commands, yet in the most important scene in the text refuses to speak, to beg for her life, or to appeal to her brothers' forgiveness. Moreover, by refusing to say *a prayer* she underlines the fact that her murder has nothing to do with religion. Her silence, then, is rendered more meaningful from the actions of Salih and Sa'ida, who follow 'Aziz's sinister scheme, notwithstanding their realization of the lawlessness and violence embodied in his actions. Knowing full well that her speech is inconsequential, the girl's only power remains in her silence and in her refusal to respond to the male voice ordering her to act in the name of wrongly interpreted religious values. Interestingly, Balbul, a male, Jewish, bourgeois writer, did not aspire to record the speech or the protest of the slaughtered woman. By recording her silence and by depicting the sociopolitical milieu that enabled the murder and its silencing, he made his most radical contribution to the discourse in which he participated.

These conflicting images regarding passivity and action, voice and silence, echo important debates conducted in the Arab public sphere of the time. Women's education was often seen as a useful venue that would rescue them from their passivity as submissive housewives and ignorant mothers, whose existence depended solely on obeying others. Education, conversely, would allow women more constructive roles as the educators of their children in the household.[9] Many nationalists argued that a society such as the Iraqi one, whose female half was paralyzed and passive, could not progress. Iraqi intellectuals in the post-war era, especially Nazik al-Mala'ika, went even further and implicitly condemned the passivity of women, all of whom were potential victims of patriarchal violence, who did not help their fellow sisters and daughters murdered by their fathers, brothers, and other family members (Bashkin 2008, 72–74). Sa'ida's role in the story should be seen in this context, as her partial passivity and vulnerability facilitate in some way the murder of a fellow woman. More generally, the text suggests that the collaboration and submissiveness of the entire Iraqi society enable such murders to take place.

To protest their passivity and victimization, women needed to regain their voices. Iraqi female intellectuals have indeed demanded suffrage (especially in the 1940s), published their works in journals and cultural magazines, and protested against their marginalization in society. In all of these venues, they insisted that their voices be heard. Balbul's text, alternatively, posits that the mere articulation of a speaking voice in such a violent context is futile, since the society surrounding these women refuses to listen. The futility involved in the mere act of speaking is exemplified by the fact that Sa'ida's voice, uttered when she talks to the brothers, pleads for mercy, asks for the protection of Allah and even screams, and is left unheard.

Although a Jew, Balbul was unhesitant to condemn certain norms perceived to be connected to Islamic law. In the short dialogues, many characters evoke the name of Allah and use his name to justify certain actions, which range from a plea for mercy (Sa'ida) to the actual murder itself ('Aziz). In fact, two people are speaking in the name of Islam: 'Aziz, who believes that his sister should be slaughtered according to Islamic law and therefore attempts to force her to pray; and the midwife, who argues that "Allah does not agree with such a thing" and knows that her acts are criminal and in contradiction with the *shari'a* (Islamic law). Significantly, Sa'ida's arguments mirror positions adopted by Muslim reformers and feminists who contended that the practice of honor killing did not represent any Islamic values but rather primitive practices that penetrated into Islam and became sanctified as holy traditions. In other words, such male killers were themselves bad Muslims and, moreover, usually conducted such barbaric acts because of their violence, sadism, desire for power, and misguided perceptions of masculinity.[10] In the text, such contentions are communicated through the voice of an ignorant midwife. Instead of presenting long arguments against the practice of honor killing, the description of the murder itself acts as a potent commentary on the brutality to which Iraqi women were exposed.

It should be noted that very few Jews dared critique directly norms and practices understood to be Islamic, fearing that a critique of the hegemonic religion by a Jew might undermine their integration efforts. Furthermore, some Muslim writers feared siding with the Muslim reformers and avoided expressing such reformist views during the 1930s lest these articulations lead to accusations of sacrilege and heresy. This move was not well received by some, and Balbul even received threats on his life because of this story and faced pressures from his publishers as well. As a Jew, then, what enabled him to speak to a Muslim audience and provide advice on the need to reform practices not typifying his own religious community? Seemingly, the only non-Muslims who preached for Islamic reform were the British that controlled Iraq in the 1920s and condemned "Islam's" treatment of Muslim women. Clearly, this was not the camp to which Balbul, a nationalist, wished to belong. Yet two intellectual moves facilitated Balbul's choice in writing about Muslim women and Islamic practices. The first was the nationalization and secularization of the Islamic past by Iraqi nationalists. Especially in the 1930s, Iraqi nationalists reread narratives relating to the Islamic past as models for the contemporary Iraqi public. The formation of the early Islamic state and the Islamic conquest of the Middle East following it became emblems of nation building, heroism, and patriotism, rather than segments in the history of the Islamic community of believers (Dawn 1988, 67–91).

The second was the familiarization of Jewish intellectuals with the Islamic tradition. Jewish students, although officially exempt from Qur'an classes, attended Qura'nic lessons in Iraqi schools. They were likewise familiar with the rich medieval Arabic literary tradition and the Arabic language that was taught in Jewish and public schools as part of the state's agenda to use Arabic language and Arab culture as the national markers of the new nation-state. Moreover, when writing about their rights as religious minorities in the Iraqi nation-state, Jewish writers used Qur'anic quotations. They often celebrated the ways in which the Islamic faith allowed Jews and Christians to coexist with the Muslim subjects of various Islamic empires and juxtaposed this tolerance with European medieval fanaticism (Kazzaz 1991, 54–158; Snir 2005, 23–246). The process of secularizing Islam, and the subsequent adoption of Islam as a national-cultural component of the identity of Iraqi Jews, encouraged Balbul to think that as a Jew he could comment on practices related to Islam. The domain in which he chose to comment on such practices was gender. The abuse of Iraqi women in the name of misconstrued religious values, in other words, seemed to Balbul the most appropriate venue to mark his national commitment to the Iraqi nation.

Balbul's critique was motivated by a sense that he was a part of the Iraqi-Muslim community and by the indignation he felt at the violence against women. His participation in the discourse about gender was, therefore, both nationalist and ethical. With much courage and compassion, he tackled a controversial topic in his community. He did so, however, by evoking a practice that many nationalists identified as a peril to the Iraqi nation. Furthermore, as the national elites often depicted the household as the most essential component of Iraqi nationhood, Balbul constructed a dysfunctional household, which was devoid of a father and a mother, and was affiliated with dark, filthy, and unknown spaces, in order to call for change and reform. As the text focuses on the uneducated and poor segments of Iraqi society, on their erroneous perception of Islam, and the ways in which it endangers the Iraqi nation, the author's gaze was turned inward. In other stories of his, however, the West, especially the colonizing West, assumed great significance.

Lydia's Voice

Balbul's short story "The Return (al-'awda)" evokes many themes that were being discussed by contemporary Arab writers, namely the effects of Western education upon Iraqi men and upon their perceptions of gender.

The story focuses on a successful merchant called Yusuf Adham. In 1910 Yusuf moves from Iraq to Istanbul to study. He returns briefly to Baghdad, where he marries his cousin, Samira, and has a son with her. Initially he marries Samira against his will, but he learns to love and respect her with the passing of time. Nonetheless, despite his blissful life in Baghdad, his loving wife, and adoring son, Yusuf decides to go back to Istanbul, motivated by greed and covetousness. World War I compels him to shift his business to Greece, where his fortune grows. He changes his name to Joseph Adam and marries Lydia, a beautiful Greek woman. Lydia, however, finds it extremely difficult to remain loyal to her Arab husband and prefers spending her nights with various lovers. Moreover, she refuses to give Joseph a child because she is afraid of the effects of childbirth on her beautiful physique, as well as on her nightly escapades.

> He had hoped for an empathetic and compassionate wife, who would distance the boredom of work and the troubles of the day from him [...]. And yet he ended up with a wife who leaves him at nighttime and returns at midnight or dawn, spending her nights at immoral dance-parties or with her lovers, who were amongst his closest friends. [...] Despite all of this, *he remained silent and speechless*, unable to criticize or scold her. He did not even have the right to ask her where she spent her nights. If he dared ask, he would hear constant grumbling. Then her tongue would commence an empty chatter; [...], attacking her pesky husband, his conduct which does not agree with the rules of civilization and culture, and his blind zealotry [...], announcing she is tired from this life, in which a husband intervenes in the private affairs of his wife, telling him that he is from the descendents of these Arabs that use women like a man uses an ox.[11] (emphasis mine)

He wonders how he could forget his Arab origins and deteriorates into a state of jealousy, helplessness, and constant humiliation. Joseph/Yusuf feels that all his wealth has become worthless in these surroundings. He longs for Baghdad, a city where he was born and grew up, and where his ancestors lived.

> He recalled his beautiful country and its features. He remembered what he heard and read about his country; that it progressed greatly;

that it revolted against the yoke of colonialism and drove the colonizers out; that it became an independent kingdom whose rulers are *pure Arabs*; and that its capital became a momentous center in the world of politics and commerce. He felt lonesome for his country and a yearning to return to it. (66, emphasis mine)

Joseph/Yusuf finally decides to return to his son and wife in Baghdad. He secretly sells all his property, leaving Lydia with the divorce papers and a letter in which he announces his disillusionment with his lifestyle. "When you read this letter, darling, I will be leaving Athens heading to my dear homeland, to Iraq, where I will meet my family and friends, my loyal wife and my beloved child." He ends the letter wishing his wife to remain "free and loved" (70).

Balbul's text appropriates gendered components of Iraqi and Arab national discourses and intertwines them with his narrative. To create the binaries between national authenticity and foreign, imperial intervention, Balbul uses the most tired convention available to the Arab writer at the time, namely, the juxtaposition of a loyal Arab woman with a materialist, hedonistic, sexually promiscuous, Western woman. Such gendered binaries (Western-licentious/Eastern-pure) appear in the works of Tawfiq al-Hakim (b. 1898) and Yahya Haqqi (b.~1905) in Egypt and Mamhud Ahmad al-Sayyid (b.1904) and Dhu Nun Ayyub (b.1900) in Iraq.[12]

Joseph/Yusuf's first wife, Samira, is connected to Iraq and is tied, in her husband's memory, with his patriotism. His homeland, more broadly, is associated with two idyllic households: his own and that of his parents, as well as to reminiscences about youth and joy. The description of family life in Iraq, however, is rather conservative: Yusuf's wife is his cousin; he is married in an arranged marriage; and Samira utters no sound during the text. We hear about her only through the memories of her husband. The product of this marriage is a healthy male boy. Lydia, on the other hand, represents all that is wrong in Western culture, in particular, an excessive freedom connoting a materialistic and meaningless lifestyle. Joseph/Yusuf thinks of her while contemplating his nation's struggle against colonialism, whereas she identifies his conservatism and demands for fidelity as reflective of his Arab mind and lack of civilized manners. Implicitly, then, the process of civilizing the Arab by a Westerner means a loss of family values related to gender, sexuality, domesticity, and propriety. Significantly, whereas in "An Accurate Portrait," the silencing voice of men oppressed Iraqi women, here the Western woman's voice silences her husband. In fact, her voice is so troubling to him that it is depicted as constant, disturbing noise. When he justly challenges Lydia on her infidelities, all that she is able to produce is a violent rant, which turns into a disturbing, even unbearable, clamor. Moreover, even at his ultimate moment of rebellion, when he finally leaves her, Yusuf simply *writes* a letter to his wife; he never speaks to her directly.

As noted, the creation of a functional and productive household was seen as an important goal of the national elites' gendered modernization efforts. Fears that excessive modernization would lead to a moral crisis and a destruction of the very same household also typified this discourse, which placed great emphasis on the perilous effects of Western modernity and Western lifestyles.[13] Balbul's story fits into this discussion and appropriates many of its features. In the context of anxieties over the ways in which middle- and upper-class Westernized Iraqi women behaved, the story addresses Iraqi, rather than European, women, as it alerts Westernized Iraqi women not to blindly follow Western cultural norms, lest their fate be similar to Lydia's. Balbul embodied these anxieties in the cardboard character of Lydia and admonished against excessive modernization, which comes at the price of long-cherished cultural values. In his final letter to his wife, Joseph/Yusuf wishes Lydia "to be free" (*hurra*). "The liberation of woman" (*tahrir al-mar'a*), as coined by Egyptian reformer Qasim Amin (1863–1908), was a call for women's education and the ending of seclusion in the discourse of Islamic religious reformers (Amin 1899). In the story, however, Lydia's freedom signals an uncontrolled sexual conduct and the abandonment of family life and the rearing of children.

Characters of Iraqis who dwelled outside their homeland populated works of prose fiction produced in the Iraq of the 1930s. Early novelists, such as Dhu Nun Ayyub and Mahmud Ahmad al-Sayyid, situated their protagonists outside Iraq as a way of reflecting on the national commitments of young Iraqis who debated the cultural mores that their country should uphold. Ayyub, in particular, focused on the immoral conduct of certain individuals who acquired a Western education abroad and then manipulated this knowledge to acquire political power in Iraq. These texts reflect a historical context in which Iraqi bureaucrats and officials like Fadhil Jamali (b.1902), Ahmad Nissim Susa (b.1902), and Matta 'Aqrawi (b.1901) returned from the United States and became part of Iraq's culture and politics.[14] Jamali and Susa also married foreign women. Regardless of the fact that the number of Iraqis who actually married European and American women was small, nationalist writers addressed this subject, warned against it, and made the issue a national symbol. Sami Shawkat, for example, warned against marrying foreign women, who resembled "foreign plants" and were consequently unfit for the Iraqi soil. The image of Lydia should be understood within this context as a woman jeopardizing Yusuf's Iraqi-ness and Arab-ness, two national markers that determine his gendered and cultural values even when he was away from Iraq.

Joseph/Yusuf's affiliation with Lydia is constructed as a betrayal of Arab, Islamic, and Iraqi norms that went even beyond gendered themes. Yusuf's first transformation is from Baghdad to Istanbul, the imperial capital to which many Iraqi elites traveled during the early 1900s in order to benefit from the Ottoman Empire's thriving educational and cultural centers. Yusuf, however, is not only disloyal to Iraq, but also to the Ottoman Empire, since he chooses to abandon the empire during World War I. The Iraqi public sphere during the interwar period cherished Turkey's secular reforms. Furthermore, despite the Arab revolt against the Ottoman Empire, many of Iraq's intellectuals supported it during World War I and identified with Turkey during its war of independence, seeing this war as a regional battle against colonialism. The transformation Yusuf undergoes between Turkey and Greece indicates a betrayal of this shared Ottoman-Arab tradition. It is in (Christian) Greece that the most profound transformation in his identity (and in his relationship to women) occurs, and it is his return to Iraq that will rectify its harmful effects.[15]

Yusuf's religious identity is unknown since his name could be Jewish, Christian, or Muslim. Although polygamous, we can assume that a Jewish or a Christian Iraqi could marry a woman in Greece without her knowing about the existence of another wife in Iraq. Crucially, the signifiers of Yusuf's identity are his Arab-ness (rather than his religion) and the ways in which he behaves with the women who surround him. The fact that he subscribes to a particular set of gendered cultural norms denotes his belonging to the Arab-Iraqi national community. Joseph Adam is a man who lives abroad, who esteems material culture, and who is humiliated and disgraced by his promiscuous Western wife. Yusuf Adham is a man who is loved by his mother and wife, who produces a son, and who is able to help his motherland. The binaries of West/East and colonizer/colonized, then, were far more important than sectarian and religious notions that separated Jews from Muslims. Differently put: the discourse about gender was used to unify members of the Iraqi *effendia* (educated urban middle classes), and served to diffuse, or at least to blur, sectarian identities, since, as the text suggests, Arab cultural values were shared by all religious communities in Iraq.

The differences between men and women as represented in the two stories correspond to different sets of representations. In "An Accurate Portrait," which is situated in the poor neighborhood of Baghdad, and whose aim is to call for religious and legal reform, women are voiceless victims. Their oppression and discrimination are rooted in their families' practices, the corruption of the Islamic faith by the urban poor, and the silent collaboration of certain female members with this oppressive and patriarchal social regime. A Jewish patriot trying to make a place for himself in the Iraqi public domain, Balbul used his writing about poor women to indicate that he, as a member of a minority community, had a say in discourses about reform and femininity current among a variety of social and ethnic groups. "The Return," in contrast, celebrates another type of woman, a bourgeois, submissive mother and wife, who patiently awaits her husband. In this story, women symbolize national authenticity, as opposed to Western colonialism, and, as such, the Iraqi household in which they live should not be reformed, but rather preserved. The voice of Western women is identified with that of the colonizers and the noise they produce. Lydia's voice is used to silence Joseph/Yusuf, and her actions to punish him for his betrayal of national values and of the motherland itself. Moreover, whereas in the first story, 'Aziz seems to be a man in control of the space he inhabits, Joseph/Yusuf, when he is in Greece, is completely incapable of deciphering the laws of his milieu and is hence condemned to a life of passivity and misery. The parallel between a nuclear bourgeois family and the nation, whose members are tied by links of Arab ethnicity, is repeated many times in "The Return." The Jewish Balbul validated his loyalty to the Arab nation by celebrating the cultural conventions and institutions he affiliated with the nation's middle-class families.

Conclusions

In postcolonial Iraq, the debate about women was never a consideration of gendered rights and citizenship alone. There was an Iraqi debate on actual issues that affected women's lives and conduct: education, entry into the labor market, honor killing, and dress codes. Parallel to this debate, however, rose a conversation about "metaphoric women," that is, cartoonlike women whose representations had very little to do with the real situation of women in Iraq, since such representations were used as a platform for deliberating a host of national concerns. Such metaphoric women, like Lydia and Samira, appear in

"The Return." Obviously, the boundaries between the "real" women and the "metaphoric" ones were never fixed, and often real concerns like honor killings, as discussed in "An Accurate Portrait," were not only realities that affected the lives of Iraqis but were also expanded (in poetry, prose fiction, and the press) into powerful emblems that echoed positions on nationalism, culture, ethnicity, and authenticity.

Balbul assumed a readership of mixed middle-class Arab readers—Jews, Christians, Shi'is, and Sunnis alike—whose interests and anxieties were not limited to any sectarian group. These interests and anxieties were, therefore, located within the framework of the Arab and Iraqi nation. Balbul chose not to tackle religious and social practices specific to the Jewish community and its relationship toward women, although other Iraqi-Jewish intellectuals at the time did attempt to do this. The category of nation managed to overcome that of religious difference since the discourses about womanhood, gender, and domesticity occurred in an Iraqi and Arab print market, which was read by many Iraqis of varying religious communities. Balbul's desire to be part of the national discourse, however, led to his participation in projects of subjugation, as his use of the submissive archetype (in "The Return") effectively undermined his attempts at reform (in "An Authentic Portrait"). In the Iraqi context, then, it was not only Iraqi men saving Iraqi women from British officials and colonizers. It was also Jewish-Iraqi men (who wanted to highlight their commitment to the nation) who saved Iraqi women from Iraqi men and saved Iraqi men from foreign women.

Notes

1. See an early favorable review of Balbul's works in the Shi'i literary magazine *al-Hatif* 4(161) (31 March 1939):1. The article complained about the fact that Iraqis do not buy works produced by Iraqi authors and novelists, and prefer Egyptian and Lebanese writers in their stead. The author then bemoaned that a talented writer like Balbul needed the aid of his father in order to publish his works. In "Introduction" in *Selections...*, 9–16, 75–79; Snir, 74–76; 112–18, 166–68.
2. On the situation of Iraqi women, see al-Shaykh-Da'ud; Ingrams; Efrati ("The Other Awakening..."), 153–83; Woodsmall; and al-'Awlaji, 'Abd al-Hamid.
3. On Iraqi nationalism in this period, see Wien; Simon; Marr, 85-99; Cleveland, 56–57; and Bashkin (*The Other Iraq...*), chap. 4, 5.
4. *Al-Istiqlal* 3669 (May 31, 1940): 4. The reference here is to the prophet's wisdom, 'A'isha bint Abi Bakr (d. 678), who was one of the leaders of a battle against the forces of the forth righteous caliph and the Shi'I iman, 'Ali ibn Abi Talib at 656.

5. The killing of a woman suspected of immoral conduct by a member of her family in order to save her family's honor.
6. Sha'ul; on Iraqi-Jewish women, see Snir 377–409; also Gabbai; Me'ir, 323–45; and Sehayek.
7. Balbul, *sura tabq al-asal*, originally published June 18, 1937, reprinted in Moreh, *Selections*, 37. (The dialogue in the text is in the Iraqi colloquial.)
8. See the story *ra'ihat al-damm* in Lutfi; also Bassun 540–41.
9. One of the earliest articulations of this position is found in Amin.
10. On gender and Islamic reforms, see Masliyah, 161–71; Ende, 1–43; and Bashkin, "Representations," 56–60.
11. Balbul, *al-'awda*, reprinted in *Selections* (originally published Oct. 5, 1937), 56.
12. Tawfig al-Hakim, *Usfur min al-sharq*. Cairo: Matba'at lajnat al-ta'lif waal-tarjama wa'l-nahsr, 1938; Yahya Haqqi, *Qindil umm hashim*. Cairo: al-Ma'arif, 1944; M. M. Badawi, "The Lamp of Umm Hashim: The Egyptian Intellectual between East and West." *Journal of Arabic Literature*, vol. 1 (1970):145–61; Mahmud Ahmad al-Sayyid *Jalil Khalid* (a novel, 1929, in *al-A'mal al-kamila li Mahmud Ahmad al-Sayyid*. Baghdad: Dar al-Hurriyya, 1978; Dhu Nun Ayyub, Duktur Ibrahim (a novel, 1939) in Dhu Nun Ayyuib, *Duktur Ibrahim, al-Athar Al-kamila li-athar Dhi Al-Nun Ayyub*. Baghdad: Wizarat al-I'lam, 1978.
13. Works of prose fiction and the press often participated in "the campaign against moral corruption" (*al-hamla 'ala al-bugha'*), cautioning against wine drinking and lack of morals. 'Abd al-Ilah Ahmad, *Nash'at al-qissa watatawwuruha fi'l-'iraq*. Baghdad: Dar al-shu;un al-thaqafiyya al-'amma, 1986, 224–28; Ja'far al-Khalili, *Al-Qissas al-'iraqiya, qaadiman wa-hadithan*. Baghdad: Maatba'at al-ma'arif, 1957, 191–92.
14. For analysis of the works of Ayyub and al-Sayyid, see Orit Bashkin, "Out of Place: Home and Empire in the Works of Mahmud Ahmad al-Sayyid and Dhu Nun Ayyub." *Comparative Studies of South Asia, Africa and the Middle East* 28(3) (2008): 428–42.
15. On the relationship between Iraqis and Ottomans, see Bashkin, *The Other Iraq*, chap. 5.

Works Cited

'Alwaji, 'Abd al-Hamid al-. 1975. *Al-Intaj al-nisawi fi al-'iraq* [Female production in Iraq]. Baghdad: Wizara al-I'lam.
Amin, Qasim. *Tahrir al-mar'a*. 1899. Cairo: al-Majlis al-a'la li'l thaqafa.
Balbul, Ya'qub. 2006. *Selections from "The First Ember" and "A Mind's Plight"/Ya'cov [Balboul] Lev, Mukhtarat min "al-Jamra al-ula" wa "Minhat al-'aql,"* (Shemuel Moreh, ed.), Jerusalem: *Agudat ha-akadema'im yoze'y 'iraq*.

Bashkin, Orit. 2008. "Representations of Women in the Writings of the Iraqi Intelligentsia in Hashemite Iraq, 1921–1958," *Journal of Middle East Women's Studies* 4(1): 52–78.

———. 2009. *The Other Iraq – Pluralism and Culture in Hashemite Iraqi*. Stanford, CA: Stanford University Press.

Bassun, Miriam al-Mulla. 1981. Ma'satuhu mathal [His tragedy is a lesson] in Shmuel Moreh, *al-Qissa al-qasira 'inda yahud al-'iraq, 1921–1978* [The short story amongst Iraqi Jews]. Jerusalem: Dar al-Nashr/Magens, al-Jami'a al-'Ibraiyya. 540–41.

Bhabha, Homi K. 1994. *The Location of Culture*. London and New York: Routledge, 157.

———. 1997. "Minority Maneuvers and Unsettled Negotiations," *Critical Inquiry* 23(3):431–59.

Cleveland, William L. 1971. *The Making of an Arab Nationalist; Ottomanism and Arabism in the Life and Thought of Sati' al-Husri*. Princeton: Princeton University Press.

Dawn, Ernest C. 1988. "The Formation of Pan-Arab Ideology in the Inter-War Years. *International Journal of Middle East Studies* 20(1) (Winter):67–91.

Efrati, Noga. 2001. "Women in Elite's Discourses: Iraq 1932–1958" (in Hebrew). PhD dissertation, Haifa University.

———. 2004. "The Other 'Awakening' in Iraq: The Women's Movement in the First Half of the Twentieth Century." *British Journal of Middle Eastern Studies* 31(2) (November):153–73.

Ende, Werner. 1980. Ehe auf Zeit in der innerislamischen Diskussion der Gegenwart. *Die Welt des Islams* 20(1–2):1–43.

Gabbai, Nilli. 2006. *Ha-isha ha-yehudit be-bagdad* [The Jewish women in Baghdad']. Jerusalem: Agudat ha-akadema'im yoze'y ' iraq.

Gharib, Rose. 1938. "The Home Economic Movement—The Factors of Its Rise and Spread in the USA." *Al-Mu'allim al-jadid* 3(3, June): 206–213 (Arabic).

Ingrams, Doreen, ed. 1983. *The Awakened: Women in Iraq*. London: Third World Centre. *"Editorial" Istiqlal* 31/May/1940 no. 3669, 4

Jawahiri, 'Imad Ahmad al-. 1984. *Nadi al-Muthana wa-wajihat al-tajammu 'al-qawmi fi al-'iraq, 1934–1942* [The Muthana Club and displays of national unity in Iraq, 1934–1942]. Baghdad: Matba'at dar al-jahiz.

Kazzaz, Nissim. 1991. *He-yehudim be-'iraq ba-ma'a he-'esrim* [Jews in Iraq during the 20th century]. Jerusalem: Yad Ben-Zvi.

Lutfi, 'Abd al-Majid. 1944. *Qalb umm* [The heart of a mother]. Baghdad: Matba'at al-sabah.

Mala'ika, Nazik al-. 1979. *Diwan Nazik al-Mala'ika*, vol. 2. Beirut: Dar al-'Awda.

Masliyah, Sadok. 1996. "Zahawi: A Muslim Pioneer of Women's Liberation." *Middle Eastern Studies* 32(3) (July):161–71.

Marr, Phebe. 1985. "The Development of Nationalist Ideology in Iraq, 1921–1941." *Muslim World* 75(3) (Spring):85–99.

Me'ir, Josef. 1989. *Hitpathut hevratit tarbutit shel yehudey 'iraq me'az 1830 ve 'ad yemeynu* [Cultural and Social Development of Iraqi Jews: From 1830 to our days], Tel-Aviv: Naharayim.

Rejwan, Nissim. 1985. *The Jews of Iraq: 3000 Years of History and Culture.* Boulder: Westview Press.

Sha'ul, Anuwar. 1984. *Qissa hayati fi wadi al-rafidayn* [My life story in the land of two rivers]. Jerusalem: Rabita al-Jami'iyin al-Yahud al-Nazihin min al-'Iraq.

Shawkat, Sami. 1939. *Hadhihi ahadafuna*, Baghdad: Majjalat al-mu'allim al-jadid.

Sehayek, Shaul. 2003. "Changes in the Social Status of Urban Jewish Women in Iraq as the Nineteenth Century Turned," *Women in Judaism: A Multidisciplinary Journal*, 3(2) at: http://jps.library.utoronto.ca.proxy.uchicago.edu/index.php/wjudaism/issue/view/37. Last accessed Feb. 13, 2011.

Shenhav Yehouda. 2006. *The Arab Jews: A Postcolonial Reading of Nationalism, Religion and Ethnicity.* Stanford, CA: Stanford University Press.

Shiblak, Abbas. 1986. *The Lure of Zion: The Case of Iraqi Jews*, London: al-Saqi Books.

Shaykh-Da'ud, Sabiha. 1958. *Awal al-tariq ila al-nahda al-nisawiyya fi al-'iraq* [The beginning of the road to the female revival in Iraq]. Baghdad: Al-Rabita.

Simon, Reeva S. 1986. *Iraq between Two World Wars: The Creation and Implementation of a Nationalist Ideology.* New York: Columbia University Press.

Snir, Reuven. 2005. *'Arviyut, yahdut, zionut: Ma'vak zehuyot bi-yeziratam shel yehudei 'iraq* [Arabism, Judaism and Zionism: An identity conflict in the works of the Jews of Iraq]. Jerusalem: Yad Ben Zvi.

Spivak, Gayatry. 1988. "Can the Subaltern Speak?" Cornel West, Cary Nelson, Lawrence Grossberg, eds. *Marxism and the Interpretation of Culture.* Chicago: University of Illinois Press. 271–313.

Wien, Peter. 2006. *Iraqi Arab Nationalism: Authoritarian, Totalitarian, and Pro-Fascist Inclinations, 1932–1941.* New York: Routledge.

Woodsmall, Ruth F. 1956. *Study of the Role of Women: Their Activities and Organizations in Lebanon, Egypt, Iraq, Jordan, and Syria, October 1954–August 1955.* New York: International Federation of Business and Professional Women.

Part III

Transnational Decentering of Human/Women's Rights

Chapter Six

Race, Gender, and Human Rights: A Glimpse into the Transnational Feminist Organization of Afro-Brazilian Women

Jessica Franklin

> The concept of human rights, like all vibrant versions, is not static or the property of any one group; rather its meaning expands as people reconceptualize their needs and hopes in relation to it. (Bunch 1990, 487)

This excerpt from feminist Charlotte Bunch identifies a critical reason for the increased prominence and usage of international human rights frameworks among social activists, nongovernmental organizations (NGOs), and governing bodies in the twenty-first century.[1] One of the most notable proponents of this framework has been the international women's movement. Framing gender inequality as a human rights issue has effectively strengthened the movement's criticisms of gender-biased domestic policy and broadened its support among other transnational social movements. Yet, in recent years growing numbers of feminist activists and legal scholars have noted the limited utility of a gender-centered viewpoint (Crenshaw 1989; Bond 2003; Lewis 2003). They have called for the development of an intersectional approach to human rights, which would effectively address the multiple forms of discrimination simultaneously faced by women. From this perspective, the multidimensionality of women's identities and the human rights abuses perpetuated against them cannot be fully revealed within a single axis framework. Gender identities and inequalities cannot be clearly delineated from those based on race, class, ethnicity, sexuality, or other identity categories, but must be viewed as manifestations of the interactions that occur between these social forces. In effect, a theoretical and legal framework of human rights that does not adequately consider the "complex and multilayered realities [of] women cannot be expected to achieve the full implementation of human rights" (Lewis 2003, 514–15).

Afro-Brazilian feminists have been at the forefront of efforts to integrate an intersectional perspective in international human rights discourse and feminist practice in Brazil. The constructs of race, gender, and class are especially salient for Afro-Brazilian women (Lovell 2006, 64). Representing 23 percent of the total Brazilian population, they are the most economically disadvantaged segment, consistently falling behind white women and men in terms of income, employment, literacy, and education levels (Barsted and Hermann 2001). Increasing rates of maternal and infant mortality, hysterectomies, and breast cancer since the 1990s reflect the barriers to reproductive health care and education faced by this community because of their low earning power and status as women and Afro-descendants.[2] Only within the past three decades has the notable imbalance between white and black populations in Brazil received considerable attention because of the significant efforts of the Afro-Brazilian women's movement. Several black women's organizations, including Geledes, the Black Women's Institute in Sao Paulo, Criola in Rio de Janiero, and Maria Mulher in Porto Alegre, developed throughout the 1980s and 1990s to address the specific challenges encountered by black women in the areas of domestic violence, reproductive health care, and education. These activists have recognized the power of the international human rights regime to legitimize and strengthen movement platforms denouncing such forms of systemic discrimination, but have also realized the historical disregard of intersectional perspectives within legal measures and conventions and limited enforcement capabilities of these instruments in the domestic realm. Through increased collaborations with the Brazilian feminist movement and political engagements at the transnational level, Afro-Brazilian feminists have looked to expand the scope of human rights, not by generalizing the experience of oppression, but by emphasizing the distinctive and compounded nature of discriminations. Their claims and strategies reflect a critical shift in the redress of the rights of marginalized women across the globe. These individuals no longer singularly seek equal status under law, but rather the right to be politically recognized and socially accepted as different (Jelin 1996, 178–79).

This essay will analyze the capacity of Afro-Brazilian feminists to challenge normative domestic discourses on race and gender through the lens of human rights and intersectionality and will consider how their heightened participation in formal international policy deliberations, such as United Nations (UN) conferences, reflects both a strategic move to expand feminist perspectives and partnerships and to influence the actions of the Brazilian government by moving outside of its borders (Telles 2004, 61). To begin, it will briefly discuss the concept of intersectionality and its significance for reconceptualizations of identity and oppression within the human rights paradigm. It will illustrate how the incorporation of an intersectional approach to human rights, identity, and collective action by the Afro-Brazilian women's movement has served to counteract the pervasive ideology of racial democracy in Brazil and will outline key moments of contestation by the black women's movement that have resulted in gradual discursive shifts at the domestic level. Following this, this essay will specifically examine the gradual synthesis of antiracist and feminist mobilization efforts in Brazil, considering the dynamics and difficulties of collaborations with the Brazilian feminist movement and the significance of this linkage for the transnational feminist practices of Afro-Brazilian women. The focus will then shift to identify two critical events in the trajectory of the transnational feminist activism of Afro-Brazilian women. These sections will discuss the extensive preparation and participation of Afro-Brazilian women for the United Nations Fourth Conference on Women in Beijing in 1995 and the United Nations Conference against Racism, Racial Discrimination, Xenophobia, and Related Tolerances, held in Durban in September 2001, and the kinds of knowledge and tensions generated in these experiences. The discussion will conclude with a few examples of the policy reforms that Afro-Brazilian feminists have been involved with and the multiple obstacles they have faced in the domestic political arena. It is hoped that this work will provide a much-needed glimpse into the processes by which women who experience multiple forms of discrimination begin to participate in a redefinition and application of human rights for their own ends and for those who have been continually silenced.

Intersectionality and the Human Rights Paradigm

The conceptualization of human rights as an instrument for political mobilization, not only as a moral underpinning, has flourished among discriminated groups seeking to combat inequalities and reveal power imbalances in their respective societies and at the global level (Dutt 1998, 226). The utopian vision of human rights, emphasizing the achievement of universal good and individual goals and fulfillment, has retained some salience in academic and activist circles, but has also faced extensive criticism from minority feminist scholars and activists for its Eurocentric proclamations, individualistic tenets, and disregard of historical and political contextuality (Ely-Yamin 1993, 658). An insightful critique comes from Celina Romany, professor of law and activist, who questions the extent to which human rights can be used as a means of empowerment because of its attachment to "frozen notions of universal good" (2001, 12). Although the premise of universality finds merit in its delineation that each person is deserving of inalienable human rights regardless of geographic, religious, or cultural factors, it reflects a somewhat static viewpoint of how the particularities of geographic location, religious beliefs, and cultural values can shape the nature of human rights abuses and protections. According to Johanna Bond, this interpretation of human rights "assumes that victims of human rights violations all experience those violations in the same way" (2003, 80). From this standpoint, the principle of universalism, in emphasizing the egalitarian application of human rights, does not adequately account for the multidimensionality or complexity of the human condition.

This serves as the critical point of entry for the concept of intersectionality. First introduced by African American law professor and feminist scholar Kimberle Williams Crenshaw to identify the factors that contributed the disproportionate levels of unemployment and domestic violence faced by black women in the United States (1989, 1991), this analytical framework suggests that axes of identity, such as race, gender, ethnicity, and class, coalesce to shape an individual's experiences. Identity is conceptualized as fluid, not static, under this framework, which looks to uncover the intersecting oppressions and discriminations that often emerge from these axes (Crooms 2003, 243–44). Intersectionality theorists recognize that interlocking identities are often the source of discriminatory practices and human rights violations. Seeking to integrate this approach in international human rights discourse, Bond encourages the adoption of "qualified universalism." She describes this perspective as recognizing "that human rights apply to all but that different groups experience human rights violations in fundamentally different ways" because of their multilayered and intersecting identities (2003, 76).

The emphasis on universality is directly linked to another common criticism of the application of the human rights paradigm by the international women's movement: the use of essentialist constructions. Hope Lewis notes that, until recently, this movement has purposefully avoided the appearance of internal distinctions or differences that could potentially threaten the achievement of "women's equality and liberation from oppression" (2003, 513), and in turn relied upon essentialist characterizations of "women" and "gender" to forge solidarity. Women were characterized as having universal attributes, sharing common experiences, and being oppressed in specific ways as women, regardless of their identity grounds. This essentialist conceptualization, however, suffers from significant limitations. As Inderpal Grewal points out, "women cannot be seen as one group with a common tradition, and the term woman carries within itself the notion of an autonomous individual" (2005, 505). This autonomy, however, does not mean that there is no basis for a shared identity or common ground in the women's human rights movement. Rather, it reflects the delicate balance that the movement must strike between "generalizing about women's oppression in a way that marginalizes critical differences along the axes of race, class, ethnicity, religion, and sexual orientation" and finding commonalities in individual experiences and understandings for the purpose of effective coalition building and strategizing (Bond 2003, 108).

For social activist and writer Barbara Schulman, the concern should not necessarily be on the shortcomings of universality and essentialism that have riddled the human rights discourse, but on the opportunities it can wield in particular domestic contexts. She suggests that despite the shortcomings of the utopian model, its general acceptance and open interpretation has served as the greatest advantage for transnational antiracist feminisms seeking to assert human rights as a source of empowerment and critical consciousness. She writes that "the disparity between the general favor directed toward human rights and the lack of concrete knowledge about it actually creates a raft of opportunities for activists working within a variety of liberatory traditions because the relatively nonthreatening language of human rights can function as the opening wedge in conversations with those who may be more resistant to more pointed critiques" (2004, 103). The opportunity to "open a wedge," or generate dialogue in exclusionary spaces, speaks directly to the Brazilian context, where for decades, state and society presented a facade of complete racial harmony and tolerance to the rest of the world while masking pervasive forms of intersectional discrimination.

Countering the Myth of Racial Democracy

Although several states have utilized inaccurate depictions of colonial encounters to legitimate postcolonial political projects, few have been as meticulous in this undertaking as Brazil. Since the mid-1930s, the myth of racial democracy, premised upon the ideals that complete racial equality exists in Brazil and that the race of an individual makes virtually no difference to his or her rights and social positioning, has structured Brazilian political discourse, cultural symbols and images, and historical accounts. Social historian Gilberto Freyre is often heralded for the development of this groundbreaking paradigm in Brazilian race relations, which effectively replaced the biological definition of race with a new domestic discourse of antiracism (Nascimento 2007, 43). According to Freyre, racial identities did not play a decisive role in the colonization of Brazil. He contended that "cosmopolitan and plastic minded" (1946, 3) Portuguese colonizers easily cohabited and mingled with indigenous and African women slaves, enchanted by their sexual allure and "begetting offspring with procreative fervor" (10). This supposedly amicable relationship and the widespread miscegenation that followed resulted in the development of a race that was not only transnational in character, but a reflection of the fluid integration of distinct races and cultures to the point where they were indistinguishable. It was during this era that "Brazil began to think of itself as a hybrid, mestizo civilization—not only European but also the product of miscegenation among whites, blacks, and Indians"—a designation that would come to define Brazil's national identity and remain largely unchallenged until the 1970s and 1980s (Guimaraes 2001, 2).

The constant associations of Afro-Brazilian womanhood with domesticity and sexual mysticism effectively manipulated processes of identity formation and the development of racial and gender consciousness for many Afro-Brazilian women. One of the most adverse stereotypes of Afro-Brazilian women is found in the depiction of mixed race or mulata women as cunning temptresses. Natasha Pravaz notes that "in Brazil, the mulata is commonly portrayed as a woman always ready to deploy her tricks of sorcery and bewitching, embodying sensuality, voluptuosity and dexterity in dancing the samba" (2000, 48). She suggests that mixed-race women will often attempt to perform or embody those features that have been eroticized by Brazilian literary and cultural interpretations in order to experience upward social mobility (Pravaz 2003).

The wide dissemination of sexualized and pejorative images of multiracial and black women in social and cultural imagery of Brazil throughout the nineteenth and twentieth centuries served not only to legitimate historical patterns of sexual exploitation and economic domination (Caldwell 2007, 57), but also to create a deep aversion to blackness among the general population. Dating back to the colonial period, a covert skin color gradient was often utilized to dictate an individual's socioeconomic position in Brazilian society, with whiteness representing the standard of idealized constructions of femininity, wealth, and intelligence. The gross distortion of the country's racial composition in Brazilian censuses in the first half of the last century reflects the internalization of these ideals by the black population.[3] Radical jumps in the white population between 1890 and 1950 were coupled with notable declines in the multiracial and black populations as these populations struggled to openly self-identify as *pardo* (brown) or *preto* (black) in a society where whiteness signified progress (Skidmore 1974, 44). Despite efforts by the Brazilian Census Bureau in recent decades to improve mechanisms of self-classification and their accuracy, the hesitancy among African descendants to classify themselves as black has continually resulted in the significant underestimation of the numbers and economic contributions of the black population and the perpetuation of notions of racial homogeneity (Nascimento 2007, 44).

As briefly noted, it was not until the transition to democracy in 1985 that efforts to counter the myth of racial democracy and reveal the extensive marginalization of Afro-Brazilians gained salience in the Brazilian political arena. As Sonia Alvarez explains, "political liberalization made a wider range of oppositional activities and discourses possible" (1990, 83). Numerous civil groups, including the women's movement, rural protest movements, and labor unions, became increasingly active and connected during democratic opening or the *abertura democratica*. They recognized that the push toward redemocratization by civilian leaders presented a crucial opportunity for the resurgence of social justice issues and that by forging a unified front they could reach greater numbers of the politically disengaged Brazilian population. Several black organizations, such as the Movimento Negro Unificado (MNU), emerged after being heavily repressed by the military dictatorship in the late 1970s to openly protest against the contemporary manifestations of discrimination that had plagued the black population: domestic violence, mistreatment by police, and limited access to health care (Davis 1999).

Resistance efforts were not unfamiliar for Afro-Brazilian women, who had long been involved in formal and informal forms of collective action for cultural and economic autonomy (Morrison 2003; Safa 2007). In their communities and neighborhoods, Afro-Brazilian women's groups challenged the perpetuation of human rights violations under the military dictatorship and questioned the ability of the regime to provide for the basic rights and needs of all its citizens. The stark realities of the discrimination faced by Afro-Brazilian women were also effectively communicated in the writings of Afro-Brazilian feminists. Leila Gonzalez's pioneering work (1982) on the exploitative relationships between black female domestic workers and white female employers exposed the complex reproductions of white superiority in Brazil (Lebon 2007, 57). Activists and scholars Sueli Carneiro and Thereza Santos (1985) followed with a comprehensive analysis of the socioeconomic and political conditions of women of African descent in Brazil, the first of its kind. These women sought not only to reveal the inaccuracies of Brazil's historical portrayals and the daily hardships faced by Afro-Brazilian women, but also to generate transformative visions of blackness and femininity.

Despite their groundbreaking works and extensive activist experience at the local and national level, black women were continually relegated to secondary roles by the male-dominated black movement (Lovell 2006, 66). The broader black movement focused on the exposure of Brazil's widespread racial inequalities, the promotion of racial consciousness among a population that had continually denied their identities, and the introduction of constitutional amendments to eliminate racism in Brazilian society. A critical intersection that the platforms of several black movement organizations did not adequately consider was the gender dimension of racial discrimination. In spite of this disregard, many black feminists remained committed to the communication of the antiracist message during the democratic transition. Recognizing the country's drive to implement a model of democracy that facilitated mutual respect, dialogue, and equality among all peoples and to sustain its international reputation for racial tolerance, black men and women came together to integrate a "racial/ethnical perspective into the ethical and moral paradigm of human rights" (Barsted and Hermann 2001, 42).

The beginnings of a significant discursive shift became visible in the 1988 Brazilian constitution, which has been described as the "most precise document vis-à-vis racial and ethnic discrimination that Brazil has ever had" (Davis 1999, 8). Civil society activists utilized the international treaties and law to place pressure on the Brazilian state (Dutt 1998), demanding the incorporation of articles from the Convention on the Elimination of All Forms of Racial Discrimination (1965), the Convention on the Elimination on All Forms of Discrimination Against Women (1979), and the Convention Against Torture and Other Cruel, Inhuman or Degrading Treatments or Punishment (1984). In an unprecedented move by Joao Figueiredo's administration, civil society representatives were invited to present their demands and concerns in a national forum and to participate in the revision process. Despite extensive involvement of black women activists and politicians in this process, such as Leila Gonzalez and Benedita da Silva, the sole black member of the National Congress, Afro-Brazilian movement leader and scholar Abidas do Nascimento was seen as the main communicator of the black movement's message (Davis 1999, 13). The extensive lobbying of Nascimento and immense pressure of black organizations culminated in the inclusion of a small number of key amendments. Article 5 assures the equality of all citizens under law and criminalizes the practice of racism, and Article 215 protects the right to cultural expression and autonomy for all groups in Brazilian society, including indigenous and Afro-Brazilians (Barsted and Hermann 2001, 58–59).

Following the wave of black militancy in the mid-1980s and the constitutional revisions, the frictions between black male activists and black feminists came to a head. Despite expectations that democratization would result in the increased consideration of their needs and demands and a shared commitment with the black movement to fight for the rights of the black population as a whole, black women's issues continued to be marginalized in favor of the restoration of male-dominated politics and institutions (Friedman 1995, 22). For Afro-Brazilian feminists, this marginalization effectively extended from the formal structures of the state to the "masculinist politics of national liberation and community struggles against racism" (Blackwell and Naber 2002, 241). These women sought a framework that would enable them to challenge locations of power even within spaces of resistance and to recognize the ways in which race is mediated by gender and other identity constructs. The following section will examine the critical linkage between the Brazilian feminist movement and Afro-Brazilian feminists and their efforts to create shared goals without pulling them away from specific issue areas and concerns (Dutt 1998, 224). While this relationship is also known for its tensions, its powerful impact on the transmission of a human rights agenda in Brazil and the transnational feminist organization of black women cannot be understated.

Finding Common Ground

Much of the literature on historical and contemporary feminist practice in Brazil has focused on the separate struggles of black and white women in Brazil (Alvarez 1990; Calderia 1990; Miller 1991; Corcoran-Nantes 1993). The initial exclusion and blatant racism experienced by Afro-Brazilian women seeking to enter the Marxist-influenced feminist movement in the 1970s and 1980s has rightfully been emphasized by Afro-Brazilian feminists and various researchers of racial and gender equality in Brazil (Carneiro 1999; Lovell 2006; Lebon 2007). Primarily focusing on the gender and class-based inequalities that led to women's subordination in Brazilian society, the predominately white and middle-class Brazilian feminist movement offered little consideration for racial prejudices that infiltrated the lives of Afro-Brazilian women or how their actions fostered their oppression (Lebon 2007, 57). As Kia Lilly Caldwell has noted, several Afro-Brazilian feminists argued that the hesitancy of white Brazilian feminists to address the relationship between racial and gender domination reflected a complicity to maintain white superiority and reinforce the inferior status of black women (2001, 222).

Yet, sufficient literary analysis has not been given to the complex relationship between antiracist and feminist struggles in Brazil that has emerged throughout the 1990s and 2000s and the strategic value of these collaborations, particularly for the advancement of an intersectional human rights platform. In her detailed study of the black women's movement in the Brazilian state of Salvador, Cecilia McCallum sheds some light on the dynamics of this relatively young and unexplored relationship, suggesting that increased interconnections among racially diverse women have become a characteristic of the Brazilian feminist movement. She argues that "the growing approximation between blacks and whites is driven by strategic needs as well as by a shared commitment to feminist ideas and demands" (2007, 63).

Afro-Brazilian feminists have widely recognized that, unlike topics of racial inequality and discrimination, efforts to achieve gender parity and equality have been more broadly accepted by Brazilian society and government (Carneiro 1999). The innovations in gender and human rights in Brazil can be traced to the 1970s and early 1980s with the heightened involvement of women in demonstrations against the authoritarian regime and later in the formal political arena. The consistent lobbying of the Brazilian women's movement resulted in critical political and legislative advancements, including the creation of state councils on women's condition in 1983, the introduction of the first women's police precincts in the world in 1985, and amendments on maternity and paternity leaves and the rights of domestic workers in the 1988 constitution (Geske and Bourque 2001, 257).

Realizing the draw of gender equality platforms across the country, Afro-Brazilian women entered the feminist movement with the purpose of increasing gender consciousness, breaking down barriers to various sources of financial and organizational support, and developing an autonomous space for women experiencing compounded forms of discrimination. Renowned social activist, psychologist, and founder of the black women's organization Fala Preta!, Edna Roland explained this "opportunity" in a 2007 interview with me:

> The fact that we are women has allowed us to interchange with the feminist movement. We have had the opportunity to participate in spaces that concern issues of gender, [which] is much more accepted in Brazil. Black women have the opportunity through this business of gender to access information, organizational and administrative experience. We were able to create relationships so we were able to get social and political capital that was more difficult for the black men. We were able to access resources through contact with foundations and governmental bodies that worked with gender. This was a key issue for us.

In effect, the partnering of the Brazilian feminist networks, such as the National Feminist Network of Health and Reproductive Rights, and Afro-Brazilian feminist organizations, including Geledes and Criola, has been a purposeful action by both sides. On the one hand, the Brazilian feminist movement has looked to assert the political subjectivity of women and to improve strained relations, introducing race and gender concerns in movement discourse and initiatives. On the other, Afro-Brazilian feminists have also sought increased influence in state bodies and to make feminist practices and demands reflective of black women through the integration of an intersectional framework. Executive director of Geledes and Afro-Brazilian feminist Sueli Carneiro describes what this process of synthesis entails:

> The unity of women's struggle in our societies depends, in general, not only on our capacity to overcome the inequalities generated by the historical masculine hegemony, but also requires that we surmount the complementary ideologies of this system of oppression, as is the case with racism. Racism establishes the social inferiority of blacks in general, and of black women in particular, and it operates as a divisive factor in the struggle of women to obtain the privileges that have been instituted for white women. (2001, 22–26)

In addition, Afro-Brazilian feminists have focused on the development of stronger transnational coalitions, an arena in which the

Brazilian feminist movement has achieved notable success. Athayde Motta, a researcher of black nongovernmental organizations in Brazil, clearly identifies this distinct strategy as central to the increased impact of black women's organizations at the national and international level. In a 2007 interview with me he explained: "What they [Afro-Brazilian women's organizations] did that very few Afro-Brazilian women's organizations did before them was partner with feminist organizations that were very much international." Afro-Brazilian feminists have realized the similarities of black women's experiences across national borders and have looked to initiate cross-border dialogue on the interconnected nature of their struggles (Collins 2000, 232). A notable example of these collaborations is the Afro-Latin American, Afro-Caribbean and Diaspora Women's Network. First established in 1992, the objective of this transnational advocacy network is to affirm the development of a black feminist identity through social activism, offering women an autonomous forum to cultivate and strengthen their struggles against sexism and racism in their individual countries and across the region (Werneck 2007, 110). Women representatives from thirty-three countries, including Brazil, Costa Rica, Nicaragua, and Honduras, hold regular regional forums to discuss the specific issues encountered by black women, including high rates of HIV/AIDS, land displacement, exclusion from political office, and the far-reaching impact of neoliberal economic mandates on their social and economic livelihoods. Sueli Carneiro states that the "internationalist vision" displayed in this network and others has encouraged cooperation among black women and increased awareness of the common concerns of health and economic and personal security faced by the black population (2001).

Central to the emergence and articulation of new feminist antiracist frameworks in Brazil have been United Nations conferences. These meetings have served as a vehicle for Afro-Brazilian feminists to expand the dialogue around the meanings and applications of human rights nationally and internationally and to encourage social movements, national governments, and the United Nations to integrate an antiracist feminist perspective into international human rights law (Carneiro 2001).

Lessons Learned: Afro-Brazilian Women in Beijing

The 1995 United Nations Conference on Women in Beijing and the regional preparatory meetings that preceded the conference marked a pivotal step in the acknowledgment of race as a determining factor in the identities, rights, and conditions of Brazilian women. For many women's rights advocates the impetus for change was laid two years earlier at the 1993 United Nations Conference on Human Rights in Vienna. It was at this conference that women's concerns were integrated into the mainstream of United Nations human rights bodies and agenda (Keck and Sikkink 1998, 187). As a result, the human rights discourse became the official language for demanding women's rights in Beijing. With more than 30,000 women converging to challenge the feminization of poverty; promote the emergence of peace, development, and equality; and demand increased support and accountability from national governments, the transformative capacity of this discourse and strength of transnational feminist solidarities was solidified.

The experience of participating in a world conference was not new for Afro-Brazilian women, who were involved in national preparations and delegations for the UN conferences on the environment in Rio de Janeiro in 1992, human rights in Vienna in 1993, and population and development in Cairo in 1994 (Htun 2004, 78). However, this conference marked the first time that the specific conditions of black women's subordination were incorporated in the official practice of the Brazilian feminist movement. More important, for Afro-Brazilian women, Beijing marked the culmination of decades of struggle to be accepted and recognized in a space of gender.

According to Sonia Alvarez, the Beijing process motivated Afro-Latin women to engage in transnationalized rights advocacy and exchanges around their specific needs and concerns (2000, 30). Black women's organizations had established extensive national and regional contracts prior to Beijing, convening the First National Encounter of Black Women in 1988 and the Second National Encounter of Black Women in 1991. More than 450 black women from various sectors and organizational backgrounds throughout Brazil participated in the 1988 meeting, despite marked opposition from the black and women's movements in the country. Participants discussed the precarious situation of black women, particularly in the labor market and institutions of higher education, and the need to be recognized as legitimate activists in the struggle to achieve social transformation, but also emphasized the importance of coalitions across social movements (Ribeiro 1995). "Organization, Strategies and Prospects" was the main theme of the second meeting held in Salvador, Brazil, in 1991. Several workshops were held to discuss the diverse identities and negative experiences of black women and girls in the health care and education system and the arena of collective action. The final report illustrated the need for different policy approaches to effectively combat discriminatory practices that derive from the institutions and structures of state (Ribeiro 1995).

The preparation for Beijing, however, provided an exceptional opportunity for Afro-Brazilian women to strategize and engage with women across the region and the world (Alvarez et al. 2002, 565). Black women were heavily involved in the regional preparations for Beijing, organizing a three-day seminar in conjunction with the NGO Preparatory Forum in Mar del Plata, Argentina, in September 1994. Participants from various Latin American and Caribbean countries converged to discuss the different configurations of racism and sexism they encountered in their respective societies and their experiences within national feminist and black movements. Alvarez et al. accurately describe these exchanges as "extra-official" processes. These allow "feminists to come together within world regions to build solidarity, devise innovative forms of political praxis, and elaborate discourse that challenge gender-based and sexual oppression" (2002, 538). As such, these preparatory meetings became critical sites for the transnational organization of Afro-Brazilian feminists.

Black feminists also became active members of the Brazilian Women's Articulation (Articulacao das Mulheres Brasileiras) or the AMB, an organization created to coordinate the feminist movement in the preparatory stages of the Beijing conference and following its conclusion (Htun 2002, 736). More than 800 women's groups participated, resulting in the development of ninety-one local advocacy coalitions and women's forums from January 1994 to May 1995 (AMB 1995). The forums played a crucial role in promoting dialogue and collaboration among diverse groups of activists and in setting the priorities for the meeting. The AMB produced the *Document of Brazilian Women*, which recommended several political measures and commitments to gender and racial equality to be adopted by Latin American and Caribbean governments. Two key priorities were the following:

> To ensure that the public sector adheres to the principle of social well being, committing itself to public policies for women, with programs to promote equal opportunities and social mobility, especially for poor women and women from ethnic and racial groups that have been victimized by social exclusion by use of legal sanctions against discrimination on the basis of race, ethnicity identity, gender, disability, or sexual preference in various spheres of social life.
>
> To guarantee the right to work for all women, adopting specific measures to monitor and prevent discriminatory practices in access to

formal labour, for young, married, black, indigenous, pregnant, and elderly women and women with disabilities (AMB 1995).

The document effectively incorporated the local perspectives and concerns of black AMB members and demanded the support of established international women's conventions and that a commitment to the universality of human rights be upheld by individual governments (AMB 1995).[4]

The increased consideration of race and forms of intersectional discrimination was also visible in the preparatory activities and official reports of the Brazilian government (Caldwell 2007, 163). Heleieth Saffioti notes that the Brazilian government was eager to integrate the positions of various feminist NGOs, contacting activists to serve as consultants and workshop leaders for a series of seminars across the country on the woman's condition in Brazil, held between April and August 1994 (1995, 200). Carneiro was asked to be the leader of the seminar on violence against women in Sao Paulo. The document prepared by the Brazilian government for the conference, titled "A General Report about the Women in Brazilian Society," acknowledged the fallacy of racial democracy in Brazil and the destructive impact of racism on the progress of black women in the national and international context (Roland 2000). A small number of Afro-Brazilian women also participated as government and NGO representatives and observers in Brazil's official delegation. They included Nilza Iraci Silva (Geledes), Wania Sant'Anna (AMB), Marta Oliveria (Institute for Religious Studies), and the country's first female black senator, Benedita da Silva.

A major triumph for these participants was the inclusion of the terms "race" and "ethnicity" in Article 32 of the Beijing Declaration, an addition that generated much controversy and criticism among delegations at the conference (Carneiro 2001). This outward support by the Brazilian government reflected an increased respect of the positions asserted by black women and their feminist allies and the long-awaited acknowledgment of racial discrimination as a serious problem at the national and international level.

Despite the extensive efforts and involvement of Afro-Brazilian women, tensions between white and black feminists still emerged. For some Afro-Brazilian delegates, attempts to unify white and black feminists effectively trumped the specificity of black women's oppressions. In her 1997 autobiography, da Silva characterized the Brazilian delegation in Beijing as progressive and unrelenting in their demands for universal women's rights. Although da Silva was one of the few black female governmental representatives at the conference, she failed to mention the advancement of race-specific claims during the conference, instead focusing on the continued struggle of all women to achieve a "true partnership with men" (117). This omission may reflect the ongoing struggle of Afro-Brazilian women to balance a commitment to a unified women's struggle, as noted by Carneiro earlier, with the recognition of the significance of intersecting forms of oppression for women, such as racism.

At the National Conference of Representatives of Black Women's Organizations in October 2000, participants from across the region acknowledged the importance of the black women's movement in the preparations for Beijing, but expressed disappointment with the minimal consideration of black women's issues in the conference proceedings and the Beijing +5. As one of the participants expressed: "Everybody acknowledges the importance of black women's issues but when formal documents are produced, the issue disappears" (Reichmann 2000). This disappointment did not result in the disengagement of Afro-Brazilian feminists from UN forums or the international political arena, but forced them to restrategize their approach for Durban in 2001. The skills they did gain from the Beijing experience, such as "the ability to articulate the local and the global, speak policy language, and negotiate consensus positions among people of diverse backgrounds", proved to be invaluable in preparation for this critical event (Htun 2004, 78).

Durban: "It Is a Journey Not Simply a Destination"

Codirector of the Global Afro-Latino and Caribbean Initiative J. Michael Turner writes that "the process of getting to Durban" was as important as the actual eight-day conference on the African continent" (2002, 31). Looking ahead to World Conference against Racism in Durban, Sueli Carneiro expressed concern with the ability of the movement's organizational structure to manage the tasks required to participate in the conference and stressed the need for further training. To address this problem, two years prior to Durban she raised funds to bring a strategist from Washington, D.C. to Sao Paulo to train Afro-Brazilian leaders in the organizational skills and lobbying practices required to successfully participate in a world conference. In an interview with me in 2007 Afro-Brazilian activist and professor Joselina da Silva described the significance of the training process:

> There is a whole process of learning. They [activists] need to understand, they need to learn how to take part in a conference. Some small things make big differences in terms of lobbying, in terms of knowing who to talk to, in terms of knowing the different languages to speak. Black women have been one of the groups that have been getting closer to this process because of their participation in the Group of Seven [World Conferences]. They got to the Durban conference understanding all of the mechanisms of taking part.

Da Silva suggests that it is the preparation for such conferences that has the most powerful influence on the strategies and cohesion of the black women's movement in Brazil. The extensive preparation process for regional meetings and United Nations conferences includes the setting of mobilization goals, selecting movement representatives, and deliberating over the fundamental issues emerging for black women at the local, national, and regional level. This kind of unique dialogue encourages the movement to coordinate its activities and share its message. Members become more in tune with the concerns and realities of the women they speak for domestically and ready to express their demands internationally (Franklin 2010).

A critical outcome of this dialogue was the creation of the Network of Black Brazilian Women's NGOs for the III Conference against Racism in 2000 (Caldwell 2009). Composed of dozens of organizations across the country, including Criola, Geledes, and Maria Mulher, the network presented an intersectional viewpoint on racism in its mandate, focused on identifying the multiple forms of social exclusion faced by black women and their significant ramifications (Carneiro 2002, 210). They produced an extensive publication in the months leading up to Durban, entitled *We, Brazilian Black Women* (Nos, Mulheres Negras), that detailed the exclusion faced by Afro-Brazilian women in the areas of education, law, health care, the media, and private enterprise and provided a series of recommendations for the inclusion and advancement of black women in these arenas in line with existing international conventions on human rights (Caldwell 2009).

For Afro-Brazilian feminists, the Durban conference was transformative on several different levels. First, the conference forced the Brazilian government to publicly acknowledge its historical mistreatment of the black population and complicity in the promulgation of the myth of racial democracy. Second, the preparation process and conference proceedings demonstrated the capacity of these activists to assume a prominent leadership role. In an unprecedented and widely heralded move, Edna Roland was appointed general rapporteur for Brazil at the meeting. Last, it illustrated that a united effort between Afro-Brazilian feminists and male leadership in the Brazilian black movement was attainable. Familiar with the extensive negotiation and lobbying processes from their previous experiences in Vienna and Beijing, black feminists were able to closely follow the official deliberations and voice the concerns of the Brazilian delegations during long and difficult debates over the conference's platform for action (Htun 2004, 78). MNU researcher David Covin notes that Afro-Brazilian male and female militants were fully aware of the national and international significance of the event and effectively put aside differences to present a strong and cohesive position (2006, 161).

Since Durban, Afro-Brazilian feminists have remained diligent in their efforts to develop and implement public policies in the areas of education, cultural preservation, religious tolerance, domestic workers' rights, and reproductive health. Some strides have been made since the commitment of the Brazilian government to adopt and implement affirmative action policies following the Durban conference. In 2003, the Special Secretariat for the Promotion of Racial Equality (SEPPIR) was created by the administration of President Lula Inacio da Silva. This government ministry is responsible for assisting the administration in the formulation, planning, and coordination of policies relating to the protection of the rights of racial and ethnic groups. With the support of the black women's movement, the National Human Rights Program proposed specific policies aimed at improving the positioning of black Brazilians, including the adoption of educational quotas by individual states to improve the access of black students to public universities (Htun 2004, 68).

In recent years, Afro-Brazilian feminists have been active participants in various regional forums on racial and gender inequalities, including the Regional Conference of the Americas held in Brasilia in July 2006. The delegation recommended the establishment of a National Commission on Truth and Reconciliation on Racism and Racial Discrimination, which would thoroughly examine the historical manifestations, expressions, and consequences of racism in Brazil. The translation of the conclusions and recommendations of the commission into a comprehensive national program for the eradication of racism and promotion of racial equality in Brazil was also strongly encouraged by the Afro-Brazilian feminists in attendance.

At the domestic level, the Brazilian government has committed to the integration of an intersectional perspective in all policy frameworks, at least in principle. An example is found in the 2008 to 2011 Multi-Year Plan presented by the Lula administration:

> The democratic environment shall be permeated by the development of relationships based on equity, without gender, race and ethnic prejudices, with equal opportunities in all aspects of social life. In the pyramid of inequality, black women are on the top followed by black men and white women. Therefore, the perspective of promoting gender and racial equality must be present at the elaboration, execution and monitoring of all government policies, incorporated as a generating principle of democracy, development and peace.

In spite of these statements, political debates over the failings of the public health system to protect young, poor black women from mass sterilization, high rates of maternal mortality, and misguided contraceptive practices remain at the forefront of black feminist agendas. While some advances have been made in the field, including the creation of the National Policy of Black Population Health and the restructuring of the Program of Full Assistance of Women's Health, the struggle to get every Brazilian state to commit to the protection of Afro-Brazilian women's reproductive rights and to recognize the statutes of domestic and international law continues. The significant lag between policy development and implementation and the minimal representation of Afro-Brazilian women in the formal political structures of Brazil only exacerbate these struggles. Since 2003, four black women have held ministerial posts within the Brazilian government: Benedita da Silva (Ministry of Social Welfare), Matilde Ribeiro (Ministry of SEPPIR), Marina Silva (Ministry of Environment), and Luiza Bairros (Ministry of SEPPIR). A critical task for Afro-Brazilian feminists in the future will be to utilize and improve upon existing political connections at the domestic level and to find new and innovative ways to challenge power hierarchies from within.

Conclusion

As the ten-year anniversary of Durban approaches, two key questions emerge for Afro-Brazilian feminists: How far have we come? Where do we go from here? Looking back at the historical and political trajectory of black feminist activism in Brazil, one cannot deny its significant impact on struggles against racial and gender injustices. Afro-Brazilian women have encountered and exposed various historical, civil, and political barriers, including pervasive colonial logics of white superiority, deeply ingrained patterns of racial and sexual discrimination masked by the myth of racial democracy, and alienation in the country's black and feminist movements. They have responded by developing autonomous organizations, rebuilding fractured relations with domestic social movement actors, and effectively conveying their message transnationally. An intersectional framework of human rights continues to be a critical instrument for the movement, with international conferences and conventions carrying significant weight in mobilization platforms and initiatives.

However, Afro-Brazilian feminists recognize that urgency of their struggle requires more than the continued pledges to democratic values and international declarations offered by the Brazilian government. More than two decades after the return to democratic rule, black women still face significant obstacles in the formal political arena and remain the most socioeconomically disadvantaged segment of the Brazilian population. As such, the next steps for black feminists will likely be as difficult as the first. What is clear is that their fervent calls for the reconceptualization and expansion of human rights and feminism in Brazil alone will not be enough to counter the intersecting oppressions of racism and sexism. Rather, they must continue to engage in a concerted effort with other feminist and social movement actors who seek to challenge racial and gender injustices in this context and across the globe.

Notes

1. The field research and interviews included in this paper were carried out with the aid of a grant from the International Development Research Centre, Ottawa, Canada.
2. For extensive demographic analysis on the socioeconomic status and rights of Afro-Brazilian women, refer to Lucila Bandeira Beato (2004) and Nathalie Lebon (2007).
3. The information collected in Brazilian censuses has historically been shrouded in controversy because of ambiguous color designations and unreliable methods of data collection utilized by the census bureau. For a detailed study of the problematic categorization of Afro-descendants in the Brazilian census, refer to Melissa Nobles (2000).
4. The AMB was also instrumental in the preparation process for Durban and continues to organize activities for female activists across the country.

For one activist the organization serves "as a kind of filter through which women from distant areas get information and find a way to take part in the national arena" (da Silva 2007).

Works Cited

Alvarez, Sonia E. 1990. *Engendering Democracy in Brazil: Women's Movements in Politics.* Princeton, NJ: Princeton University Press.

———. 2000. "Translating the Global: Effects of Transnational Organizing on Local Feminist Discourses and Practices in Latin America." *Meridians: A Journal of Feminisms, Race and Transnationalism* 1(1):29–67.

Alvarez, Sonia E., et al. 2002. "Encountering Latin American and Caribbean Feminisms." *Signs: Journal of Women in Culture and Society* 28(2) (Winter):537–79.

Articulacao de Mulheres Brasileiras. 1995. "Synthesis of Brazilian Women." Paper Presented at the Fourth World Conference on Women, Beijing, China. Sept. 4–15.

Barsted, Leila Linhares and Jacqueline Hermann. 2001. "Black and Indigenous Women: Law vs. Reality." *Brazil: Women and Legislation against Racism.* Eds. Leila Linhares Barsted, Jacqueline Hermann, and Maria Elvira Vieira de Mello. Rio de Janeiro: Cepia. 39–84.

Beato, Lucila Bandeira. 2004. "Inequality and Human Rights of African Descendants in Brazil." *Journal of Black Studies* 34(6) (July):766–86.

Benjamin, Medea, Maisa Mendoca, and Benedita da Silva. 1997. *Benedita da Silva: An Afro-Brazilian Woman's Story of Politics and Love.* Oakland, CA: Food First Books.

Blackwell, Maylei, and Nadine Naber. 2002. "Intersectionality in an Era of Globalization: The Implication of the UN World Conference against Racism for Transnational Feminist Practices–A Conference Report." *Meridians: Feminism, Race, Transnationalism* 2(2):237–48.

Bond, Johanna E. 2003. "International Intersectionality: A Theoretical and Pragmatic Exploration of Women's International Human Rights Violations." *Emory Law Journal* 52(1) (Winter):71–186.

Bunch, Charlotte. 1990. "Women's Rights as Human Rights: Towards a Re-vision of Human Rights." *Human Rights Quarterly* 12(4) (Nov.):486–98.

Calderia, Teresa Pires de Rio. 1990. "Women, Daily Life and Politics." *Women and Social Change in Latin America.* Ed. Elizabeth Jelin. London: Zed Books, Ltd. 47–78.

Caldwell, Kia Lilly. 2001. "Racialized Boundaries: Women's Studies and the Question of Difference in Brazil." *Journal of Negro Education* 70(3) (Summer):219–30.

———. 2007. *Negras in Brazil: Re-envisioning Black Women, Citizenship, and the Politics of Identity.* New Brunswick, NJ: Rutgers University Press.

Caldwell, Kia Lilly. 2009. "Transnational Black Feminism in the Twenty-first Century: Perspectives from Brazil." *New Social Movements in the African Diaspora: Challenging Global Apartheid.* Ed. Leith Mullings, 105–120. New York: Palgrave Macmillan.

Carneiro, Sueli. 1999. "Black Women's Identity in Brazil." *Race in Contemporary Brazil: From Indifference to Inequality.* Ed. Rebecca Reichmann. University Park: Pennsylvania State University Press. 217–28.

———. 2001. "Rendering Feminism Blacker: The Situation of Black Women in Latin America from a Gender Perspective." Trans. Manuel de Freitas. *Lola Press* 16 (Nov.). http://www.lolapress.org/index/authors.htm. Last accessed April 22, 2008.

———. 2002. "A Batalha de Durban." *Revista Estudos Feministas* 10(1):209–14.

Carneiro, Sueli, and Teresa Santos. 1985. *Mulher Negra.* Sao Paulo: Nobel/Conselho Estadual da Condicao Feminina.

Collins, Patricia Hill. 2000. *Black Feminist Thought: Knowledge, Consciousness, Politics of Empowerment.* 2nd ed. Abingdon: Routledge.

Corcoran-Nantes, Yvonne. 1993. "Female Consciousness or Feminist Consciousness? Women's Consciousness Raising in Community-Based Struggles in Brazil." *Viva: Women and Popular Protest in Latin America.* Eds. Sarah Radcliffe and Sallie Westwood. London: Routledge. 136–55.

Covin, David. 2006. *The Unified Black Movement in Brazil: 1978–2002.* Jefferson, NC: McFarland & Co.

Crenshaw, Kimberle. 1989. "Demarginalizing the Intersection of Race and Sex: A Black Feminist Critique of Antidiscrimination Doctrine, Feminist Theory and Antiracist Politics." University of Chicago Legal Forum. 139–167.

———. 1991. "Mapping the Margins: Intersectionality, Identity Politics and Violence against Women of Color." *Stanford Law Review* 43 (6) (July):1241–1299.

Crooms, Lisa A. 2003. "To Establish My Legitimate Name Inside the Consciousness of Strangers": Critical Race Praxis, Progressive Women-of-Colour Theorizing, and Human Rights." *Howard Law Journal* 46(2):229–68.

da Silva, Joselina. 2007. Interview by author. Juazeiro do Norte, Brazil. Oct. 31.

Davis, Darien J. 1999. *Afro-Brazilians: Time for Recognition.* London: Minority Rights Group International.

Dutt, Mallika. 1998. "Reclaiming a Human Rights Culture: Feminism of Difference and Alliance." *Talking Visions: Multicultural Feminism in a Transnational Age.* Ed. Ella Shohat. Cambridge: Massachusetts Institute of Technology. 224–26.

Ely-Yamin, Alicia. 1993. "Empowering Visions: Toward a Dialectical Pedagogy of Human Rights." *Human Rights Quarterly* 15(4) (Nov.):640–85.

Franklin, Jessica. 2010. "Afro-Brazilian Women's Identities and Activism: National and Transnational Discourses." *Latin American Identities After 1980*. Eds. Gordana Yovanovich and Amy Huras. Waterloo, ON: Wilfrid Laurier University Press. 97–115.

Freyre, Gilberto. 1946. *The Masters and the Slaves: A Study in the Development of Brazilian Civilization*. New York: Alfred Knopf.

Friedman, Elizabeth. 1995. "Women's Human Rights: The Emergence of a Movement." *Women's Rights Human Rights: International Feminist Perspectives*. Eds. Julie Peters and Andrea Wolper. New York: Routledge. 18–35.

Geske, Mary, and Susan C. Bourque. 2001. "Grassroots Organizations and Women's Human Rights: Meeting the Challenge of the Local-Global Link." *Women, Gender, and Human Rights: A Global Perspective*. Ed. Marjorie Agosin. New Brunswick, NJ: Rutgers University Press. 246–64.

Gonzalez, Leila. 1982. "A mulher negra na sociedade brasileira." *O Lugar Mulher*. Ed. M. T. Luz. Rio de Janiero: Edicoes Graal. 87–106.

Grewal, Interpal. 2005. "On the New Global Feminism and the Family of Nations: The Dilemmas of Transnational Feminist Practice." *Talking Visions: Multicultural Feminism in a Transnational Age*. Ed. Ella Shohat. Cambridge: Massachusetts Institute of Technology. 501–30.

Guimaraes, Antonio Sergio Alfredo. 2001. "Racial Inequalities, Black Protest and Public Policies in Brazil." Paper prepared for the United Nations Research Institute for Social Development Conference, Durban, Sept. 3–5.

Htun, Mala. 2004. "From Racial Democracy to Affirmative Action: Changing State Policy on Race in Brazil." *Latin American Research Review* 39(1):60–89.

———. 2002. "Puzzles of Women's Rights in Brazil." *Social Research* 69(3) (Fall):732–51.

Jelin, Elizabeth. 1996. "Women, Gender and Human Rights." *Constructing Democracy: Human Rights, Citizenship and Society in Latin America*. Eds. Elizabeth Jelin and Eric Hershberg. Boulder, CO: Westview Press. 177–224.

Keck, Margaret E., and Kathryn Sikkink.1998. *Activists beyond Borders: Advocacy Networks in International Politics*. Ithaca, NY: Cornell University Press.

Lebon, Nathalie. 2007. "Beyond Confronting the Myth of Racial Democracy: The Role of Afro-Brazilian Women Scholars and Activists." *Latin American Perspectives* 34(6) (November):52–76.

Lewis, Hope. 2003. "Embracing Complexity: Human Rights in Critical Race Feminist Perspective." *Columbia Journal of Gender and Law* 12(3):510–20.

Lovell, Peggy A. 2006. "Race, Gender, and Work in Sao Paulo, Brazil, 1960–2000." *Latin American Research Review* 41(3):63–87.

McCallum, Cecilia. 2007. "Women Out of Place? A Micro-historical Perspective on the Black Feminist Movement in Salvador da Bahia, Brazil." *Journal of Latin American Studies* 39(1) (Feb.):55–80.

Miller, Francesca. 1991. *Latin American Women and the Search for Social Justice*. Hanover: University Press of New England.

Morrison, Judith. 2003. "Afro-Brazilian Women's Organizations and Their Influence: Leadership from the Grassroots." Paper presented at the annual meeting of the Latin American Studies Association, Dallas, Mar. 27–29.

Motta, Athayde. 2007. Interview by author. Rio de Janeiro, Brazil. Oct. 3.

Nascimento, Elisa Larkin. 2007. *The Sorcery of Color: Identity, Race, and Gender in Brazil*. Philadelphia: Temple University Press.

Nobles, Melissa. 2000. *Shades of Citizenship: Race and the Census in Modern Politics*. Stanford, CA: Stanford University Press, 2000.

Pravaz, Natasha. 2000. "Imagining Brazil: Seduction, Samba and the Mulata's Body." *Canadian Women Studies* 20(2) (Summer):48–56.

———. 2003. "Brazilian Mulatice: Performing Race, Gender, and the Nation." *Journal of Latin American Anthropology* 8(1) (Mar.):116–47.

Reichmann, Rebecca. 2000. Report from the National Conference of Representatives of Black Women's Organizations. Brasilia, Brazil. Oct. 30–Nov. 1.

Ribeiro, Matilde. 1995. "Mulheres Negras Brasileiras: de Bertioga a Beijing." *Revista Estudos Feministas* 3(2):446–57.

Roland, Edna. 2000. "O Movimento de Mulheres Negras Brasileiras: Desafios e Perspectivas." *Tirando a mascara: Ensaios sobre o Racismo no Brasil*. Eds. Antonio Sergio Alfredo Guimaraes and Lynn Huntley. Sao Paulo: Paz e Terra. 237–56.

———. 2007. Interview by author. Sao Paulo, Brazil. Oct. 11.

Romany, Celina, ed. 2001. *Race, Ethnicity, Gender and Human Rights in the Americas: A New Paradigm for Activism*. Washington, D.C.: Race, Ethnicity and Gender Justice Publications.

Safa, Helen I. 2007. "Racial and Gender Inequality in Latin America: Afro-descendant Women Respond." *Feminist Africa* 7 (Dec.):49–66.

Saffioti, Heleieth I. 1995. "Enfim, sos: Brasil rumo a Pequim." *Revista Estudos Feministas* 3(1):198–202.

Schulman, Barbara. 2004. "Effective Organizing in Terrible Times: The Strategic Value of Human Rights for Transnational Anti-Racist Feminisms." *Meridians: Feminism, Race, Transnationalism* 4(2):102–8.

Skidmore, Thomas E. 1974. *Black into White: Race and Nationality in Brazilian Thought*. New York: Oxford University Press.

Telles, Edward E. 2004. *Race in Another America: The Significance of Skin Color in Brazil*. Princeton, NJ: Princeton University Press.

Turner, J. Michael. 2002. "The Road to Durban—and Back." *NACLA* 35(6):31–35.

Werneck, Jurema. 2007. "Of Ialoades and Feminists: Reflections on Black Women's Political Action in Latin America and the Caribbean." *Cultural Dynamics* 19(1) (Mar.):99–113.

Chapter Seven

Shaping Political Discourse on Women's Rights: The Role of Women in the Amendment of Gender Policies in Turkey

Gul Aldikacti Marshall

Since the early 2000s, gender policies have undergone a remarkable change in Turkey.[1] Although one might rightfully argue that the Turkish state initiated these policy changes as part of an effort to become a European Union (EU) member[2] (Muftuler Bac 2005), it is my contention that grassroots feminism played an important role in this process. The European Commission (EC), the executive body of the EU, criticized Turkey for not complying with its requirements, especially the "political criteria" that were put forward by the EC at the 1993 Copenhagen Summit (Karluk 2003). These criteria encompass the stability of institutions guaranteeing democracy, the rule of law, human rights, and respect for and protection of minorities. They also include the requirements regarding gender equality. In order to comply with the criteria and with the hope for receiving a date from the EC to begin the accession negotiations, Turkey amended its civil and penal codes, the labor law, and the constitution after 2000.

Most studies that deal with Turkey's EU membership process in relation to the fulfillment of the "political criteria" do not provide an in-depth account of the political efforts of women's groups to influence the amendment process of gender policies. To give a few examples, Muftuler Bac's study mentions the importance of "internal pressure" for political reforms (18), yet it primarily explains the role of the EU and EU-Turkey relations at the institutional level in this process. Although Goksel and Gunes mention the influence of women's nongovernmental organizations (NGOs) on changes to the penal code (2005), they focus on the ARI movement, which aims to consolidate democratization in Turkey by training young leaders and educating the youth to be informed citizens about issues such as human rights and political participation. In another example, Tocci (2005), who argues that the external pressure from the EU and the internal pressure from the civil society within Turkey worked together for the reforms, does not provide an explanation for how mostly feminist-oriented women's groups "make use of the EU context to advance their claims" (Diez 2005, 10). There are only a few works, such as Kardam's (2005) insightful book on Turkey's engagement in global discourse of women's human rights, that pay significant attention to women as agents of gender policy changes.

Here, rather than examining the implementation of EU provisions and directives at an institutional level, which would focus on top-down measures and the relationship between the state and the supranational entity of the EU, I aim to unearth grassroots agency. While an institutional analysis would ignore the role of Turkish feminist organizations as extrainstitutional actors (that is, establishments outside of traditional political bodies such as political parties, government, and parliament) and highlight the role of the EU in policy changes in Turkey, an analysis of the role of women in the implementation of EU stipulations in the Turkish political cultural context will reveal their agency.[3] As Román-Odio and Sierra have pointed out in the introduction of this volume, fragmentary processes of globalization open up borderland spaces within which marginalized groups organize against hegemonic discourses. The task, when contributing to knowledge on gender and transnationalism, is to reveal the way in which women's groups claim power. However, this would provide a partial picture if it is limited to the analysis of the opportune moment without taking into account the history of struggle. I conceptualize the national and international efforts of Turkish feminists and other women's rights activists who collaborated with feminist groups, sometimes on an issue basis, as a discursive struggle launched against the official framing of women's rights in law. This conceptualization recognizes the diligent efforts of feminist groups to influence gender policies, not only in the early 2000s because of the conducive environment created by the EU's stipulations for Turkey's EU membership, but also in the 1980s and the 1990s during which the feminist movement developed and institutionalized. This discursive struggle, which has been part of feminist activism since the early years of feminism, is tied to the question of who will determine the definition and scope of policies pertaining to women and gender.

The official framing is couched within a strong patriarchal ideology that governs the symbolic field of politics. It has been developed by the state elites, most of whom are men. Using the French sociologist Bourdieu's terms, feminist groups' framing of women's rights has symbolically disturbed the official legal frames constructed by the patriarchal state establishment. As expected, this disturbance received internal opposition, but at the same time support from external political bodies, such as the EC and the European Parliament (EP), and internal forces, such as a small number of sympathetic and influential politicians in the Turkish parliament.

An analysis of political discourse on women's rights in Turkey benefits from the concept of "conditionality," borrowed from political science, and discourse theory, as applied in feminist literature, to public policy. Political conditionality refers to "the linking, by a state or an international organization, of perceived benefits to another state (such as aid), to the fulfillment of conditions relating to the protection of human rights and the advancement of democratic principles" (Smith, quoted in Schmid 2004, 397). Gender equality policies are packaged within this conditionality in the current context of EU integration and Europeanization. Candidate countries are expected to comply with this conditionality in order to be considered for EU membership (Schmid 2004; Williams 2004).

While the concept of conditionality explains the influence of the EU on the Turkish state's efforts to amend its existing laws, feminist discourse theory provides tools to explain the attempts of Turkish feminists to participate in changing public policy on women's rights (Mills 2004; Brenner 1998; Fraser 1997, 1989; Isanberg 1992). Feminist discourse theory calls attention to power relations in society and argues that the notion of dominance within gender regimes cannot be revealed without this focus (Isanberg 1992). More specifically, this theory utilizes Gramsci's concept of hegemony as "the term for the discursive face of power" (Fraser, 381). Hegemony

> points to the intersection of power, inequality, and discourse. However, it does not entail that the ensemble of descriptions that circulate in society constitute a monolithic and seamless web, nor that dominant groups exercise an absolute, top-down control of meaning. On the contrary, 'hegemony' designates a process wherein cultural authority is negotiated and contested. (Fraser, 381)

Thus, shaping of political discourse involves multiple actors among whom actors with less power contest the power of dominant groups. The public arena is where "discursive struggles" (Fraser, 381) to influence political discourse take place. A discursive struggle for securing gender equality would require questioning the ideology of masculinity and femininity that is entrenched in culture and reflected in political discourse (Isanberg 1992). Feminist conceptualization of discourse, therefore, does not treat women as passive victims of male oppression. Rather, it underlines women's engagement in discursive struggles to negotiate power and takes women's efforts to render the personal as political into account (Mills 2004).

The EU conditionality for Turkey's membership has provided an opportunity for feminist groups to intensify their discursive struggle against institutionalized actors who had the duty and power of amending policies. When Turkey accepted the task of aligning its laws with the European Union laws after 1999, the civil and penal codes, the labor law, and the constitution went under the scrutiny of not only parliament members who made and voted for the changes, but also of feminist groups who knew that this was the time to pressure the government and parliament. Their insistence on participating in the reshaping of women's rights on a policy platform was about questioning and challenging the long-standing patriarchal and family-oriented gender policies.

In the summers of 2007 and 2008, I conducted in-depth, face-to-face interviews in Ankara and Istanbul with activists from ten feminist organizations and three Kemalist women's organizations.[4] Kemalist women's organizations did not use feminism as an identifying mark in their founding principles; yet, these three organizations aimed at improving women's rights and had some members who identified themselves as feminist. Among women who represented these three organizations, two of the interviewees described themselves as both Kemalist and feminist. One interviewee said she simply sees herself a Kemalist, not a feminist, although she was an important figure among women whose goal was the amendment of the gender discriminatory laws. Kemalist women from these three organizations were interviewed because these women worked with radical and socialist feminists in their common goal to change the gender discriminatory laws and gave considerable support to feminist efforts during the amendment process of the civil and penal codes. Several Kemalist women, whether feminist oriented or not, were involved in and helped feminist organizations with understanding and interpreting the legal documents because they had law degrees. In the summer of 2008, I also interviewed an Islamist activist from Capital City Women's Platform, the only large Islamist women's organization that collaborated with secular-oriented feminist organizations during part of the policy amendments. These multiple identifications[5] highlight the complexity of women's identities and their social, cultural, and political ideologies, as well as social links, in Turkey.⁶

In addition to the interviews, I examined the websites of two leading feminist organizations, Flying Broom [Ucan Supurge] in Ankara and Women for Women's Human Rights/New Ways [Kadinin Insan Haklari ve Yeni Cozumler Vakfi] in Istanbul. I conducted a newspaper archive analysis using two newspapers with the highest circulation rates. One newspaper, *Zaman*, was in the Islamist spectrum, while the other, *Hurriyet*, was in the secularist. I also examined Turkey's country progress reports issued by the EU since 1999. In the following, I provide insight into the ways in which feminist groups have persistently used various venues to pressure the state toward making gender policy changes in the direction they envisioned.

Shaping Political Discourse on Women's Rights Is an Abiding Feminist Project

It would be a mistake to see the feminist effort to amend the existing laws as limited to the late 1990s and early 2000s during which time the EU pushed Turkey to align its laws with EU laws in order to start the accession negotiations. Feminist groups have continuously pressured the state to amend its laws pertaining to women since the beginning of the feminist movement in the early 1980s. They launched a campaign in the late 1980s to pressure the state to implement the Convention on the Elimination of All Forms of Discrimination against Women (CEDAW) and to eliminate the discriminatory articles in the civil and penal codes. This campaign did not result in a success for feminists, but it raised public awareness about their cause. Another campaign was mounted in the early 1990s to amend the civil code. As a Kemalist feminist activist and a lawyer from the Istanbul Union of Women's Organizations pointed out during a personal interview on May 16, 2007, feminist and Kemalist women's groups came together during this campaign. Some Kemalist women used their law background to provide legal advice. The campaign was not enough to amend the civil code, but created an alliance between feminist and Kemalist women and received media attention.

A limited success was achieved by feminists when they became effective in the elimination of an article in the penal code that stipulated a reduced sentence for a man who rapes a prostitute, as well as an article in the civil code that stated that a woman has to have her husband's permission to work outside of the home. Even though these judicial successes did not lead to the amendment of the civil and penal codes in parliament, the partial success gave feminists the courage to continue launching campaigns until a favorable environment emerged in the early 2000s. Their role in the passage of the family protection law, which was enacted in 1998 to combat violence against women, especially domestic violence, was also an important boost for the feminist effort to influence public policy.

The 1999 Helsinki Summit, at which Turkey was officially recognized as a candidate for EU membership (Karluk 2003), prompted the Turkish parliament to comply with the Copenhagen criteria, which included gender conditionality. The government and parliament members decided to amend the civil and penal codes, the labor law, and the constitution. Turkish officials' eagerness for Turkey's EU membership brought an opportunity for feminist groups to be effective in the amendment of the civil and penal codes and the constitution in the early 2000s.[7] Skilled with experience from previous years and equipped with a set agenda, these groups were ready to push their demands into the parliamentary discussions during the revision of the civil and penal codes. They collaborated with some Kemalist women during the amendments and received support from a large Islamist women's organization, Capital City Women's Platform, during the revision of the penal code.

The primary target of feminist organizations such as Flying Broom, Women for Women's Human Rights/New Ways, and the Association for Support and Education of Women Candidates [Kadin Adaylari Destekleme ve Egitme Dernegi] was the principal philosophy of the existing laws. This philosophy was couched in a governing model, which may be called "family-centered patriarchal morality," a model that was the target of feminist criticisms and efforts to bring change. Feminist groups emphasized the fact that many articles in the civil and penal codes were treating women as the parcel of the family and society rather than as individuals. For example, the existing civil code stipulated that the head of the family is the husband and that in the case of a disagreement between husband and wife, the husband decides where the family lives and which schools the children can attend. In the penal code, which also reflected the family-centered patriarchal morality, crimes against women were treated as crimes against the moral order of the collective Turkish society. The penal code allowed a man who killed his female relative for dishonoring him or the family to receive a reduced sentence. Furthermore, the code postponed for five years the sentence of a man who kidnapped or raped a girl or single woman if he married her. The sentence was lifted if the marriage lasted for five years. It was not uncommon that the relatives of both sides saw the marriage as a way to solve the problem without any moral blemish on their families. The penal code supported the patriarchal family and emphasized its role in upholding the moral structure of society. This was also evident in a clause that stipulated a reduced sentence for a woman who killed her baby that was born out of wedlock.

The aim of the feminists, including some Kemalist feminists, was to eliminate these discriminatory clauses and change the way the law treated women. They especially focused on what they called "the property regime," which, if passed by the parliament to be included in the amended civil code, would give women the right to half of the assets gained by the couple during marriage. They heavily criticized the clauses that gave men the right to make decisions on family matters and demanded that the clause that recognized the man as the head of the family be abolished. Feminists pleaded that the penal code be changed to recognize women as individuals rather than the parcel of the moral collective. They asked for heavy punishment for honor killings and insisted that the word "honor" be included in the amended penal code when judging a crime based on disturbance of honor. Virginity examinations, which could be ordered by the parents or school officials to find out whether a girl is a virgin, were also condemned by these women's groups, who proposed a clause be added to the penal code that would ban the examinations without the girl's consent.

Persuading the lawmakers to amend the laws in the direction they wanted was a struggle for feminists, considering that the majority of parliament members who needed to be pressured to vote for the changes were conservative men who saw nothing wrong with some of the existing laws. They even treated these laws as necessary building blocks to keep the foundation of society strong. As a result, feminist activists clashed with conservative parliament and government members. For example, during the changes to the penal code, the prime minister, who was reelected in 2007 from the religious conservative Justice and Development Party, the party that initiated most of the policy changes toward an EU membership, called feminists a group of "marginal women who do not represent Turkish women." He blamed feminists who protested in front of parliament for being against moral values of society that, according to him, already "empower women" (Sen 2004, 6). In another case, the woman minister of the Directorate General on the Status and Problems of Women at the time sued a group of feminist women from several feminist organizations for condemning her for her "outworn discriminatory behavior" after she had voted against the inclusion of a positive action measure toward women in the amended constitution (Armutcu 2006).

Still, feminists sometimes successfully turned these oppositions around. For instance, during the parliamentary discussions on the division of property in the case of divorce, some parliament members, especially some members of the Nationalist Action Party, who were against the EU stipulations and saw the attempts to change the laws as a sign of a decline in Turkish state's sovereignty, were against this proposal, stating that they would not let women gain possession of property. According to a statement on the webpage of Women for Women's Human Rights/New Ways (2001), rather than being disheartened, representatives from forty-five feminist organizations visited Nationalist Action Party members and convinced some of the key names to keep the property regime in the draft law.

To influence the amendment of gender policies, feminist groups used their ties with the EC's delegation to Turkey, the United Nations Commission on the Status of Women (CSW), and sympathetic bureaucrats from the EC and the EP. For example, in 2000 representatives from women's organizations, both feminist and Kemalist, were in the Turkish delegation that went to the United Nations (UN) meetings on status and problems of women. During these meetings, the representatives were able to convey their concerns about the civil and penalcodes to the CSW. Afterwards, their concerns were cited by the CSW in reports on Turkey's performance. As Ilkkaracan (2000), a member of Women for Women's Human Rights/New Ways, stated, representatives from the EU were also present at the meetings, hearing the concerns of the women in the Turkish delegation. Later, these concerns were evident in EC's progress reports on Turkey. Turkish feminist organizations were visited by representatives from the EC and EP. The interviews I conducted with the members of some prominent feminist organizations reveal that during the visits, discriminatory laws and violence against women were two significant issues that were raised by feminist activists.

One specific event especially highlights the support Turkish feminist groups received from the bureaucrats in the EC and EP. During the amendments to the penal code, some parliament members from the governing Justice and Development Party proposed that adultery, which was abolished as a crime in the late 1990s, be included in the revised penal code as a punishable crime. When feminist and some Kemalist women's groups protested the proposal, arguing that this would only increase honor crimes, the supporters of the proposal from the governing party defended it by saying that "this was a request from the women in Anatolia." The statement was made to imply that women who are outside of urban areas of the three big cities of Istanbul, Ankara, and Izmir constitute the "authentic" Turkish women, as opposed to "western-influenced" activists who were protesting the proposal. It was during this conflict between activists and parliament members and the government, who supported the proposal, that the EC and the EP pressed the Turkish parliament and government to withdraw the proposal. When supporters resisted the pressure from the European bureaucrats, they were told abruptly and firmly that this might halt the opening of the accession negotiations (Mercimek and Lule 2004, 24).

Another significant tool that Turkish women's rights activists used in their discursive struggle to reframe the laws was the utilization of CEDAW. Since the signing of CEDAW by the Turkish state in 1985, leading feminist groups have pointed to it as a reference to ask for amendments in the civil and penal codes. In the early 2000s, when they found out that parliament was to change the penal code as a result of the pressure from the European Union, prominent feminist and Kemalist women's groups got together and sent the report they had already prepared, taking CEDAW as a reference, to the parliamentary commission in charge of reviewing the proposals for amendments. Although the commission did not ask feminist groups for their views, feminists made an effort to contact them through their connections with a few sympathetic parliament members (Women for Women's Human Rights/New Ways 2003). They also used the media, especially the secular print media, effectively to convey their demands to the members of the commission and the larger parliament. According to these activists, Turkey's membership prospects were tied to compliance with EU conditionality, and this was the time that the government and parliament paid attention to the voices that came from women's organizations (Duzel 2004). The importance of the media as a tool to reach the public was emphasized numerous times by the feminist activists during my interviews with them. As a member of a feminist organization Amargi, which means "freedom" in Sumerian, specified during a personal interview on May 14, 2007, "feminists have a very good relationship with the print media, especially with the women journalists"; yet, some feminists also stressed that this positive relationship is primarily with the secular-oriented print media.

During parliamentary discussions on the civil and penal codes in the early 2000s, feminist groups often used press releases, street demonstrations (especially in front of the Turkish parliament), fax campaigns, and signed petitions. The leadership of some of the feminist organizations, especially Women for Women's Human Rights/New Ways and Flying Broom, became pivotal in the organization of some of the activities. For example, during the amendment of the civil code, the former organized more than 126 women's organizations to push for desired changes. The latter also organized women's groups, held meetings about the laws, and initiated contacts with parliament members.

My interviews with the representatives of feminist and other women's organizations underscore the significance of the Internet as a new and revolutionary tool in communicating with each other. Feminist groups believe that organizing women under one umbrella as a large forum increases their power. They argue that the Internet gives them the ability to manage these large forums on a momentary basis. As one feminist activist from Women for Women's Human Rights/New Ways explained during a personal interview on May 16, 2007: "E-groups quickly organize. There are always some NGOs who have some expertise on the matter under scrutiny. These NGOs send a document to all other women's groups instantly and ask them to give an input by a certain date. The Internet helps us tremendously."

One might argue that without the push from the EU and the carrot of prospective EU membership, Turkish government and parliament would not have amended the civil and penal codes as quickly as they did in the early 2000s, but it was exactly this change-oriented atmosphere created by the process that helped feminists have an influence on the content of the amended laws despite some opposition and remaining legal loopholes. Several of the resulting changes in the civil code included the removal of the clauses that recognized the husband as the head of the family and as the representative of the family unit in all matters, including financial decisions. The code treats both men and women as equal partners on decision making within the family. Feminists especially focused on the divorce law in the civil code and managed to influence the decision on the division of property in the case of divorce. The amended law now stipulates equal division of property acquired during marriage in the case of divorce.

The new penal code treats women as individuals rather than as part and parcel of the moral collective run by men. It considers violence against women as violence against an individual rather than society and increases punishment for honor killings and rape. The definition of rape is now extended to include rape within marriage. Marrying the rape victim is not a way out of punishment for male perpetrators anymore. Moreover, women who kill their out-of-wedlock babies will be sentenced to life in prison, according to the amended penal code.

There are remaining loopholes and problems with the existing laws. The new law on property ownership in the civil code covers the property acquired after January 1, 2002. According to feminist and some Kemalist women's groups, this limitation excludes an important number of women who married before this date, especially housewives who lack economic resources and wealth of their own and depend on their husbands for their livelihood. These women's groups are still struggling to make sure that the law covers the period before this date as well. Moreover, the clause on virginity examinations was not eliminated altogether in the penal code. Although the article does not allow fathers and school principals to send girls arbitrarily to hospitals for virginity exams anymore, it allows for a virginity examination with a court order and does not ask for the consent of girls who are subjected to this examination. The revised penal code includes a clause that forbids the consensual sexual relationship between two young people within the age bracket of fifteen and eighteen. Regarding honor killings, the word "customs" as a motive for murder is not replaced by the word "honor"; there is still room for an interpretation of the law that would reduce the punishment. A man can claim that he murdered his female relative if he proves "unjust provocation."

There is significant discrimination toward people who are not heterosexuals in Turkey. Feminist groups pushed for a clause that would define discrimination on the basis of sexual orientation as a crime that should be treated in the same way as the discrimination cases based on language, religion, sex, and ethnicity; yet, their demands were not met in the amended penal code. Most parliament members simply ignored the issue of discrimination based on sexual orientation. Despite these loopholes and problems, the early 2000s were fruitful years for Turkish feminists, who managed to push the gender policy-making process away from the family-centered patriarchal morality model toward a woman-centered model.

Conclusion

The literature on Turkey's integration into the EU and the Europeanization process within Turkey primarily emphasizes the role of the EU in pressing the Turkish state to make changes in its policies regarding human rights, including women's rights. Though the EU's role in pushing for changes is undeniable, the efforts of women, especially feminist activists, in gender policy changes have not received adequate attention. This gap leads to picturing women's activism toward the policy amendments as tangential when compared to the influence of the EU.

It has been my argument that conditionality for EU membership provided an opportunity for feminist groups to have an impact on the gender policy-change process in Turkey. Through their alliances inside and outside of the Turkish parliament, as well as in the EC, EP, and the UN, these groups influenced the shape of the laws, which now signal a more egalitarian legal approach to men's and women's status and conduct. Yet, an account of the feminist activism toward changing the discriminatory laws should not be limited to the early 2000s. Feminist discourse theory allows us to see this activism as an ongoing discursive struggle from the early years of the feminist movement. This has been a struggle against the hegemonic patriarchal legal discourse and political attitude toward women's rights in Turkey—a struggle that bore most of its fruit within an auspicious environment created by Turkey's EU membership process. The opposition these groups faced from parliament members regarding a number of their demands and recent attempts by the current Islamist Justice and Development Party toward reversing some of the laws are signs that the feminist discursive struggle toward challenging patriarchal hegemony on political grounds is far from over.

Notes

1. This research was partially funded by an Intramural Research Incentive Grant from the office of the vice-president for research at the University of Louisville.
2. Even though Turkey's relationship with the European Economic Community dates back to 1963 and Turkey officially applied for EU membership in 1987, Turkey still has not been admitted to the EU.
3. See Liebert (2004) for a discussion of the discourse and agency in the EU contest.
4. Kemalist women are strong supporters of the reforms led by Mustafa Kemal Ataturk in the beginning of the twentieth century. They believe that religion is a private matter and should have no authority in governing the country. They also support Turkey's policies toward Westernization and modernization.
5. Radical and socialist feminists, who have been the building blocks of the feminist movement, usually are secular oriented, but not as strictly as

the Kemalist women, who see themselves as the guardians of the existing secular regime. While feminist organizations have a limited relationship with Islamist women's organizations, Kemalist women, including the ones who identify themselves also as feminist, despise Islamist women, perceiving them as a danger to the secular establishment. Women who employ Islam politically often identify themselves as Islamist. Only a handful of these women also identify themselves as feminist. As the representative I interviewed from Capital City Women's Platform on June 16, 2008, said, "Although we work with feminists on certain women's issues, our organization's name is not under every event because some slogan-like events or activities on certain women's issues can be misunderstood by our constituents. We do not want to clash with our constituents." The supporters to whom she refers are typically Islamist women who are not feminist.
6. In this essay I mainly focus on political efforts of radical and socialist feminists and refer to socialist and radical feminists when I use the term "feminist," "feminists," or "feminist groups." If a Kemalist or an Islamist woman or a women's group is also a feminist, I specify her or the group as "Kemalist feminist" and "Islamist feminist." Although the names of the organizations I visited for the interviews are revealed, the names of the interviewees are concealed in order to comply with the Human Subject Protection Protocol of the University of Louisville.
7. The interviews I conducted and the documents I analyzed reveal that the labor law was amended without much input from the feminist groups.

Works Cited

Armutcu, Emel. 2006. "Kadin orgutleriyle degil, bazi kadinlarla sorunum var" [Not with women's organizations, I have a problem with some women] (Feb. 12). www.turkhukuksitesi.com/showthread.php?t=4562. Last accessed Sept. 20, 2007.

Brenner, Johanna. 1998. "Feminist political discourses: Radical versus liberal approaches to the feminization of poverty and comparable worth." *Contemporary Feminist Theory*. Ed. Mary Rogers. Boston: McGraw-Hill. 204–14.

Diez, Thomas, Apostolos Agnantopoulos, and Alper Kaliber. 2005. "Turkey, Europeanization and Civil Society." *South European Society & Politics* 10(1):1–15.

Duzel, Nese. 2004. "Yasayla, flortu de yasakliyorlar" [Flirting is being forbidden by law] (Sept. 6). www.ucansupurge.org. Last accessed Sept. 11, 2005.

Goksel, Diba, and Rana Gunes. 2005. "The Role of NGOs in the European Integration Process: The Turkish Experience." *South European Society & Politics* 10(1):57–72.

Fraser, Nancy. 1997. "Structuralism or Pragmatics? On Discourse Theory and Feminist Politics." *The Second Wave: A Reader in Feminist Theory*. Ed. Linda Nicholson. New York: Routledge. 379–95.

Fraser, Nancy. 1989. *Unruly Practices: Power, Discourse, and Gender in Contemporary Social Theory.* Minneapolis: University of Minnesota Press.
Ilkkaracan, Ipek. 2000. "Kadin haklari mucadelesinin temel talebi: Demokrasi" [The primary demand of the women's rights struggle: democracy]. (Aug.). www.kadinininsanhaklari.org/?id=414. Last accessed Nov. 10, 2004.
Isanberg, Nancy. 1992. "The Personal Is Political: Gender, Feminism, and the Politics of Discourse Theory." *American Quarterly* 44(3):449–58.
Kardam, Nuket. 2005. *Turkey's Engagement with Global Women's Human Rights.* Burlington, VT: Ashgate.
Karluk, Ridvan. 2003. *Avrupa Birligi ve Turkiye* [The European Union and Turkey]. Istanbul: Beta.
Liebert, Ulrike. 2004. "Between Diversity and Equality: Analysing Europeanization." *Gendering Europeanization.* Ed. Ulrike Liebert. Brussels: P.E.I.-Peter Lang. 11–45.
Mercimek, Ali, and Zeynel Lule. 2004. "Resti cekti" [He made his final point]. *Hurriyet* Sept. 20.
Mills, Sara. 2004. *Discourse: The New Critical Idiom.* 2d ed. London, New York: Routledge.
Muftuler Bac, Meltem. 2005. "Turkey's Political Reforms and the Impact of the European Union." *South European Society & Politics* 10(1):17–31.
Schmid, Dorothee. 2004. "The Use of Conditionality in Support of Political, Economic and Social Rights: Unveiling the Euro-Mediterranean Partnership's True Hierarchy of Objectives?" *Mediterranean Politics* 9(3):396–421.
Sen, Erdal. 2004. 'Turk kadinini marjinal bir kesim temsil edemez' [A marginal group cannot represent Turkish women]. *Zaman* Sept. 25.
Tocci, Nathalie. 2005. "Europeanization in Turkey: Trigger or Anchor for Reform?" *South European Society & Politics* 10(1):73–83.
Williams, Andrew. 2004. *EU Human Rights Policies: A Study in Irony.* New York: Oxford University. Press.
Women for Women's Human Rights/New Ways. 2003. "Kadin bakis acisindan Turk Ceza Kanunu [Turkish Penal Code from woman's perspective]." *Cumhuriyet* June 4, 2003 www.kadinininsanhaklari.org. Last accessed Nov. 30, 2004.
———. 2001. "Son dakika atagi" [Last minute effort]. *Aksam* March 20, 2001 www.kadinininsanhaklari.org. Last accessed Nov. 30, 2004.

Chapter Eight

Trouble in the Global Village: A Snapshot of LGBT Community in Eastern Europe

Anna Kłosowska

Decentering Homophobia: Links to Anti-Semitism and Conspiracy Theory

In *Feminism Without Borders: Decolonizing Theory, Practicing Solidarity,* Chandra Talpade Mohanty calls for "definitions, descriptions, and interpretations of Third World women's engagement with feminism...[to] be simultaneously historically specific and dynamic, not frozen in time in the form of a spectacle" (2003, 48).[1]

Like other decentering approaches in postcolonial studies, Mohanty's appeal for a nonsolidified, destabilized, dynamic study of Third World feminism may be traced to the pluralism of the 1980s, particularly the work of Gilles Deleuze and Félix Guattari. In *A Thousand Plateaus* (1980), Deleuze and Guattari propose plateaus, rhizomes, *bricolage,* nomadic thought, and packs as conceptual models to counter dyads and triads of Hegelian and Freudian systems. Their optic is decentered: not focused on an individual as the humanistic subject of inquiry, but rather looking above and below the level of the individual at the configurations of collectivities accessible through multiple innovative points of view. Using the same terms (above, below) in a different context, Deleuze and Guattari talk about the difficulty and the importance of seeing things "in the middle" instead of a generalizing bird's-eye view from above or a distorting view from below. Bringing together these two examples helps define the difference between "applying a theory" and dynamic decentering that Mohanty advocates, a creative process that borrows from experience to establish speculative models.

Along these lines, in *The Fold: Leibniz and the Baroque* (1988), Deleuze borrows examples from philosophy, mathematics, and the arts to describe complex nonlinear relationships configured as folds. Among the images he evokes are soft fabric folds, a wave breaking on itself, and origami—objects that serve as models to practice and analyze new nonlinear modes of thought. This intellectual game allows us to see connections and correlations that we have trained ourselves not to see when we entered the space of "spectacle," to borrow Mohanty's metaphor, of traditional academic disciplines, including the history of sexuality. New connections emerge where folds meet, new areas of inquiry open in their interstices.

Guided by Mohanty's call and mental games proposed by Deleuze, this chapter gathers data, historical landmarks, and personal testimonies concerning lesbian, gay, bisexual, and transgender (LGBT) populations in northeastern Europe (Poland, Lithuania, Latvia, Estonia, Belarus) to create new spatial, theoretical, and temporal connections in order to understand the delay in recognizing LGBT rights in these countries, compared to Western Europe. Stalling legislation is concurrent with lower social tolerance for gay couples, a high rate of closeted gays (about 70 percent), persistent perception that LGBT sexuality is illegal and deviant, and absence of basic rights, "from picking up a [partner's] package at the post office to inheritance."[2]

As Mohanty suggests, "unfreezing" time can bring out similarities between geographically, politically, and economically foreign contexts. Therefore, I will preface the discussion of the current LGBT situation in Eastern Europe by a collage representing the attitudes toward male homosexuality in 1950s mainstream journalism in the United States at the height of the Cold War. A series of articles in 1958 in *Time* magazine reported on decriminalization of same-sex acts in Britain. One article highlights an "alarmingly" high incidence of gay scoutmasters: " 'This suggests,' say the [authors of the British study] guardedly, 'either that scouting strongly activates latent homosexuality or that homosexuals...join the scouting movement because of the...opportunities' "(*Time* 1958).

Moving back in *Time*, a 1956 article in the Medicine section entitled "A Curable Disease?" cited *Homosexuality: Disease or Way of Life?*, a book authored by a psychoanalyst specializing in "curing" homosexual men by "leading [them] to normal sexual enjoyment." The book put into question "common misconceptions" based on the findings of the Kinsey report ("homosexuality is an incurable, hereditary condition...'normal' for an unspecified proportion of the population") and alleged that

> [t]he full-grown homosexual...wallows in self-pity and continually provokes hostility to ensure himself more opportunities for self pity....He

is generally unreliable, in an essentially psychopathic way...he must give up his habit of using homosexuality as a weapon against his family, which (unconsciously) he always hates. (*Time* 1956)

The 1954 *Time*, featuring Roy Cohn and Joe McCarthy on the cover, broke the story about Cohn's alleged boyfriend David Schine, leading to the Army-McCarthy hearings focused on the alleged preferential treatment of Schine (March 16 to June 1954), eventually bringing down McCarthy and Cohn. The *Time* issue, largely devoted to this controversy, was thus breaking a detailed story on Cohn and his alleged boyfriend relatively early, in the second week of the Army-McCarthy hearings (March 22):

> Cohn's important Manhattan legal friends had been telling him for a long time that he should meet young David Schine.... Cohn's old boss, Irving Saypol, got Dave and Roy together at a luncheon in a restaurant in downtown Manhattan in 1952. Dave Schine turned out to be a pleasant, articulate young man with the build and features of a junior-grade Greek god. (*Time* 1954)

These citations illustrate mainstream attitudes toward male homosexuals in the 1950s. The topic of homosexuality is introduced as a foreign affair in Britain, an "essentially psychopathic" medical issue, or a way to bring down one of the most powerful public figures at the time. Homosexuality is denounced as the key that allows the magazine's mainstream public to read the otherwise secret code of widely disparate public and private pathologies that affect the most trusted institutions, concerning the entire population, and not contained by or limited to the same-sex minority: Boy Scouts infiltrated by sexual predators, families ruined by hostility, federal government and the army in the throes of nepotism.

There are structural similarities between these 1950s mainstream U.S. examples and contemporary mainstream discourse on LGBT rights in Eastern Europe, a discourse that denounces grassroots LGBT rights movements as foreign intrusions in a country's affairs. It is a phenomenon known from the fight for women's rights. When an oppressed group stands up for its rights, it is often labeled as unpatriotic, unnatural, "other" in terms of ethnicity, race, language, religion, or politics. In this hostile optic, nongovernmental organization (NGO) stands for "foreign funding for foreign value systems." Conspiracy theory becomes an all-purpose explanation, allowing the majority to process the inevitable, impending change by representing itself as the victim of covert operations. In the case of LGBT rights, the Catholic majority in Poland presents itself as the oppressed victim of the LGBT conspiracy. Simultaneously, the Polish Catholic minority in Europe sees itself as the victim of the globalized majority enforcing an incompatible system of values. An alliance arises between homophobia and populism, nationalism, fear of globalization, and "Euro-skepticism" (opposition to unified Europe). Thus, conservative Polish Catholics see themselves at the same time as victims of a minority conspiracy (by LGBT individuals) and of majority oppression or "open conspiracy" (by European Union [EU] and Western nations that support LGBT rights). This corresponds to two kinds of conspiracy identified by Timothy Melley (2000): the "classic" version ("covert operations") where conspiracy is an impenetrable secret perpetrated by a mysterious group of unidentifiable conspirators—here, the unrecognizable LGBT individuals—versus the "open conspiracy" whose rise Melley (2000) associates with the post–World War II increased awareness of the ways in which public opinion and individual viewpoint can be manipulated by such overt operations as advertisement, politics, government policy, and other factors. The paradox of double victim—Catholic majority victim of LGBT minority at home is also the Catholic minority victim of Western democratic majority on the European scene—is consistent with the "bipolar" functioning of conspiracy rhetoric in the political forum, as I will show in the next section.

The connection between homosexuality and foreign conspiracy is exploited by Eastern European politicians, including the president of Belarus, Alyaksandr Lukashenka: "We have to show our society... what... [European Union and the United States] are doing here, how they are trying to turn our girls into prostitutes, how they are feeding our citizens illicit drugs, how they are spreading homosexual perversion here, which methods they are employing" (September 28, 2004; cited in Kuhar and Takács 2007, 365). The Belarus president's remarks linking homosexuality with organized crime, human trafficking, sexual slavery, and the rise of the drug economy and characterizing same-sex orientation as a foreign perversion, reflects nationalist, populist, and religious family values of the Eastern European mainstream. The association between foreignness and LGBT made by Lukashenka was echoed a few months later in the Belarus TV coverage of the expulsion of a Czech diplomat: "our neighbours' [that is, Czechs'] understanding of democracy is peculiar: intoxication of youths, debauchery, and pornography. Do they, who are spreading the worst, vile predilections in our country, have the moral right to tell us how to live?" (January 21, 2005; Kuhar and Takács 365). Along the same lines of gay conspiracy, the election of Klaus Wowereit, the first openly gay mayor of Berlin (2007), was described by the mainstream Polish weekly *Wprost* as a proof that "against the popular opinion, in many countries, declaring that you are gay makes it easier to reach higher offices."[3] This conspiratorial revelation was qualified in the same article by the focus on murders and attempted murders of openly gay Western politicians in two sections darkly subtitled "The Price of Coming Out" and "Slave to His Orientation." The article accomplished, on its limited scale, the twin rhetorical goals of conspiracy theory: alienating and terrorizing. It also paradoxically combined irreconcilable positions: is being gay good or bad for a politician? In the next section, I will focus on mechanisms of thought that enable conspiracy theory to seamlessly combine such extreme opposites and to relate apparently mutually exclusive beliefs (being gay is either good or bad for a politician) in such a way that far from excluding, they mutually reinforce each other.

In order to understand how conspiracy theory works, it is also important to know the milieu in which it circulates. In Poland, one of the most prominent conservative groupings that circulate different variants of conspiracy theory (anti-Semitic, homophobic) is the so-called Mohair Berets, or "blue rinse brigade," prominently covered in national news. The Mohair Berets are not formally organized but are defined by gender (female), age (retired), economic status (blue collar), religion (practicing Catholics), and culture (target audience of a popular radio talk show *Radio Maryja* hosted by a Redemptorist priest Father Rydzyk, openly homophobic, and anti-Semitic). The label *Mohair Berets* is an affectionate pun on the Green Berets: the postmenopausal Mohair Berets are as deadly and as fierce as the elite storm troops. Mohair berets, sometimes homemade, are a marker of social standing, contrasted with the boutique felt or fur hats worn by the middle class, similar to the pre–World War II sartorial opposition between women in scarves versus hats. The Mohair Berets' core characteristic is piety, connoted by a condescending Polish term *dewotka* ("church lady"). They continue the tradition of peaceful and often brilliant collective acts of civil disobedience and social affirmation that thrived under the repressive communist regime after World War II. A recent (2009) collective happening was the distribution of hundreds of thousands of miniature mohair berets knitted by the sympathizers of *Radio Maryja* at the annual national pilgrimage to Częstochowa on July 12. According to the *Radio Maryja* blog, the miniature berets worn as badges "signify, 'I love Our Lord, the Church, and Poland'" (*Głos Rydzyka*). The Mohair Berets are impervious to liberal attacks because they embody categories that liberals hold sacred: working and retired lower-middle-class women, the elderly, mothers. One of the few weapons capable of deflating them is satire, for instance, a hit song under the eponymous title "Mohair Berets" by the Polish Beastie Boys, a band named Big Cyc ("Big Tit").[4] As a line of the song explains, Mohair Berets "drink tea and fight evil."

Heading Mohanty's appeal, as I analyze the discourse of homophobia in Eastern Europe, I am reluctant to rely on the predictable dichotomy that associates the academia with gay rights on one hand and the Church with homophobia on the other. In reality, there is accommodation on both sides; for instance, in Belarus in 2003, when the screening of *Outlawed* (a film on LGBT rights) at the European Humanities University in Minsk, was cancelled by the organizers of the Amnesty International Belarus Film Festival under pressure from the Russian Orthodox Church.[5] Another example is a recent conference on LGBT topics at a top university in Poland, which was displaced by the university's president from the central campus to the city's periphery.[6] Neoconservative rhetoric had its day on the same campus in a conference entitled "Mouth Wide Shut," critiquing politically correct speech. That conference appealed to "pick up the gauntlet before the Academia becomes the preserve of the 'reality challenged'" (Basiuk et al. 2006, 11). Thus, while intellectual milieus in Eastern Europe are more empowered than the general public to privately speak out against homophobia, the academia/Church dichotomy does not reflect the consensus-based functioning of the public sphere and the coexistence of both liberals and conservatives in the academia as well as in the Church. As Mohanty has warned, predictable dichotomies such as gender studies/populism, high culture/low culture, academia/Church do not always apply locally. Looking exclusively through their sightlines can cause us to overlook mutual accommodations that characterize the actual situation. Other, often not explicit thought structures organize the discourse on homophobia in Eastern Europe and dictate the decisions regarding the accommodation of the LGBT presence in the homophobic majority cultures of that region. Conspiracy theory is one of the most persistent among these operative thought structures.[7]

The Cultural Work of Conspiracy Theories

The label *foreign* and the concept of *the enemy within* are two transnational discursive structures well known from the history of European anti-Semitism that are currently applied to marginalize LGBT grassroots activists. The accusation of foreignness undercuts the rootedness of the LGBT movement in Eastern European soil and represents them as an intruder wreaking havoc on the vulnerable, pure, natural, local ecosystem. In order to uncover the way this conspiracy theory is constructed, it is useful to look at allegations of foreignness in a transnational context. The LGBT rights agenda could be foreign to Poland; there could even exist a conspiracy. However, a transnational reading allows us to see that foreign conspiracy theory is a discourse that can be found across state, ethnic, and language divides.[8] We come to realize that there exists a limited range of discourses and thought operations at our disposal to conceptualize that which we do not want to accept, a range so limited that it is both transnational and ahistorical. The discourse of degeneracy, foreignness, and conspiracy constitutes a true universal. Analyzing the cultural work of conspiracy theory allows us to gain insight to the universal grammar of hegemonic cultural resistance to minority pressures.

As a guide to conspiracy theory in post–World War II society, I cite Timothy Melley's *Empire of Conspiracy: The Culture of Paranoia in Postwar America*. Melley opens by emphasizing that the "notion that a network of agents may be operating 'beneath the surface' is not specific to the postwar era in the United States and "nervousness about the supposedly extraordinary powers and dangerous motives of large organizations has long been a feature of U.S. political culture" (2000, 1). He gives two examples that demonstrate, paradoxically, that identical discourse is used to warn against conspiracies motivated by either capitalist or communist principles:

> The question...is why these accounts of national crisis look so similar when they seem to be at ideological cross-purposes....The postwar model of conspiracy...is dependent upon a notion of diminished human agency...one index of this shared anxiety is that [accounts sympathetic to drastically different ideologies, for example, capitalism and communism] each posit a secret effort whose real goal is the mass reingineering of persons. (2–3)

Melley adds: "My interest lies less in the widely accepted idea that social and economic systems affect individual action than in a particularly nervous expression of this idea, an expression that gravitates toward representations of paranoia, conspiracy, and agency-in-crisis" (5). Melley calls this "nervous tendency" *agency panic*: "the frightening 'discovery' " of the obvious: that "human behavior can be regulated by social messages and communications: part of the paradox in which a supposedly individualist culture conserves its individualism by continually imagining it to be in imminent peril" (5–6).

There is a similarity between conspiracy theory as a symptom of *agency panic* and the branding of LGBT movements as foreign as a symptom of *moral panic,* defined as the reaction of conservative Eastern European constituencies, including the Catholic Church, to the "frightening discovery" that there exist LGBT communities in Eastern Europe. Human rights watch groups note a spike in hate crimes, especially violent crimes targeting LGBT individuals, coinciding with the fall of communism and greater visibility of LGBT groups and persons. As the editors of a recent (2006) Polish LGBT studies volume note:

> Increased visibility of the alternative [LGBT] community [coincides] with moral panic about the homosexual question, sexual harassment, pedophilia, and AIDS.... As we were sending the manuscript to press, two important events took place: the entire stock of *Homophobia à la polonaise,* the first book entirely devoted to this issue in Poland, published in October 2004, sold out, and on November 20, the *bojòwki* [guerilla groups of a political party] of All-Poland Youth attacked and dispersed the Equality March in Poznań. (Basiuk et al., 9)

There exists a confirmed relation between the more public and open LGBT presence and the rise of homophobic violence.

In his history of twentieth-century conspiracy theories in the United States, Melley links the emergence of a new kind of conspiracy theory, "the open conspiracy," with post–World War II era's agency panic and other signs of the demise of an integrated and unified humanistic perception of self or subject. The humanistic subject is undermined not only by the Holocaust but also by the realities of post-war economy and culture. Citing Frederic Jameson's remark that conspiracy theory is "a degraded attempt—through the figuration of advanced technology—to think the impossible totality of the contemporary world system" (1991, 38), Melley deepens Jameson's understanding of the cultural work of conspiracy theories by asking what is the reason to "conserve a sense of *intentionality* when explaining the manipulation of individuals by huge social and economic networks, labyrinthine webs of power?" (9–10). Melley answers:

> Conspiracies are understood to be hermetically sealed, marvelously efficient, and virtually undetectable.... [They] typically serve to conceptualize the relation between individuals and larger social bodies.... Conspiracy is often understood as a structure that curtails

individuality, or that is antithetical to individualism itself.... This way of thinking is rooted in long-standing Western conceptions of self-hood.... Its widespread appearance in the cultural landscape cannot be simply explained as a response to some *particular* political issue, historical event, or social organization...conspiracy discourse has considerable political effects, the most important of which stem from its usefulness to both the disempowered *and* the powerful. (10–11)

Melley points out that the proliferation of conspiracy theories and the emergence of "open conspiracy" narratives are symptoms of agency panic, a "nervousness or uncertainty about the causes of individual action" that can take various forms, from the belief in brainwashing to the fear of being manipulated by forces outside of our control, forces of which we are often unaware, as if we were "acting out parts of a script written by someone else" (12). Conspiracy theory proponents often invest these subterranean controlling forces with the individuality that they abstracted from the individuals they control: "*post-modern transference* in which social regulation seems to be the intentional product of a single consciousness or monolithic 'will'" (13). Even as the individuals are robbed of their essential humanness by conspiracies, the conspiracies grow into monstrous assemblages that concentrate the stolen valuable: free will.

An important and often overlooked aspect of the cultural work of conspiracy theories, according to Melley, is "that it develops from the refusal to accept someone else's definition of a universal social good or a universally sanctioned truth." Conspiracy theories "seem to be logical responses to technological and social change...to 'future shock,' 'global village' and 'postindustrial society'" (13–14). For Melley, "agency panic" is a symptom of the changing concept of humanness, from liberal individualism, that is "a view of the individual as a rational, motivated agent with a protected interior core of beliefs, desires, and memories," to a model or concept that accounts more fully for social regulation, for example, models based on post-structuralism and postmodernism inflected by sociology: "[a]gency panic...may be understood as a nervous acknowledgment, and rejection, of post-modern subjectivity" (14–15). By "postmodern subjectivity" Melley means these theories and experiences of subjectivity that, in opposition to the liberal humanism's image of the individual as a discrete whole centered on itself and operating by essentials and dichotomies, *celebrate* fragmentation, decentering, multiplicities, performance, as in Mohanty's description of an ideal approach to Third World feminism cited in the opening of this chapter. Further, for Melley, conspiracy theories are not social detritus emptied of meaning by their obvious absurdity, but rather means of insight into the least accessible recesses of postmodernity. Agency panic "bears an important likeness to sociological thinking" (15–16). Conversely, "'institutional analysis' is often dismissed as mere 'conspiracy theory' by those who believe our institutions...are supremely fair" (16).

Indeed, Melley points out that one of the most interesting aspects of conspiracy theory and paranoia is the impossibility to separate them from interpretation on any grounds other than the *presence of a consensus* (for a discussion of *consensus* and *dissensus*, see the last section of this chapter). Melley brings up the fact that in psychoanalysis, "cases of paranoia take the form of interpretive contests between analyst and patient, each of whom claims to have unearthed the hidden truth about the patient's (apparent) persecution.... Freud's description of paranoia has [much] in common with paranoia itself" (17). This consensus-based, not ontological nature of the distinction between paranoia and analysis translates into one of the strengths of conspiracy theory as it serves its cultural function.

The Enemy Within: Conspiracy Theory and Homophobia

In the nation-states of Eastern Europe twenty years after the fall of the Berlin Wall, the discursive structures of paranoia and conspiracy theory applied to the LGBT community seem directly transferred from the anti-Semitic tradition of Jewish conspiracy strongly present in these countries. The ideological continuity between anti-Semitism and homophobia is facilitated by genealogies of political parties and dynasties of civil servants. For instance, in Poland the leader of the right-wing League of Polish Families, appointed minister of education in 2006, notorious for homophobia in the context of the discussion of a law that would bar LGBT individuals from teaching positions, is the grandson of a politician active in the anti-Semitic Greater Poland Party of the 1930s (Kuhar and Takács, 327–34). Similarly, "All-Poland Youth, an anti-Semitic nationalist organization declared illegal in the 1930s, has been reborn as a weapon against sexual minorities" (Basiuk et al., 8). Such institutional and familial dynasties of intolerance are a conduit of "equal opportunity hate" and help explain the persistence of homophobia in spite of the proximity to Western multiculturalism and the proud, local traditions of tolerance in Eastern Europe.

Another conduit of "equal opportunity hate" is ideological rather than institutional and dynastic: "[T]he language of public debate often superposes" LGBT issues, "moral panic" issues (the existence and spread of AIDS, sexual harassment, pedophilia) and "other, more shameful problems, for instance anti-Semitism" (Basiuk et al., 9). These issues can stand in for each other in the public debate; to quote but one example, "This confusion of issues is evident... in the case of a priest whose anti-Semitic public statements and ostentatious lavish lifestyle were well known but rarely criticized, until he was accused of seducing an altar boy and lost his parish" (Basiuk et al., 9). The institutional homophobia of the Church is used as leverage to punish sexual predation; meanwhile, anti-Semitism and corruption are overlooked until a public figure is brought down by a sexual abuse scandal. These examples draw a thematic continuum where homophobia and anti-Semitism contradictorily assist the protection of minors and prosecution of sexual harassment and abuse. The bundle of issues clustered around homophobia and anti-Semitism in Eastern Europe are not part of a stable, ontological, or universally recognized system of values, but rather are fluid and shift to fit the demagogic or political needs of the moment and the case. Such fluidity is a symptom of the coexistence of multiple grounds of reference and systems of value.

As Melley points out, building up straw men to justify violence is part of the arsenal of conspiracy theory, where the victim is recast as aggressor. The "phantom of political correctness," described by the conservatives as a powerful social force, is not so powerful in reality if it cannot stop the bricks flying at the Gay Pride Parade (Basiuk et al., 10–12). Victims of stigmatization are required to act as if their burdens were not significant so that the majority could pretend that there is no discrimination. The University of Chicago sociologist Erving Goffman, who worked on the concept of stigma in the 1960s, termed this phenomenon "phantom acceptance."[9] For instance, in Poland "Jews were accused of bringing anti-Semitism upon themselves," and violence against Jews was considered "a basically sound defensive reaction by the Polish nation."[10] Similarly, when Gay Pride Parade was met with bricks and bottles in Cracow in 2004 and again in 2005, the bishop of Cracow commented: "if you bait someone, then no wonder!" and "the fault lies on both sides," while the aging cardinal Stanislaw Nagy called the Tolerance March "a shameless provocation" that "humiliated the city of a hundred churches" (Ostolski 2005).

There is a relation between conspiracy theory as a way to dismiss the legitimacy of the LGBT rights movement on one hand and the "communal option" of democracy on the other hand. The "communal option" consists in privileging the communal *sanctity* of the nation, the family, the Church over the rights of the individual, and its ultimate test, privileging the rights of the majority over minority. Community and integrity are the slogans of the ultranationalist, Church-based, and populist parties and formations. These constituencies use the term *sanctity* frequently as if it were a self-evident justification, similar to the use of the term *universal rights* or *human rights* in secular Western democratic political forums. The existence of an LGBT conspiracy is belied by the facts, taken seriously only by a small fringe, but paradoxically present in the thought processes of many. The claim that there exists a foreign conspiracy is not true, but facts do not matter if people think and act "as if"; as in the slogan cited by Melley, "It's not paranoia if they are *really* out to get you" (17). We could account for the rise of conspiracy theories as a pathological reaction to the pressure of an unresolved conflict between two constituencies. The victims of aggression are cast as the true aggressors, which justifies their victimization. The added bonus of the projection of hostility onto its victims is that a conspiracy calls for secret, stricter, illegal measures of repression; it justifies extreme violence. I will discuss strategies to dismantle the rhetoric of the "communal option" in the last part of this chapter, centered on Jacques Rancière's notion of *dissensus*.

Foreigners in Our Own Body: Acculturation to Homophobia

Public opinion studies demonstrate the complex layering of attitudes toward LGBT rights in Eastern Europe. On one hand, Eastern Europe self-identifies as democratic and devoted to the idea of universal human rights. On the other, the majority rejects LGBT rights. This contradiction is encapsulated, among countless other examples, in a comment of a Polish member of the parliament (MP) representing the political party Catholic-National Movement at the House Meeting of the Education, Science, and Youth Commission in 2005: "We are not hunting [LGBT] people, because we are clearly not at that stage of the civilized life."[11] Poland prides itself on half-a-millennium-long tradition of democratic institutions, including general elections since the 1500s, and the creation of the first ministry of education in Europe in the 1700s, but homophobia paradoxically coexists with Poland's self-definition as a trendsetter of democracy in Europe.

Similarly, a Lithuanian study (2006) showed that while 70 percent of respondents "would never personally approve of discrimination based on the grounds of sexual orientation," 61 percent "would not like to belong to any organization which has homosexuals among its members."[12] The authors of the study, sociologists Jolanta Reingarde and Arnas Zdanevičius, explain the apparent contradiction as a chasm between two incompatible cognitive systems used simultaneously by their subjects; simultaneous in the sense that they are always available but are applied discreetly, in different contexts or at different times. We rely on multiple and often contradictory systems of value and meaning as we negotiate social and internal pressures. We could cite the struggle between passion and reason, reality and appearances, private and public, soul and body, or the psychoanalytic distinction between the super-ego and the id, among many models, to account for the fact that we constantly negotiate between contradictory but coexisting systems. We try to reconcile them positively by personal and social action, but there often remains an irreconcilable part. The Lithuanian sociologists distinguish between *normative homophobia* (normative attitudes toward homosexuality) on the wane versus *empirical homophobia* (related to value systems of individuals), which persists. That schizoid status of homophobia, unacknowledged but persistent, corresponds to the schizoid social status of LGBT individuals. In Lithuania and in Eastern Europe in general, "LGBT people have a right to exist as long as they suppress their own identity" (Kuhar and Takács, 56). The work of reconciling incompatible positions and bridging the gap between perception and reality falls onto the shoulders of the LGBT population. Remaining closeted, LGBT individuals pretend not to exist so as to avoid challenging the belief that LGBT people are not "natural," are rare or absent from the society, and are not traditionally "Lithuanian." Polish LGBT activist Anna Gruszczyńska echoes this logic: "the average lesbian [believes] in a fairy tale world where (1) everyone is heterosexual, and (2) if you are not heterosexual, look under (1)."[13]

Advances in LGBT legislation in Eastern Europe that are often the prerequisite or the result of membership in the EU may hide an unchanged homophobic social reality. Although nondiscrimination legislation was "incorporated into Lithuanian national law before joining the EU in 2004," and Vilnius, the capital of Lithuania, was the site of 2007 International Lesbian and Gay Association (ILGA) annual conference, Lithuanian society is far from gay-neutral. In a self-selected sample of thirty-eight LGBT respondents in Lithuania, seven were "completely open about their sexuality at work," a further ten were out to selected individuals, while the majority (twenty-one) pretend to be heterosexual, have to "think, talk and be silent that way" (Kuhar and Takács, 56). The mayors of the two biggest Lithuanian cities prohibited the EU antidiscrimination truck from parking on the municipal territories (parking was found in private supermarket lots). In 2004 in Poland, the mayor of Warsaw denied three times the permit for the Gay Pride Parade; the triple prohibition was necessary because each time the mayor's decision was overturned by the governor of the region (Basiuk et al., 8). The chair of Lithuanian Gay Leagues responded: "We know that it takes time to build a non-homophobic, inclusive, and tolerant society...the mayors...are sending a clear message that LGBT people are still not welcome in their diverse communities and they are creating a kind of twenty-first century apartheid. Homosexuals who find it impossible to live in this situation are forced to emigrate to more tolerant European cities," that is, to the West (*Euro-Letter* 2008, 10).

The closet is not just a place one inhabits; it is a place built with one's own language and thinking, resulting in the self-realization that one is a *dead body* or *a permanent foreigner in one's own land*, two metaphors repeated throughout the Eastern European studies on the subject. LGBT people are aware of the damage self-inflicted in the process of acculturation to the heterosexual norm. One of the participants in the Lithuanian study says: "sometimes, it seems that *even if I leave for a foreign country*, the same insecurity will stay with me" (Kuhar and Takács, 56). The LGBT people describe themselves as "dead," "abnormal," "evil somehow," their lives a "lie," "vanishing," "alienation," "self-discrimination":

> "I immediately become something of a dead person...it means that from the beginning you have to become some dead person."
>
> "This is a constant lie, an eternal one...sometimes I even get confused."
>
> "I am a very lively person by nature, but when I get to my working place I immediately become something of a dead person."
>
> "I feel as if I am somehow vanishing from the inside."
>
> "I have to destroy myself from the inside in order to please them. So how can one live that way? And our lives are too short—understand?"

In a Polish study with 214 gay male participants, two-thirds did not have a partner, and among the one-third of couples 45 percent lived in urban areas with more than 1 million inhabitants.[14] Homophobia is more acute in the countryside, home to 25 to 40 percent of the Polish population. Forty-nine percent of the study's respondents (all the respondents were gay men) were against gay adoption and agreed that children should be brought up only in heterosexual marriages. A large group (30 percent) agreed that the child adopted by a gay couple would be a victim of social aggression, commenting that "it would be a prejudice to the child, perhaps even a humiliation and a source of ridicule in the eyes of other families. It could warp the child's psyche, making him/her unhappy" (Basiuk et al., 55–56). The majority of respondents (73 percent) thought Poles are homophobic (Basiuk et al., 56). Most respondents were not out to their closest family and friends, and most of them named the fear of their family as the main reason ("they are not tolerant"), while 20 percent named "easier life" as the main reason. Seventy-three percent were not out in the workplace, "mostly because of fear of discrimination ('they would eat me alive')"; 20 percent of respondents could describe a specific example of discrimination, frequently from their own experience (Basiuk et al., 57). Classifieds in Polish gay magazines frequently list "100% guy," "normally functioning as a hetero" in men's ads or "not part of the tribe" in women's ads as attractive or desired traits (Basiuk et al., 56, 127–36). The poignant comments reveal that LGBT people perform a disproportionate amount of work for social consensus. And yet, it is far from all the work they are asked to do. In addition, LGBT individuals are constantly harassed for undermining that consensus by their very presence. The effort to maintain both the pretense and one's own identity while being harassed "makes you feel abnormal…evil somehow." One participant in the Lithuanian study compares this to living under the totalitarian regime: "I feel the same way…as a dissident during the Soviet era who used to live a double life" (Kuhar and Takács, 53). The effort of finding out how much disclosure is socially acceptable is also placed on LGBT individuals' shoulders, as these comments from the participants of the Lithuanian study reveal: "When somebody asks me about that I look into this person's eyes and try to tell as much as she or he can stand" (Kuhar and Takács, 57); "certainly, you choose whom to tell and what to tell them" (58).

Only very little can be told, as a 2003 poster campaign against homophobia has shown in the neighboring Poland. The posters represented one lesbian and one gay couple, photographed holding hands in the street, with a red stamp saying "Let Them See Us" in the corner. In a few days all the posters were torn down or covered with paint (Basiuk et al., 7–8). To come out is "to be something like a kamikaze. Our society will not change its attitudes, and there is no point in sacrificing your life" (Kuhar and Takács, 62). The authors of the Lithuanian study sum up: "The perpetual angst…generates a form of constant self-surveillance of sexuality" (63).

Outing historical figures and contemporary public figures is also taboo. In the nineteenth and twentieth centuries, publishing constituted one of the few professions open to unmarried women, a fact that may explain a relatively high incidence of lesbians. Some of the most important Polish authors of that period were lesbian, including poet, novelist, and beloved children's book author Maria Konopnicka (1842–1910) or popular novelist, playwright, and journalist Maria Dąbrowska (1889–1965). Konopnicka was an important figure of the patriotic Polish underground whose works played a major role in preserving national identity during the century-long occupation of Poland, and Dąbrowska was a prominent human rights activist during the pre–World War II period. Most readers ignore lesbian aspects of the biography of these major, canonical authors.

Another symptom of homophobia concerns contemporary artists and authors whose LGBT orientation is not explicitly discussed even though their work focuses on LGBT contexts. This is the case of the most important living Polish Ukrainian poet, Eugeniusz Tkaczyszyn-Dycki. Although Dycki's poetry abounds in homosexual motifs, there is little reference to them or to the author's sexual orientation in criticism or anthologies devoted to him. The poet himself frequently and explicitly focuses on same-sex acts, for instance: "an eighty-year-old / and he will also desire as many / young men, so that he could take / at least one with him to eternity, / and caress their members / with his member as if there were no death" (*Peregrynarz*, cxxxvi. *Genetliakon*).[15] A similar silence envelops the work of Krzysztof Jung, an important visual artist (d. 1998) who exhibited homoerotic drawings and whose important and well-known happenings consisted of male couples sewing their clothes together, gazing into each other's eyes, or lying together naked. Jung's happenings involved stringing webs, weaving thread between performers and the audience, sewing, and cutting apart: "The meditative and ritual aspects of plastic theater protected these happenings from the impact of ridicule reserved for homoeroticism in Polish culture" (Basiuk et al., 192–93). Only those familiar with Western art could read Jung's frequent references to gay painter David Hockney as self-identification or coming out:

> [Jung's] alternative sexuality…could not be revealed other than through encoded language at the limit of articulation, but at the same time it was omnipresent, like a net in a gallery. Tied and released men in Jung's performances take on a new meaning in this context. They can be a transposition, a performance of his own, powerful need to tell the truth about himself, a ritual coming out, which the artist played

out in his own body or transferred onto the roles assigned to his actors. (Basiuk et al., 192–93)

While Lithuania and Poland are mostly Catholic, their neighbors Latvia and Estonia are largely Lutheran, self-identify as Nordic, and perceive tolerance as a specifically Scandinavian cultural value. Latvia and Estonia also culturally self-define as leaders in the international music culture, from folk to classical and avant-garde. The fall of the communist regime in Latvia was called the "Singing Revolution." It began with a lyrical act of civil disobedience later repeated elsewhere, including in the United States: a human chain holding hands throughout the three Baltic states, Latvia, Estonia, and Lithuania, to protest against post–World War II annexation of Baltic regions to the Soviet Union and redrawing of borders that ignored ethnic, religious, and linguistic regional boundaries. The protest against Soviet expansionism was thus a personal gesture translated into a grassroots effort on an international scale. It amplified an intimate gesture between two people into an international affirmation of a hidden Baltic identity, and by this means it emphasized the individual states' identity whose expression was forbidden under the Soviet rule. This tradition of nonviolent lyrical protest makes homophobic violence in these countries even more scandalous. Similar to Poland, the "events following the Pride Parade in [Latvia's] capital Riga in 2005 surprised and shocked Latvian society" when a coalition of left- and right-wing reactionaries "mobilized hundreds of people" to attack the parade.[16]

As does Mohanty, Latvian sociologist Aivita Putnina emphasizes the importance of local history in her account of the LGBT movement. She warns against premature generalizations that would portray Latvian homophobia as the result of an atrophy of democratic institutions, violently repressed under the Soviet regime. Instead, homophobia is a reaction to this repression and draws on the tools used in protesting against the Soviet rule. Putnina shows that although issues related to "patriarchy...are different in Old and New Europe...the main difference between both 'Europes' lies in the relationship of the dominant discourse to the dominated" (Kuhar and Takács, 315). By "discourse" she also means the absence of verbal debate on sex, sex roles, and practices, and the prevalently silent enactment of sexual practices that characterize Latvian population, including the youth: double standards for gender-specific behavior, lack of sex education, infrequent condom use, and other cultural practices connected to patriarchal hegemony. Putnina argues that LGBT issues are bound with culturally institutionalized shame about sexuality in general and

LGBT sexuality in particular, and thus are a weak link in the chain that links Latvia to its Nordic ideal, its cultural heritage, and the democratic institutions of the EU. Attitudes toward sex, gender hierarchy, and women, as well as political and economic issues, would have to change in order to modify the symbolic value of LGBT identity. A comment cited by Putnina shows a connection between women's rights and LGBT rights:

> If the husband beats his wife at home and she accepts it—this is a matter for their family. If he starts beating his wife in Riga city centre—it becomes a social matter and society expresses its opinion by putting that man into jail. Society has spoken on the gay demonstration, and it is accepted that in democracies the minority submits to the will of the majority. (Kuhar and Takács, 324)

I interpret the connection between a man publicly beating his wife and a gay demonstration, not as a metaphor for the difference between private and public behavior, the way it is intended by the homophobic speaker, but as a metonymy, a thematic affinity. The callous use of the image of an abused wife is an instance of verbal aggression. Similar violence echoes in the speaker's attitude toward gay rights. At the same time demonstrations are valued as an expression of autonomy and democracy: "society has spoken." The "communal option" of democracy serves to condemn gay rights, as in the Polish examples earlier. The protest against the gay minority is conflated with the protests against the Russian minority that oppressed Latvia during the Soviet era. Thus, the tradition of public protest is redeployed to fight against LGBT rights.

Ranciere's Dissensus vs. the "Communal Option" of Democracy

The slippage from democracy as a system based on the *rights of man* to democracy as the way to uphold the rights of the community and the majority (*human rights*) against a minority is a telling symptom. The slippage from the concept of the individual subject to the communal subject—a subject to the rule of the majority, a Polish subject, a subject that embodies the principle of Polonization, and heterosexually produces heterosexual Polish children—alerts us to the shift from democracy to totalitarianism. This is not to say that the communal model of democracy cannot be used to advocate feminist issues. The power balance of the feminist fight is often the inverse: women fight against globalization, locally protecting the interests of a disenfranchised majority against the powerful few. But if an argument can be used for the good, that doesn't make it intrinsically a thought structure that automatically generates democracy.

Rancière's concept of *dissensus* can be used to dismantle the "communal option."[17] Writing on Hannah Arendt and Giorgio Agamben, Rancière attempts to overcome what he sees as the impasse of democracy by challenging the way we think about human rights and the operations of politics. Traditionally, we perceive two separate interacting spheres, public and private. We understand democracy as a contest between the two that results in compromise or consensus. In opposition to consensus, Rancière's *dissensus* does not smooth out the differences between individuals or constituencies in a social relation, but rather it establishes a *third term* through which they can communicate. Instead of the binary consensus/conflict, there is a two-step process that begins with the inscription of rights "of the community as free and equal"; the second step is to claim, exercise, or apply these written rights: "the Rights of Man are the rights of those who make something of that inscription" (Rancière 2004, 303). According to Rancière, the litigation and negotiation of these rights does not take place in the political sphere, as Arendt proposed, but rather on the intersection of the private and public spheres: "this is what I call dissensus: putting two worlds in one and the same world. A political subject, as I understand it, is a capacity for staging such scenes of dissensus" (303). The rights of man are implemented at the theoretical and juridical location that corresponds to the conjunction "and" in the phrase *The Declaration of the Rights of Man and Citizen*: "it is the opening of an interval for political subjectivation" (304). Instead of opposing the public to the private sphere, Rancière distinguishes between *police,* the sphere of entitlements based on collective qualifications, and the *political process,* defined as that which cannot be subsumed to entitlements/police. The political process, not the entitlements, is the source of the rights of man. Consequently, consensus and conflict are not the only two possible outcomes of politics: "consensus is the reduction of democracy to the way of life of a society, to its *ethos*" (306). In a paradoxical departure from the traditional way of thinking about democracy, Rancière concludes that the *less* consensus there is between different constituencies, the *more* political space and opening for the rights of man. A perfectly consensual society, in Rancière's theory, is the totalitarian society. For instance, in a polemic on gay civil unions between gay and Catholic conservative voices published by a mainstream Polish newspaper *Gazeta Wyborcza*, the sociologist Jacek Kochanowski writes:

> The absence of legally regulated definition of same-sex couples is an act of social injustice, because it discriminates...lesbians and gays have a right to respect for their unions, just as Christians have a right to demand respect for their tradition, and the business of the state and of democratic institutions is to reconcile both rights so that the social order formed as a result can be called a just order. (Cited in Basiuk et al., 124)

Rancière's emphasis on *dissensus* in the democratic process can serve as an argument against the "community option" that would justify the rule of the mainstream majority against the rights of the LGBT minority in Eastern Europe. His argument for *dissensus* and social standing of rights resonates with the arguments of Eastern European gay rights activists.

Notes

1. I thank Clara Román-Odio and Marta Sierra, the editors of the volume, and the anonymous readers for invaluable comments and suggestions for revisions. Work on this article has been supported by a sabbatical research appointment, conference, and travel grants from Miami University.
2. Iza Desperak, "Homofobia, czyli dwuglos o prawach gejow I lesbijek na łamach "Gazety Wyborezej," in Basiuk, Ferens, and Sikora, 113–26. All translations are mine unless otherwise indicated.
3. Pawel Białobok. 2007. "Gej na kanclerza," [A gay for a chancellor] *Wprost* 41. www.wprost.pl/ar/115281/Gej-na-kanclerza/?O+115281&pg+1/.
4. One of the Big Cyc's posters proclaims, "The *Big Cyc* is the work of Satan."
5. *Outlawed* was produced by Amnesty International Netherlands and portrays LGBT discrimination in India, Nicaragua, South Africa, Romania, and the United States (Kuhar and Takács, 364).
6. The conference took place at the Jagiellonian University in Cracow: Basiuk et al., 11.
7. Gregory E. Czarnecki, "Analogies between Pre-war Anti-Semitism and Present-day Homophobia in Poland," in Kuhar and Takács 327–44.
8. I acknowledge conversations with Bruno Chaouat and Sante Matteo, following Chaouat's lecture "Monstrosity in Post-Cold War France at Miami University (Oct. 2008).
9. Goffman, cited in Kuhar and Takács 338. Goffman also proposed the term *institutionalization* to describe the effects of confinements on inmates and focused on the role of framing/spin in the media. More recent work on stigma includes Link and Phelan (2001) and Major and O'Brien (2005).

10. Ostolski, cited in Kuhar and Takács, 343. Many sources singled out that quote from Nagy's broadcasted sermon. Reporting for the Polish section of *Radio Vatican,* Dobrzyniak used it to highlight Nagy's call to "bravely confront godless Europe."
11. Cited in the epigraph by Ostolski. On the same Internet site as Ostolski's article appears an earlier "equal opportunity hate" blogger's suggestion on how to sabotage the LGBT Tolerance March (April 21, 2004): "We have to make it known that there is some Itzak from Israel, and some Arab will jump out with a grenade," illustrating the seamless confluence of openly anti-Jewish, anti-Arab, and anti-gay hate speech in Polish mainstream.
12. Jolanta Reingarde and Arnas Zdanevičius, "Disrupting the "(Hetero) Normative: Coming-Out in the Workplace in Lithuania," in Kuhar and Takács 49–64, 55.
13. Anna Gruszynska, "Lesbijki w sieci. Zadyminony pokòj I ucieczka od branży," in Basiuk et al., 127–36, 132.
14. Artur Krasicki, "Homosexualiści w Polsce. Studium środowiska (Fragmenty)," in Basiuk et al., 51–60. This chapter is based on Krasicki's 1999 MA thesis.
15. Cited by Przemysław Pilarski, "Obsesje Dyckiego. Homoseksualność na tle pozostałych problemòw tożsamosci bohatera wierszy autora *Przewodnika dla bezdomnych...,*" in Basiuk et al., 252–61, 257.
16. Aivita Putnina, "Sexuality, Masculinity and Homophobia: The Latvian Case," in Kuhar and Takács 313–26.
17. For a discussion of the history of human rights and a summary of positions of Arendt, Agamben, Jean-François Lyotard, Jacques Derrida, and Jürgen Habermas on the rights of man, see Kłosowska and Reynolds.

Works Cited

Basiuk, Tomasz, Dominika Ferens, and Tomasz Sikora, eds. 2006. *Parametry Pożądania: kultura odmieńcow wobec homofobii* (Cracow: TAiWPN Universitas).

Białobok, Paweł. 2007. "Gej na kanclerza," [A gay for chancellor] *Wprost* 41. www.wprost.pl/sr/115281Gej-na-kanclerza/?O=115281&pg=1. Last accessed Sept. 2009

Deleuze, Gilles. 1988. *The Fold: Leibniz and the Baroque.* Foreword and trans. Tom Conley. Minneapolis: University of Minnesota Press.

Deleuze, Gilles, and Felix Guattari. 1980. *A Thousand Plateaus.* Trans. Brian Massumi. London, New York: Continuum, 2004. Vol. 2 of *Capitalism and Schizophrenia.* 1972–1980. Trans. of *Mille Plateaux.* Paris: Les Editions de Minuit.

Dobrzyniak 2004. "Poles Against God-Less Europe," *Radio Watykanskie* (Sept. 5). http://74.125.95.132/search?q=cache:4mlAKcqNVy8J:www

.oecumene.radiovaticana.org/pol/Articolo.asp%3Fc%3D7807+bezwstyd
na+prowokacja+nagy&cd=2&hl=pl&ct=clnk&gl=pl.
Euro-Letter. 2008. Aug. (vol. 156). www.ilga-europe.org/europe
/publications/euro_letter.
Glos Rydzyka. http://glosrydzyka.blox.pl/2009/06/350-tysiecy-moherowych
-beretow.html.
Goffman, Erving 1963. *Stigma: Notes on the Management of a Spoiled Identity.* New York: Prentice-Hall.
Jameson, Frederic. 1991. *Postmodernism, or, the Cultural Logic of Late Capital.* Durham: Duke University Press.
Kłosowska, Anna, and Bryan Reynolds. 2009. "Civilizing Subjects, or Not: Montaigne's Guide to Modernity, Agamben's Exception, and Human Rights After Derrida," in Bryan Reynolds, *Transversal Subjects: From Montaigne to Deleuze after Derrida.* New York: Palgrave Macmillan. 203–61.
Kuhar, Roman, and Judit Takács, eds. 2007. *Beyond the Pink Curtain: Everyday Life of LGBT People in Eastern Europe.* Ljubljana: Peace Institute.
Link, Bruce G., and Jo C. Phelan. 2001. "Conceptualizing Stigma," *Annual Review of Sociology* 27(1):363–85.
Major, Brenda, and Laurie T. O'Brien. 2005. "The Social Psychology of Stigma," *Annual Review of Psychology* 56(1):393–421.
Melley, Timothy. 2000. *Empire of Conspiracy: The Culture of Paranoia in Postwar America.* Ithaca: Cornell University Press.
Mohanty, Chandra Talpade. 2003. *Feminism Without Borders: Decolonizing Theory, Practicing Solidarity.* Durham, NC: Duke University Press.
Ostolski, Adam. 2005. "Zydzi, geje, i wojna cywilizacji," http://kobiety
-kobietom.com/queer/art.php?art=2249. Last accessed Sept. 2009
Rancière, Jacques. 2004. "Who Is the Subject of the Rights of Man?" *South Atlantic Quarterly* 103(2/3) (Spring/Summer):297–310.
Time. 1958. Medicine: "What Is a Homosexual?" June 16, www.time.com. Last accessed Sept. 2009
Time. 1956. Medicine: "A Curable Disease?" Dec. 10, www.time.com. Last accessed Sept. 2009
Time. 1954. National Affairs: "The Self-Inflated Target." Mar. 22, www
.time.com. Last accessed Sept. 2009
Tkaczyszyn-Dycki, Eugeniusz. 2008. *Peregrinary.* Trans. Bill Johnston. Brookline, MA: Zephyr Press.

Part IV

Pedagogies of Crossing and Dissent

Chapter Nine

The Vagina Monologues: *Theoretical, Geopolitical, and Pedagogical Concerns*

Kimberly A. Williams

> In order for the human race to continue, women must be safe and empowered. It's an obvious idea, but like a vagina, it needs great attention and love in order to be revealed.
>
> —Eve Ensler (2001, xxxvi)

This essay explores the pedagogical possibilities and pitfalls inherent in using Eve Ensler's *The Vagina Monologues* and its attendant antiviolence organization, V-Day, as an example of transnational feminist antiviolence organizing and activism. While acknowledging the importance of the play and V-Day in antiviolence fund-raising efforts and in generating awareness of the global ubiquity of gender-based violence, I contend that the play, as well as the global antiviolence movement that has grown up around it, relies almost exclusively on U.S.-based feminist epistemologies, subjectivities, and theoretical perspectives that are embedded within an American nationalist discourse[1] that positions the United States as the "rescuer" of poor, brown women from the global South, who, as many feminist scholars have convincingly argued over the course of the last twenty years or so, are repeatedly depicted in American media—and by mainstream U.S. feminism—as a singular, powerless, and passive group (Mani, 1990; Mohanty, 1991; Narayan, 1997; Dell, 2002). This depiction has been reified and exaggerated since the days immediately following 9/11 when the Bush administration strategically (and successfully) justified the U.S. invasion of Afghanistan by arguing that the United States must "save" the women of Afghanistan from their (racialized, male) Muslim oppressors.

I argue that U.S. feminism's embeddedness in American nationalism affects how and why *The Vagina Monologues* is used, both formally and informally, as a pedagogical tool in U.S. women's studies classrooms. I conclude that the play has the potential to serve as an important antiracist pedagogical tool through which women's studies students can learn to engage in critically productive transnational feminist critique that avoids ethnocentrism, but that feminist educators who use the play must be willing to incorporate analyses of capitalism, the historical legacies of colonialism, and the contemporary consequences of U.S. imperialism and to acknowledge U.S. feminism's position as part and parcel of American nationalism.

My work here is part of a much larger project-in-progress that relies on what Román-Odio and Sierra in their introduction to this volume term "transnational feminist practices" (2011, 1) to interrogate the intersection of government/elite discourse *on* and popular representation *of* "violence against women" as a category separate and apart from other kinds of violence. The term "violence against women" is in quotation marks on the page and in my head in order to draw attention to its constructedness as a category separate and apart from other forms of violence. The category "violence against women" did not always exist, and to acknowledge its discursivity inherently requires learning about its evolution: How, why, and when did the category develop? What is "violence," broadly conceived, and why/how is it different from "violence against women"? What counts as "violence against women," for whom, where, and under what circumstances?

It is this series of questions that fuels my continued ambivalence toward *The Vagina Monologues*. As feminist theorists have made clear, not all women are the same, nor, I maintain, is all "violence against women." The term is defined differently in different contexts, and *The Vagina Monologues* reproduces universalisms that do not acknowledge this crucial point. However, given the play's impressive political efficacy and extraordinary global popularity, these questions also make an acknowledgment of its (and Eve Ensler's) importance to feminist antiviolence activism crucial to any transnational feminist critique. Essentially, my concern about *The Vagina Monologues* is threefold:

1. **Theoretical:** I argue that a largely U.S.-based liberal/mainstream feminist framework is being used in *The Vagina Monologues* to define "violence against women" globally. This framework assumes that "equality" (to men) is the key to ending women's oppression, and it promotes an individualistic approach to achieving that "equality." Most important for my work here, however, is that liberal/mainstream feminism (and the feminists who advocate this approach) not only works *within* extant state

structures and institutions without seeking to alter them, but also frequently *with* them.² Consequently, its issues and agendas are easily co-optable by those same state structures and institutions.
2. **Geopolitical:** Co-optation is precisely what has occurred with regard to U.S.-based liberal/mainstream feminist antiviolence organizing and advocacy. The issue of "violence against women" has been co-opted by the U.S. government in support of the "rescuer" rhetoric of American nationalism, and to legitimate a neocolonial foreign policy agenda that includes global economic restructuring and increasing militarism.
3. **Pedagogical:** The embeddedness of liberal/mainstream U.S. feminisms in American nationalism reifies a cultural rhetoric of ethnocentrism and xenophobia,³ which not only draws attention to the "racial and imperialist implications of feminist discourses" in the United States (Román-Odio and Sierra, 2011), but concomitantly serves to (re)enforce what U.S. women's studies students think they already know about "other" women around the world. This problem is exacerbated by the implicit obligation that women's studies departments at least endorse *The Vagina Monologues,* if not actually use it in their classrooms as a core pedagogical tool.

The Vagina Monologues: A Brief History

In the early 1990s, self-identified feminist actor and playwright Eve Ensler began interviewing women in the New York City metro region about their vaginas; she was concerned about the health risks that were the consequence of the ignorance, embarrassment, and shame associated with women's sexual health. The negative feelings that her interviewees had concerning their vaginas were being reinforced by the medical community, by popular culture, and by other powerful social institutions. What Ensler found by doing these interviews, which later turned into a series of monologues about vaginas, was that an overwhelming number of these women—just in the New York City metro area alone—were survivors of gender-based violence, particularly rape, battery, and incest.

Ensler, herself a survivor of childhood sexual abuse, became aware of the magnitude of the problem of "violence against women" through her interviews. Although she had been performing versions of *The Vagina*

Monologues around the United States since the mid-1990s, she decided to put what she had learned to use in an attempt to raise awareness and money. In 1998 the play was performed at a star-studded fund-raiser for New York City–area antidomestic violence organizations. A number of celebrity feminists performed *The Vagina Monologues* at this event, including Glenn Close, Whoopi Goldberg, Susan Sarandon, Winona Ryder, Marisa Tomei, Margaret Cho, Gloria Steinem, and Rosie Perez. This fund-raiser, and this performance of *The Vagina Monologues*, marked the founding of an organization called V-Day (Victory over Violence Day), which describes itself on its website as "a global movement to end violence against women and girls" (www.vday.org).

What is interesting about this description, though, is that V-Day did not start out with a global focus. Rather, Ensler's concern was *U.S.-based* violence against women and girls committed by men, normally termed "domestic violence" or "intimate partner violence." In these early days of V-Day, Ensler defined "violence" against women and girls quite narrowly as the three I already mentioned (rape, battery, and incest), because it was those types of gender-based violence that were being talked about by the (mostly heterosexual) U.S.-based women she interviewed. Interestingly, those "domestic" types of gender-based violence were also how the U.S. Congress, in several hearings between 1987 and 1994, defined the term "violence against women," and I will return shortly to a discussion of the dynamic relationship between Ensler's evolving definition of "violence against women" and that of Congress.

In the decade since that time, however, V-Day has quite literally gone global. It has expanded its scope to incorporate a more inclusive critique of gender-based violence, particularly the sexualized violence that occurs in conflict zones, and what the organization terms "sexual slavery" and "female genital mutilation." In addition, its foundational text, Ensler's *The Vagina Monologues*, has been translated and performed royalty-free across the United States, Europe, Africa, the Middle East, and central and east Asia as part of local feminists' struggles to pass antiviolence legislation in their own communities and to bring attention to the frequency and variety of gender-based violence perpetrated against women and girls around the world.[4] And Ensler herself has become a celebrity feminist advocating for women's rights as human rights.

The Problems

As I mentioned earlier, I have theoretical, geopolitical, and pedagogical concerns about all of this. There is no denying that, in any number of ways, V-Day is accomplishing its three stated objectives to empower women, raise money, and raise awareness of "violence against women" (www.vday.org). Testimonials by performers suggest that *The Vagina Monologues* can be, and has been, empowering for the women who perform it (Obel 2001). Performances of the play raise millions of dollars every year to support local community antiviolence organizations, and through its annual Spotlight Campaigns, V-Day is building awareness of the global prevalence of gender-based violence.[5] But the play's theoretical foundation in U.S.-based liberal/mainstream feminist approaches and perspectives seems to have been co-opted by the U.S. government to support an American nationalist rhetoric of exceptionalism (that is, the notion that the United States has a divinely inspired duty to spread its vision of freedom and democracy to the rest of the world) and to validate its neocolonial foreign policies. I argue that this affects how and why the play is used, both formally and informally, as a feminist pedagogical tool.

I am wary, too, of Ensler's celebrity status as a prominent media spokesperson on the issue of "violence against women," particularly because I am skeptical about the dynamic relationship between Ensler's definition of "violence against women" and that used by Congress. Has the evolution of "violence against women" as a policy priority for the U.S. government over the past two decades followed the lead of feminist theorists and activists, or has the United States set the antiviolence agenda, expecting that feminists (and the United Nations) will step in line? Although impossible to answer within the framework of this essay, this question has broad implications within the larger context of transnational feminist antiviolence activism, particularly when feminist scholar-teachers are considering the pedagogical disadvantages of using Ensler, *The Vagina Monologues,* and V-Day as an example of successful transnational feminist organizing.

Although inherently interconnected, the three reasons for my ambivalence about *The Vagina Monologues* are more readily understood if considered in turn.

Theoretical

The Vagina Monologues has two overarching messages. The first encourages women to claim bodily autonomy and sexual awareness/agency. The play's focus on vaginas not only theoretically positions Ensler as a liberal/mainstream feminist, but also serves to reify a biological essentialism that assumes "woman" as a singular, universal discursive category while ignoring the argument long made by intersectional, postcolonial, and, more recently, transnational feminist theorists that such a category cannot remain unaffected by hierarchies of power based on other simultaneously occurring identities such as skin color, age, ethnicity, religion, socioeconomic status, sexual orientation, nation, and so on. However, this potentially troublesome theoretical framework is of less concern to me than the play's second message.

Since expanding her definition of "violence against women" to encompass "other" forms of gender-based violence that (apparently) occur less frequently in the United States (such as sex trafficking and female genital surgeries), Ensler seems to be using *The Vagina Monologues* to argue that the experience of and/or potential for sexual violence is an issue that affects and connects all women globally (Ensler 2001). This liberal/mainstream feminist trope of "sisterhood," particularly as it pertains to "violence against women" (Stapleton 2002) is what the editors of this volume term an "imaginary formation" whose ahistoricism and decontextualization has been justifiably critiqued by postcolonial and Third World feminists (Román-Odio and Sierra, this volume, 00), who have repeatedly pointed to the ways in which the universalizing agenda of mainstream U.S. feminisms have been co-opted to serve an American neocolonial agenda, both within the United States and abroad.

Historian Antoinette Burton has called attention to the complicity of British feminists in the British Empire's attempts to "civilize" India by imagining Indian women as helpless colonial subjects (1994), and it is not difficult to make a conceptual leap to the contemporary "war on terror" to argue that mainstream U.S. feminism has been co-opted (willingly or not) for the same sort of imperialist project. Clear evidence of this occurred in the weeks after 9/11 when the Bush administration conducted an "unusual international offensive [...] to publicize the plight of women in Afghanistan" (Bumiller 2001). As part of a strategy designed by Bush public relations adviser Karen Hughes, high-ranking administration officials from the Pentagon, State Department, and White House, including Hughes and National Security Advisor Condoleezza Rice, met with leading (and long-time) feminist advocates of Afghani women's rights Mavis Leno and the feminist majority's Eleanor Smeal. In addition, First Lady Laura Bush was positioned in an uncharacteristically high-profile role in an attempt to bring public attention to the status of Afghani women under the Taliban (Lynch 2001). And, as Kelly Oliver points out, in the years since the commencement of the "war on terror,"

Muslim women in Afghanistan and Iraq have been at the center of an American nationalist rhetoric that insists that the "freedom" being brought to them by U.S. military intervention and corporate colonialism is figured as "sexual freedom, imagined as the freedom to expose the female body, to wear any clothing, and to shop for that clothing" (2007, 47). The complexity of colonial projects, though, is that there are material benefits that are given to colonial subjects (such as suffrage, access to education, infrastructural "development," and so on), but these benefits almost always come with problematic contingencies that render the "freedoms" largely ineffective and inadequate for the people whom they are intended to benefit.

The complicity of liberal/mainstream U.S. feminisms in maintaining the ethnocentricism and xenophobia of American nationalism is manifest in Ensler's work. For example, a 2004 documentary about V-Day, called "Until the Violence Stops," positions sex work and what it terms "female genital mutilation" as always already negative without attending to postcolonial, poststructuralist, and Third World feminist arguments regarding the homogenizing discourse about these issues.[6] And the documentary negatively stigmatizes sex trafficking without considering the role of U.S.-led "development" policies and increased global militarization in *causing* the economic hardship that feminist scholars argue is a significant factor pushing women into the global sex trade in the first place (Farr 2005).[7]

Geopolitical

In the United States, the naming of "violence against women" as an issue of concern, and the evolution of what counts as "violence against women," paralleled the increasingly global focus of V-Day and *The Vagina Monologues*.[8] U.S. congressional hearings on the issue began in 1987 before the House Committee on Children, Youth, and Families, which confined definitions of "violence against women" to physical and sexual "domestic partner violence." At the same time, Ensler started her interviews with women in New York City about their vaginas and learned that an overwhelming number of them had had violent sexual experiences involving incest, battery, and rape. By 1990, the Senate Committee on the Judiciary took up the issue. Led by then-Senator Joe Biden, a liberal Democrat from Delaware (and Barack Obama's vice-president), the committee's goal was to develop an antidomestic violence law. But not only was the resulting legislation (the 1994 Violence Against Women Act) focused entirely on "family violence," it was also, as Inderpal Grewal (1998) points out, heavily skewed toward providing funding and support for law enforcement rather than to emergency shelters and recovery programs that would directly assist survivors and their children.

During the lengthy congressional proceedings through which the Violence Against Women Act was finally enacted into federal law in 1994, Biden's Senate committee held a hearing that considered the possibility that "domestic violence" may not be the only kind of gender-based violence, that "violence against women" may well extend beyond the family structure. By 1999/2000 (possibly as a result of similar conversations at the United Nations), this resulted in a series of congressional hearings that debated whether or not to include sex trafficking as "violence against women" in the reauthorization of the 1994 law.[9] In the end, the Violence Against Women Act was reauthorized with the original definitions of "violence against women" essentially intact, and a separate law, the Trafficking Victims Protecting Act, was passed in 2000 to deal with sex trafficking. Interestingly, the 2000 reauthorization of the Violence Against Women Act formally established the Violence Against Women Office as part of the State Department, thus signaling for the first time that "violence against women," as an official part of the U.S. foreign policy agenda, had become conceptualized as one more global problem that the United States should rightfully address.

Meanwhile, Ensler founded V-Day, and *The Vagina Monologues*, too, began incorporating "global" kinds of "violence against women," including female genital surgeries (which Congress began discussing as early as 1993 [Gunning 1998]), sex trafficking (which, as I discussed earlier, Congress took up in 2000), "violence against women" in the military (Congress, 2006),[10] and rape as a weapon of war (Congress, 2008).[11] Ensler also kicked off V-Day's 2003 Spotlight Campaign at a massive press conference at Pine Ridge in late 2002—a full five years before Congress held a hearing concerning the particular circumstances and effects of "violence against women" on Native women.[12]

Of course, raising public awareness of the exploitation and abuse of women is crucial, and feminist interventions into U.S. domestic and foreign policy have great potential to effect much-needed, progressive change. However, a consequence of the constructedness of the term "violence against women" is the fluidity and multiplicity of its definition(s), and, thus, the multiple (political) uses to which those definitions can be put. "Violence against women" seems to me to be similar to racially motivated violence in that it is fairly universally regarded as a negative practice throughout the global West. And because positioning oneself in opposition to "violence against women" is not controversial, U.S. legislators and policymakers across the political spectrum nod in agreement and sympathy with U.S. liberal/mainstream feminists that "violence against women" is bad, and everyone is similarly appalled. In other words, it is politically efficacious for a liberal Democrat like Biden and a conservative Republican the likes of Strom Thurmond (who served on the Senate Foreign Relations Committee during Biden's chairmanship) to support legislation that makes illegal the hitting, raping, and killing of women.

But when the far right and the far left can agree, both with each other and with a select(ed) group of feminist antiviolence advocates, I cannot help but experience apprehension. Ideological accord between these three constituencies is a sure sign that compromises are being made that are likely to at least undermine, if not entirely negate, any kernel of social justice advocacy that may have been the catalyst for such discussions in the first place. This has certainly been the case with both the U.S. Violence Against Women Act (Grewal 1998) and the Trafficking Victims Protection Act (Williams 2011). Those involved in antiviolence advocacy in the United States, whether legislators and policymakers on Capitol Hill or professional feminists from liberal/mainstream think tanks, are unable to solve a problem they cannot concretely define or articulate. They have wrongly imagined the causes, consequences, and types of "violence against women" as universal, regardless of geographic location or cultural context. This has resulted in the simultaneous simplification and erasure of the harsh reality of men's "violence against women" globally within the American nationalist rhetoric of "human rights," which is discursively deployed to justify unilateral U.S. (military) engagement abroad. As a result, "violence against women" can be (and has been) effortlessly co-opted in the service of more sinister American nationalist agendas, such as to defend and legitimate the "war on terror" (particularly the invasions and occupations of Afghanistan and Iraq) as a "civilizing" mission to "rescue" abused Islamic women from their male oppressors, while simultaneously insisting that American women are "lucky" to enjoy the "freedoms" that come with living in a "modern," "civilized" "democracy" (and vilifying those U.S. feminists who disagree with both arguments).

As Grewal (1998) rightly points out, these epistemologies, subjectivities, and perspectives are, themselves, embedded within what she refers to as the "moral superiority" of American nationalism, the rhetoric of which not only sustains ethnocentricism and xenophobia, but also situates the United States—and liberal/mainstream American feminists—as the saviors and rescuers of "oppressed" Third World women. In addition, because it makes invisible the gender-based exploitation and abuse of women in the global West and fails to acknowledge the neocolonial practices and policies of the United States that create exploitation elsewhere, this rhetoric also creates impunity for the United States, making impossible the inclusion of the United States as a global human rights violator in its own right.

Pedagogical

The popularity and success of V-Day's College Initiative, which began in 1999 as a way for V-Day to get its antiviolence message to communities throughout the United States, means that *The Vagina Monologues* is performed annually on U.S. college and university campuses as part of V-Day celebrations (Obel 2001). And this is the context in which women's studies instructors, as the de facto feminist representatives on campus, are pressured by both students and administrators to unproblematically teach and support campus productions of the play. My concern as a feminist educator located within women's studies as an institutionalized space of academic knowledge production is that the play may well undermine my efforts to discourage ethnocentrism and promote inclusive transnational feminist critiques and perspectives in my classes.

If it does, it is probably not (only) the fault of the play, particularly because the hundreds of annual performances of *The Vagina Monologues* in dozens of countries worldwide have helped V-Day to "increase awareness, raise money and revitalize the spirit of existing antiviolence organizations" as feminist activists around the world seek to end gender-based violence (www.vday.org/about/more-about, par. 1). A self-identified advocate of feminism and a passionate antiviolence advocate, Ensler is, at worst, guilty of universalization in her conceptualization of "violence against women." And, yes, this theoretical approach does make the play and its oversimplified antiviolence message easily co-optable by American nationalism as a legitimate reason for U.S. neocolonial expansion.

But the political application of her ideas by the clueless and/or willfully malevolent is surely beyond Ensler's control. The play is about "violence against women" globally *as well as* U.S.-based sexual violence; Ensler's point, after all, is that the experience and/or threat of sexual violence is a commonality that connects all women globally—and that necessarily includes women living in the United States. But, in my own experiences using the play as a pedagogical tool in my women's studies classrooms, those monologues describing the types of violence that occur most often elsewhere (such as "female genital mutilation" and sex trafficking) seem to stand out to my students as particularly horrific because, in the play, they are culturally and geographically decontextualized. Unfortunately for my attempts at an inclusive transnational feminist pedagogy, it is those monologues my students remember most clearly at the expense of the monologues that draw attention to other types of "violence against women" that occur with similarly alarming frequency right "here" "at home" in the United States. Nonetheless, neither Ensler nor the play should be held responsible for the frequency with which American students, particularly since 9/11, (usually) unwittingly come to *The Vagina Monologues* with the ethnocentric and xenophobic notion, first, that "violence against women" happens "over there" and not "here" in the United States, and, second, that if "violence against women" does occur "here," it is somehow different, justifiable, or not as severe.[13]

Why, I wonder, does this happen? First (and this is no great revelation), I think it is about self-preservation; it is significantly easier to admit that an anonymous "someone else," "over there" is being oppressed and exploited. Second, it is also easier for earnest women's studies undergraduates taught to be wary of their own privileges to enact strategies for change when they are able to identify someone to help, and, further, are given permission to do so by U.S. feminism's embeddedness in American nationalist discourses. Third, recognizing the "global" nature of "violence against women" is a good way to establish one's antiracist credentials, which is quite different from actually *engaging* in antiracist feminist praxis. Each of these is connected to ongoing efforts to make U.S. women's studies curricula transnational, which is a good, necessary project that I heartily support and am absolutely a part of. But it must be done for the most appropriately strategic and efficacious reasons.

In my opinion (at the foundation of which are the "engaged pedagogies" and "pedagogies of crossing" as advocated by bell hooks [2003] and Jacqui Alexander [2005], respectively[14]), our most fundamental responsibilities as feminist educators are, first, to complexify and problematize what our students think they already know; second, to draw attention to the existence of power hierarchies; and, third, to help our students learn to interrogate why and how those hierarchies operate. Consequently, an inability to avoid the theoretical, geopolitical, and pedagogical pitfalls inherent in *The Vagina Monologues* is not the fault of the play; rather, the fault lies in the way it tends to be used as a pedagogical tool in women's studies classrooms. If *The Vagina Monologues* had been written by a man, the play would likely not be considered "feminist." On the contrary, feminists of all ideological persuasions would have a jolly time critiquing the text for being potentially (heterosexually) titillating and/or for discursively positioning women as always already "victims" (rather than survivors) of men's violence.

But Ensler is a self-professed advocate of feminism, and *The Vagina Monologues* is arguably the most widely popular "feminist" play ever written in English. So, even if we wanted to, or thought we should, feminist educators cannot ignore it, as is evidenced by continued student and administrative interest in incorporating the play into campus-wide antiviolence initiatives during February and March each year. What we *can* do is continue to teach the play and encourage productions of it. But we must confront and finally excise the ethnocentric "rescuer" rhetoric that currently (still) exists in women's studies pedagogy, and then reinforce its absence. As Heather S. Dell suggests, "Texts must find a difficult balance between emphasizing the oppressiveness of particular practices and yet not allowing them to be used as emblematic of an entire nation's culture" (2002, 277).

One way to achieve this balance might be to ask students to interrogate Ensler's production and use of the first-person monologue through a project in which they re-create for themselves Ensler's process of interviewing a woman about her vagina and then creating a monologue based on that interview. Such an activity would not only encourage active, engaged learning, but also force students to contextualize their monologue in time, space, and place, thus helping them to understand the specific cultural and geographic contexts of the individual monologues that comprise Ensler's text. Another strategy may be to include supplemental materials that highlight the local, community-based antiviolence activisms of which Ensler's work may or may not be a part, thus reinforcing the idea that *The Vagina Monologues* is not a U.S.-exported catalyst for antiviolence activism "over there," but a potential tool for raising awareness of and much-needed financial resources for long-established indigenous feminist antiviolence movements.

In addition, creating and/or utilizing the existence of cross-campus institutional alliances to hold teach-ins or workshops as part of annual

V-Day celebrations is another potentially powerful and effective approach. Speakers and facilitators could use these student-centered spaces to clearly demonstrate the fallacy of ethnocentrism, that "violence against women" is rampant even in the "civilized," "free" West, as well, albeit in (arguably) different forms. The difficulty, though, is to accomplish this by making analogies that are historically and culturally contextualized in order to avoid universalizing the experience of "violence against women" (Grewal and Kaplan 2002).

Feminist educators should endeavor to go global in our classrooms only if there is a clear connection to the local. The pedagogical materials of U.S. women's studies must include an unambiguous critique of American nationalism and U.S. neocolonialism. It has become impossible for me to teach my women's studies students to be antiracist and to avoid ethnocentrism without asking them to first examine the structures of "violence" that undergird the underlying precepts of American nationalism and then to interrogate the complex ways in which American nationalism remains constitutive of mainstream U.S. feminism.

Conclusion

This essay has asked a lot of questions about Eve Ensler, *The Vagina Monologues*, V-Day, the evolution of definitions of "violence against women" in the United States, and my concerns about using Ensler's work as an effective and/or appropriate example of successful transnational feminist antiviolence activism. *The Vagina Monologues* rightly argues for a recognition of the global ubiquity of "violence against women," but that statistically supported *ubiquity* should not be manipulated to generate theoretical universalism, geopolitical oversimplification, or pedagogical decontextualization. *The Vagina Monologues* draws on the epistemologies of liberal/mainstream U.S. feminism to universalize "violence against women," offering no clear analysis of capitalism, the historical legacies of colonialism, or the contemporary consequences of U.S. neocolonialism and militarization. Such a simplistic theoretical frame thus makes the play's antiviolence message, which is also the antiviolence message of U.S. liberal/mainstream feminists, easily co-optable by U.S. policymakers into the "rescuer" rhetoric of American nationalism. If, as feminist educators, we continue to use the play and Ensler's work in our classrooms, we must do so with critical awareness, not only of its extraordinary ability to bring widespread public attention to the issue of "violence against women" and to empower those who perform in and attend productions of *The Vagina Monologues*, but also of its problematic aspects that tend to reify and support the ethnocentrism and xenophobia of American nationalism and, consequently, the neocolonial rhetoric of the "war on terror."

Notes

1. For more on the constitutive elements of American nationalism, see Anatole Lieven 2004, *America Right or Wrong*.
2. For more on liberal/mainstream feminist approaches and perspectives, please refer to bell hooks (2000).
3. U.S. foreign relations historian Michael Hunt (1987) contends that existence and maintenance of a racial hierarchy, along with the promotion of liberty and an expressly antirevolutionary political positionality, is constitutive of the American nationalist ideas that have historically shaped U.S. foreign policy.
4. In their introduction to this volume, Román-Odio and Sierra offer an excellent discussion of the usefulness of both hooks and Alexander for transnational feminist approaches to pedagogy (15).
5. Permissions fees are customarily paid by the producers of a given play for the temporary rights to production. In other words, the play's copyright holder essentially rents production rights to the play for a certain length of time, and the play's credited author is then given a contractually negotiated percentage of those permission fees, which are "royalties." Although there are specific rules and requirements to which producers of *The Vagina Monologues* must adhere, that Ensler does not collect either permissions fees or royalties (www.vday.org/organize-event, par. 14) is evidence of her commitment to feminist antiviolence activism. Given the number of annual productions of *The Vagina Monologues* globally, Ensler is certainly in a position, as the play's credited author, to receive an extraordinary amount of money through royalties and permissions fees.
6. V-Day's annual Spotlight Campaigns focus on "a particular group of women who are experiencing violence with the goal of raising awareness and funds to put a worldwide media spotlight on this area and to raise funds to aid groups who are addressing it." Previous campaigns have included Afghani women (2002), Native American and First Nations women (2003), Korean "comfort women" (2006), and women in the Democratic Republic of Congo (2010). www.vday.org/spotlight+history. Last accessed Dec. 5, 2009.
7. For critical feminist analyses of "female genital mutilation," see Gunning 1992; Gunning 1998; Grewal and Kaplan 2002; and James 2002. On the politics of sex trafficking, prostitution, and sex work, see Kempadoo and Doezema 1998; Doezema 2000; Outshoorn 2004; and Kempadoo 2005.

8. See Tickner 2001; Rai 2002; and Steans 2006 for detailed information concerning the overwhelmingly negative effects of "development" policies on women.
9. I use the term *geopolitical* to refer to the means by which "dominant and powerful sovereign nation-states have tried to make sense of and represent their global spatial environment [...] with a view to facilitating their foreign policy making" (Debrix 2008, 9).
10. For more information concerning the conversations about and debates over sex trafficking at the UN, see DeStephano 2007.
11. House Subcommittee on National Security, Emerging Threats, and International Relations, *Sexual Assault and Violence against Women in the Military and at the Academies,* June 27, 2006.
12. Senate Subcommittee on Human Rights and the Law, *Rape as a Weapon of War: Accountability for Sexual Violence in Conflict,* Apr. 1, 2008.
13. Senate Committee on Indian Affairs, *Examining the Prevalence of and Solutions to Stopping Violence against Indian Women,* Sept. 27, 2007.
14. As just one among many postcolonial and Third World feminists to expose this fallacy, Uma Narayan famously demonstrates in *Dislocating Cultures* (1997) that, despite the rhetoric to the contrary, the number of domestic violence deaths in the "civilized, modern" United States is equivalent to the number of "dowry murders" in "backward, traditional" India.

Works Cited

Alexander, M. J. 2005. *Pedagogies of Crossing: Meditations on Feminism, Sexual Politics, Memoir, and the Sacred.* Durham and London: Duke University Press.

Bumiller, E. 2001. "First Lady to Speak about Afghan Women." *New York Times,* Nov. 16. http://www.nytimes.com/2001/11/16/politics/16BUSH.html. Last accessed Dec. 4, 2009.

Burton, A. 1994. *Burdens of History: British Feminists, Indian Women, and Imperial Culture, 1865–1915.* Chapel Hill: University of North Carolina Press.

DeStephano, A. M. 2007. *The War on Human Trafficking: U.S. Policy Assessed.* Rutgers, NJ: Rutgers University Press.

Debrix, F. 2008. *Tabloid Terror: War, Culture, and Geopolitics.* New York: Routledge.

Dell, H. S. 2002. "Making 'Racialized Misogyny' Visible: Internationalizing Women and Violence." *Encompassing Gender: Integrating International Studies and Women's Studies.* Eds. Mary M. Lay, Janice Monk, and Deborah S. Rosenfelt. New York: Feminist Press. 272–86.

Doezema, J. 2000. "Loose Women or Lost Women? The Re-emergence of the Myth of 'White Slavery' in Contemporary Discourses of 'Trafficking in Women.'" *Gender Issues* 18 (1):23–50.

Ensler, E. 2001. "Introduction." *The Vagina Monologues.* V-Day edition. New York: Villard Press. xxiii–xxxvi.

Farr, K. 2005. *Sex Trafficking: The Global Market in Women and Children.* New York: Worth Publishers.

Grewal, I. 1998. "On the New Global Feminism and the Family of Nations: Dilemmas of Transnational Feminist Practice." *Talking Visions: Multicultural Feminism in a Transnational Age.* Ed. Ella Shohat. New York: MIT Press. 201–530.

Grewal, I., and Kaplan, C. 2002. "Transnational Practices and Interdisciplinary Feminist Scholarship: Reconfiguring Women's and Gender Studies." *Women's Studies on Its Own.* Ed. Robyn Weigman. Durham, NC: Duke University Press. 66–81.

Gunning, I. 1992. "Arrogant Perception, World-Traveling, and Multicultural Feminism: The Case of Female Genital Surgeries." *Columbia Human Rights Law Review* 23(2):189–248.

———. 1998. "Cutting Through the Obfuscation: Female Genital Surgeries in Neoimperial Culture." *Talking Visions: Multicultural Feminism in a Transnational Age.* Ed. Ella Shohat. New York: MIT Press. 203–46.

hooks, b. 2000. *Feminist Theory: From Margin to Center.* Cambridge, MA: South End Press.

———. 2003. *Teaching Community: A Pedagogy of Hope.* New York and London: Routledge.

House Subcommittee on National Security, Emerging Threats, and International Relations. 2006. *Sexual Assault and Violence against Women in the Military and at the Academies.* 109th Cong., 2nd sess., June 27. Washington, DC: U.S. Government Printing Office.

Hunt, M. 1987. *Ideology and U.S. Foreign Policy.* New Haven, CT: Yale University Press.

James, S. 2002. "Listening to Other(ed) Voices: Reflections around Female Genital Cutting." *Genital Cutting and Transnational Sisterhood: Disputing U.S. Polemics.* Eds. Stanlie James and Claire Robertson. Urbana: University of Illinois Press. 87–113.

Kempadoo, K., ed., with Jyoti Sanghera and Bandana Pattanaik. 2005. *Trafficking and Prostitution Reconsidered: New Perspectives on Migration, Sex Work, and Human Rights.* Boulder, CO: Paradigm Publishers

Kempadoo, K., and J. Doezema, eds. 1998. *Global Sex Workers: Rights, Resistance, and Redefinition.* New York: Routledge.

Lieven, A. 2004. *America Right or Wrong: An Anatomy of American Nationalism.* New York: Oxford University Press.

Lynch, Dotty. 2001. "Women United on Afghanistan." CBS News, Dec. 3. http://www.cbsnews.com/stories/2001/12/03/politics/main319887.shtml. Last accessed Dec. 4, 2009.

Mani, L. 1990. "Multiple Mediations: Feminist Scholarship in the Age of Multinational Reception." *Feminist Review* 35:24–41.

Mohanty, C. T. 1991. "Under Western Eyes: Feminist Scholarship and Colonial Discourses." *Third World Women and the Politics of Feminism.* Eds. Chandra Talpade Mohanty, Ann Russo, and Lourdes Torres. Bloomington: Indiana University Press. 51–80.

Narayan, U. 1997. *Dislocating Cultures: Identities, Traditions and Third-World Feminism.* New York: Routledge.

Obel, K. 2001. "The Story of V-Day and the College Initiative." *The Vagina Monologues*, V-Day edition. New York: Villard Press. 129–44.

Oliver, K. 2007. *Women as Weapons of War: Iraq, Sex, and the Media.* New York: Columbia University Press.

Outshoorn, J., ed. 2004. *The Politics of Prostitution: Women's Movements, Democratic States and the Globalisation of Sex Commerce.* New York: Cambridge University Press.

Rai, S. M. 2002. *Gender and the Political Economy of Development.* Malden, MA: Blackwell Publishers Inc.

Román-Odio, C., and M. Sierra. 2011. "Introduction." *Transnational Borderlands in Women's Global Networks: The Making of Cultural Resistance.* Eds. Clara Roman-Odio and Marta Sierra. Palgrave Macmillan. 3–20

Senate Subcommittee on Human Rights and the Law. 2008. *Rape as a Weapon of War: Accountability for Sexual Violence in Conflict.* 110th Cong., 2nd sess., Apr. 1. Washington, DC: U.S. Government Printing Office.

Senate Committee on Indian Affairs. 2007. *Examining the Prevalence of and Solutions to Stopping Violence against Indian Women.* 110th Cong., 1st sess., Sept. 27. Washington, DC: U.S. Government Printing Office.

Stapleton, J. 2002. "Six Degrees of Separation." *Women, Gender, and Human Rights: A Global Perspective.* Ed. Marjorie Agosín. New Brunswick: Rutgers University Press. 219–33.

Steans, J. *Gender and International Relations: Issues, Debates, and Future Directions.* Second ed. Malden, MA: Polity Press.

Tickner, J. A. 2001. "Gender in the Global Economy." *Gendering World Politics: Issues and Approaches in the Post-Cold War Era.* New York: Columbia University Press.

V-Day: A Global Movement to End Violence against Women and Girls. http://www.vday.org/home. Last accessed Dec. 4, 2009.

Williams, K. A. 2011. "Crime, Corruption, and Chaos: Sex Trafficking and the 'Failure' of U.S. Russia Policy." *International Feminist Journal of Politics* 13.1:1–24.

Chapter Ten

The Long Table Model: Bringing Transnational Feminist Debates to a Small Midwestern University

Katy Strzepek, Beatrice Jacobson, and Katherine Van Blair

In a recent edition of *College English*, Lisa Eck described the challenges students encounter in a global literature course. Initially, students might identify with a figure from another culture, emphasizing the similarities and the universals, as traditional humanism would encourage: "This text is really about you," as Eck summarizes this perspective (2008, 579). Yet, soon students shift to the comparative/relativistic response: "This text was never about you" (579). Then Eck describes a final shift, informed by the understanding that "the legacy of colonialism is everybody's business": "this is *also* about you" (579). The journeys of Eck's students through these responses parallel the challenges many students face as they explore global women's studies and begin to ask questions about power dynamics across national and cultural borders.

This paper explores our efforts to bring transnational feminist perspectives to a diocesan Catholic school of about 3,600 students. Our university is traditionally Midwestern: many of our students are white; many come from the rural areas in our region; many are from the suburbs of Chicago, or the city itself. Fewer than 9 percent of the students identify themselves as minorities, and international students represent 1 percent of the student body. Over the years, our program has sought ways to meet some of these challenges and to create spaces on our campus for transformative and transnational thinking about issues of women and gender.

Our model builds upon theories of feminist educators who have focused on the importance of fracturing the agent/victim dichotomy often present in media narratives of globalization (Alexander 2005; Hesford and Kozol 2005; hooks 2003; Mohanty 2003). We want to move from merely exposing our students and community members to global perspectives toward building relationships across borders and questioning transnational power dynamics based on race, class, gender, and colonial heritage. As we teach our students to be agents of change, we contend that we must teach them to be socially conscious advocates and to critique the ways "new contexts and cultures of human rights" are related to "liberal and neoliberal formations and to new modernities at different sites and regions" (Grewal in Hesford and Kozol 2005, viii). As Nancy Naples has argued in *Teaching Feminist Activism: Strategies from the Field,* we need to move past the second-wave model of consciousness raising that proved useful, but sometimes produced limited outcomes because of the homogenous nature of many consciousness-raising groups and classrooms. We need to move toward a model that hooks and others have proposed that demands that we provide a "context for recognizing how the history of capitalism, colonialism, or racism, shape our experiences" (hooks 1994; Naples 2002, 10). As we seek to transform our university and community, we remember hooks's advice that "Whenever we love justice and stand on the side of justice we refuse simplistic binaries" (10).

The model we have used to create a space for transnational feminist dialogue and activism on our campus is suggested by Diana Taylor in her exploration of the metaphorical possibilities of Lois Weaver's performance installations called "The Long Table." Weaver is a performance artist, director, writer, and teacher known for her commitment to using performance to advance human rights. Her "Long Table" program is an open public event, "an experimental public forum…a hybrid performance-installation-roundtable discussion-dinner party designed to facilitate dialogue" on serious topics (Taylor 2007, 1427). For each program a series of dinner tables are set out in an open space, sometimes outdoors, sometimes indoors. Participants are invited to take a chair at any of the tables. Often there is a theme: women in prison, human rights, violence, or the politics of representations. The etiquette of the gathering ensures that guests exchange ideas and experiences in a setting in which everyone is equal and all share responsibility for engaging and effective communication (Taylor, 1427–28).

Weaver's project inspires us because the long table model creates a space for what Roman-Odio and Sierra in the introduction to this volume refer to as emancipatory knowledge building that fractures the typical creation of knowledge and invites everyone to participate as learners. Our duty as professors is to show students that we all come to the table with different histories shaped by the legacies of colonialism and neoliberal capitalist policies and that building partnerships at long tables of feminism is not a given, but a complex process that requires work and respect for differences (Hesford and Kozol 2005).

First, we focus on our efforts to transnationalize our curriculum. Next, our discussion focuses on cocurricular programming, sponsored by Women for Social Justice (WSJ), a group formed to bring transnational feminist perspectives to campus and to foster local and transnational alliances. The last section demonstrates how integrating transnational feminist issues into classes and service projects can move students from an abstract understanding of transnationalism toward thoughtful transnational feminist activism. We offer our suggestions for scholars, community activists, and those who function as both, who aim to engage in transnational inquiry: how and why do people, ideas, and commodities cross borders and how do race, class, gender, and history impact animosities and alliances between people from different nations and cultures (Grewal and Kaplan 2006, xxii)?

When we began to design our women's studies program in the mid-1990s, we realized that transnational concerns must be integral to the curriculum. Initially, this criterion brought some practical and theoretical challenges: How might a women's studies program negotiate binaries (us/them; local/global) that fail to encompass "the complex intersections of identity, community, region, nation and world" (Lay et al. 2002, 9)? We were also determined that transformation via conscientization needed to be an initial objective. Peggy Antrobus reminds us that "the link between consciousness-raising and conscientization (relating personal experience to a structural analysis) takes feminist consciousness-raising to a new level, transforming the person into action that reaches beyond personal concerns" (Antrobus 2002, xiv). Thus, we are all challenged: students need to grow into theory(ies), and use it (them) as a tool for action as well as for scholarly inquiry. Further, as Naomi Scherman reminds us, critical reflection on our practices, of action and of theorizing, is key (2002, 235). Finally, activism and service should play key roles in the transnationalizing of women's studies.

As we began our program, we were aware that theory, and traditional academic systems in general, need to be anchored in service and activism. We also recognized that serious inquiry is needed to link the local to the global. Moreover, we wanted to organize a program of activism and service that would include an analytical component to help students understand that activism is not a "given" but has a history in itself tied to the legacies of colonialism and neoliberal capitalist policies (Hesford and Kozol 2005). As we developed our new curriculum and related service projects, we wanted students to consider the complicated nature of transnational relationships and to avoid casting themselves as saviors of "those other women." The task of gaining even a foothold on transnationalism can be daunting. How could we bring, as Deborah Rosenfelt describes, "disciplinary perspectives—in theorizing the complex relations among local experiments—to bear in theorizing the complex relations among local experiences and political formations; the unequal movement across borders of capital, technology, peoples, and culture, and the forms of feminism emerging both within and across borders" (2002, 170)?

All of us—faculty, staff, and students—have been challenged to develop our skill set and knowledge base and to venture into other intellectual terrains: language, anthropology, politics, environmentalism, economics, sociology, cultural differences, arts, literature, environmentalism, top-down approaches (such as the United Nations) and bottom-up mechanisms (micro-enterprise, cooperatives, communal soup kitchens), and many more. As a feminist teacher, Helen Johnson aims "to enable students to feel at ease in contesting established ideas" (2002, 288). She encourages intellectual study within what Mary Louise Pratt calls "contact zones...social spaces where disparate cultures meet, clash, and grapple with each other" (288). We contend that feminist faculty can empower and equip our students to negotiate such contact zones by creating long tables of feminism at our universities. Our women's studies curriculum aims to introduce students to these essentials and to offer support, building confidence while empowering a student to relate her individual context and experience of the world to that of women from around the world.

Women's studies at our university has, over the past fourteen years, sought to bring a transnational presence to a small Midwestern campus. By now, we have campus and community allies, but early on, the transnational focus of the campus was scattered and uneven. While we raised consciousness in the classroom, we still felt we were relying on the old second-wave model and needed to better integrate the voices of women from transnational perspectives. We hoped to change the limited second-wave model by inviting many people to the table to plan events that would generate discussions about transnational issues with participants from many cultures.

Helping our students realize their connections to women from around the globe has taken place within a continuum of contexts and developments, both on our campus and around the world. As Mary M. Lay, Janice Monk, and Deborah S. Rosenfelt, the editors of *Encompassing Gender: Integrating International Studies and*

Women's Studies, observe, such a process has entailed a series of questions:

> How do we think and teach comparatively and relationally about women's lives and gender arrangements in locations around the world? And how do we bring international perspectives to bear on women's lives and gender arrangements in any given location, including the U.S.?...and further, how do we think about the relation between the local and the global, both as objects of inquiry and as dimensions of subjectivity, as ways of knowing, seeing, and acting? (Lay et al., 2–3)

As our minor began, we anchored transnational perspectives in our introductory course: Women's Studies: A Cross-Cultural Introduction. On one level, this was a pragmatic decision: we did not have funding to offer many different courses, so infiltrating the introductory course with concerns from other parts of the world was, simply, efficient. However, this course was first offered just as the Fourth World Conference on Women in Beijing in November of 1995 was getting underway, so the energy generated by the conference made such a design both urgent and appropriate. Most important, however, we wanted students to understand that women from other parts of the world were not "another category" studied in "another class," but, rather, central to even an introduction to women's studies.

The interest and enthusiasm evoked by the Beijing Conference inspired us in other ways as well. In November 1995 a local conference, sponsored by a local foundation, was held in our region. Faculty and students attended "Bringing Beijing Back," an event that brought local, regional, and national leaders to the table to discuss with Midwesterners the proceedings and the promise of the Beijing Conference. Two other related Beijing events were later hosted at our university. A workshop, "Bringing Beijing into the Classroom," encouraged faculty to consider ways to foreground the issues and controversies of the conference in their courses. In 1996 our women's studies program hosted a satellite telecast from the President's Interagency Council on Women, focusing on progress made since the conference. Following the telecast, a panel of women leaders from the area discussed the report. This event encouraged us to explore opportunities for transnational discussions and alliances offered by new technologies.

As the "Bringing Beijing Back" project ended, we tried to compensate, still bringing a few speakers but also accomplishing our goals by creating study-abroad opportunities within women's studies.

"Latin American Women's Issues" was a course developed specifically to bring a women's studies presence to the university's annual study-abroad program in Ecuador. A half-dozen years later, a course in women and Irish film was added to our program. Thus, the two women's studies designated electives with specific international focus addressed the two areas of the world where our university has long-standing institutional ties: Ecuador and Ireland. These transnational connections, pioneered by women's studies, have encouraged our colleagues in graduate programs to follow suit. Our School of Social Work also offers a cross-listed graduate and undergraduate class in Ecuador on international social work and social welfare, which asks students to critically analyze the impact of globalization, colonialism, and racism on community projects in Ecuador. Exchange students from Ecuador have also participated in women's studies classes at our university, thus enhancing transnational feminist discussions about migration and colonialism. As well, our Occupational Therapy program sponsors a class on social and occupational justice in health care in Ilheus and Itabuna, Brazil, and offers rich opportunities for our students to discuss the issue of health care in a transnational context and to learn from their peers in Brazil.

Our alliances with other cognate areas both within and outside the College of Arts and Sciences, as well as our transnational connections, helped us build a major in women's studies. We kept a women's studies topics course that was part of our minor curriculum and have used that to cross-list additional courses such as "Women in Africa," "Asian Women," "U.S. Latina Culture and Literature," and "Liberation Theology" to ensure that our students will learn about transnational concerns through the lens of specific disciplines. Moreover, we have worked to make many of these courses count as general education credits so that students outside of women's studies will learn about the ways race, class, gender, colonial history, and neoliberal policies have intersected to impact people's lives around the world. We have fought hard to change our university's general education policy to require classes that focus on transnational issues and have recruited new faculty in a variety of disciplines whose research interests are anchored in transnational feminist concerns, thus expanding our long table of feminism. For example, a recently hired faculty member in social work, who does research with survivors of the tsunami in Southeast Asia, has provided community workshops on disaster relief, demonstrating that good intentions are not enough and that disaster capitalism can have disastrous consequences ("Good Intentions Are Not Enough"). As Grewal has argued, when we engage in service, we need to ask who is empowering whom? (Grewal in Hesford and Kosol 2005, viii). We must demand that transnational activists avoid reinscribing colonial practices that profited the privileged and failed to listen to and partner with colonized women and men.

While we are a small school, the transnational is present in our own backyard. We suggest that most women's studies programs, regardless of their size, can save money and build community by connecting with neighboring schools or community groups. Collaborating with a neighboring university, we have been able to bring women writers from around the world to our campus; we have also worked with other schools in our region to share speakers' transportation fees. We have hosted breakfasts with the local China Friendship Association, worked with local Latina groups, and invited speakers from neighboring institutions to campus. We also started partnering with campus organizations, especially Campus Ministry's peace and justice programs, as well as Amnesty International, on a variety of projects.

In sum, the women's studies program has capitalized on three approaches: 1) The heart of transnationalizing efforts is the curriculum, with course dedication or orientation to global issues and building awareness of dynamics of power. 2) Study-abroad and local activist/service opportunities have provided students with invaluable experiential learning and the opportunity to analyze activist practices. And 3) coalitions with on-campus entities and off-campus organizations have strengthened and deepened transnational opportunities and relationships in our women's studies program and beyond our campus.

One step toward achieving this vision and setting a long table at our university has been the creation of WSJ. We believe WSJ could serve as a model for other women's studies programs across the nation who are coping with budget cuts, a backlash against feminism, and a post-9/11 mass media that bell hooks says has "created a context of vulnerability and rage where folks were eager to simplify everything to make a common enemy" (2003, 12). WSJ was born in the fall of 2003 when dedicated faculty and staff from across the university collaborated to bring Barbara Ehrenreich to campus to speak about living or "not getting by" on minimum wage. Other WSJ events have been richly informed by the critical transnational feminist issues, such as labor rights and migration, examined in Ehrenreich's edited collection, *Global Women*. WSJ pursues social justice locally, regionally, and globally, understanding that the connectedness of economic, social, communication, and political systems calls for strategies that move across the borders of culture, race, class, state, and gender in creative and imaginative ways.

Prior to the creation of WSJ, bringing transnational feminist speakers to campus was largely the purview of the women's studies program. To expand the long table of feminism and to show that those most knowledgeable about transnational feminist issues are not always academics, our group sought to cross departmental borders and reach out to community groups. Faculty members from multiple disciplines, including women's studies, business, theology, social work, international studies, nursing, languages, and exercise science, created WSJ in order to expand the conversation to include the presence of feminists from many disciplines and perspectives on our campus. Connecting with groups outside the university has been key to our programming. Attendance at WSJ events has ranged from 150 to 800 people, including participation from the larger community, local colleges and high schools, civic organizations, trade unions, and churches. WSJ programs encourage participants to use the knowledge gained through a lecture or workshop to build local and transnational alliances. We do this by modeling "just advocacy" and by emphasizing the importance of building relationships before assuming partnerships exist (Hesford and Kozol 2005).

Yet, initiatives that reach out to the community beyond the campus are only possible due to a series of political strategies on campus that have strengthened WSJ and established its presence as a recognized university venue for social justice programming. Some actions have been as basic as linking the organization's mission statement to the university's mission and values, where diversity and social justice are emphasized; thus, WSJ has come to be seen as integral to the university's vision. Further, WSJ members have volunteered or been elected to serve on various of the university's strategic planning committees, giving the group a voice in multiple discussions of revenue prioritization. Moreover, the large numbers of participants from both the campus and the community have demonstrated that transnational feminist issues were not the concerns of feminist scholars alone. All of these steps provided the groundwork for securing an annual programming budget from the university. While we have been successful in securing external funding, the presence of a reliable fiscal base facilitates long-range planning of events and programming.

In addition to funding, however, these efforts to develop into an established and integral dimension of the university have enabled WSJ to respond to local criticism. On one or two occasions early on, when plans for specific speakers were challenged as controversial, WSJ members were able to respond, presenting reasoned arguments based on the principles of academic freedom and the Catholic Intellectual Tradition. In these cases, those raising the questions were convinced and decided to support WSJ. Although reason won the day in these instances, it is also clear that the integrity of WSJ's commitment to social justice was becoming both recognized and respected because of its evolving strategic position within the university. Ironically, the process of responding to challenges and making the case for our programs not only formulated, for ourselves and others, a clearer vision of our goals, it also galvanized WSJ's commitment to future programming.

The first WSJ event, which featured Barbara Ehrenreich, author of *Nickel and Dimed* (2002), an exploration of the challenges facing people attempting to live on the minimum wage, provided a model for some of these future events. To stimulate community and academic dialogue, a regional conference on topics of social justice, economics, and the causes of and solutions to poverty preceded her presentation. Through guided discussions, participants reflected on and critiqued Ehrenreich's assumptions, moving toward possible solutions both locally and nationally. Significant interest in the project came from many community groups, including the local labor movement, political action organizations, and other universities and community colleges. Additional extracurricular programming and the integration of Ehrenreich's ideas in many classes also introduced labor issues to many audiences.

In our debriefing about the Ehrenreich lecture, consensus was clear that, although the event was extremely successful, WSJ should present labor and other human rights issues from transnational perspectives to teach our students and community how U.S. policies affect people across borders. The next WSJ event focused on the problems of AIDS, poverty, and human rights abuses in Kenya. Clearly, we did not want to reify the "save the poor African woman" paradigm often presented to students. Often insulting and infantilizing, this paradigm leads to poor policymaking decisions and to human rights documents that deem women need protection (Scully 2009). To avoid this, we worked with a transnational feminist group, MADRE, that partners with women in Africa and insists that African women can and should speak for themselves. We offered a day-long symposium, "Indigenous Women Defending Human Rights," that featured presentations by two indigenous women from Kenya, Lucy Mulenkei and Rebecca Lolosoli, along with Vivian Stromberg, executive director and a founding board member of MADRE. Lolosoli and Mulenkei helped break down many essentializing media images and stereotypes about "exotic indigenous women" or "helpless African women" and showed our students that there is a long history of women working for change throughout the world (Mohanty, 237). Vivian Stromberg, an Anglo activist, demonstrated that MADRE's transnationalist work is based on solidarity and that, although women in the United States didn't build the table of women's rights, they can and should sit at it to help dismantle destructive U.S. policies.

Lolosoli, Mulenkei, and Stromberg explored the relationships between AIDS, economic underdevelopment, and women's inequality and described MADRE's collaborative projects with the Indigenous Information Network that offers training sessions in rural areas of Kenya with high rates of HIV infection. In follow-up classroom discussions, students began to ask transnational questions about, for instance, the impact of U.S. policies such as the global gag rule on women in Kenya and around the world.

To make our students more educated participants at the long table modeled by WSJ events, we insist they start with history. We attempt to use what Chandra Mohanty calls the "Comparative Feminist Studies model," where we are often moving between the personal/local and the political/global, "show[ing] the interconnectedness of the histories, experiences, and struggles of U.S. women of color, white women, and women from the Third World/South" (2003, 242). In collaboration with the university library, WSJ provides extensive reading lists related to the events in order to inform students and community members of an issue's historical context. For example, before the MADRE speakers came, students in the Modern Africa class read about colonialism and imperialism in Kenya and its relationship to female genital mutilation and other cultural practices. (During these discussions, we point out that cultural body modification/mutilation also occurs in the United States.) The students also read the more recent history of Kenyan indigenous women, who were abused by soldiers during the colonial era and are now demanding compensation. Through these readings and class discussions, students learn about how indigenous groups in Kenya came to be impoverished, how this poverty has been gendered, and how women have resisted this oppression. Students and community members also read about Lolosoli's creation of a women's village for women fleeing abuse and early marriages (Wax 2005). Further, we discussed how this was similar to women's shelters in the United States. Finally, we asked our students to write position papers about the causes of poverty in Africa in order to help them consider American policies that impact poverty in other countries.

We hope to teach our students that when we sit at the long table of feminism, we may all come with different pasts, but we should view each other as equals and should also admit when we know less than activists who lack formal degrees but are formidable feminist educators nonetheless. One goal of the long table approach, and the goal of many service projects, is to gather people who would not normally sit at the table together. One student in the Modern Africa class, Nina, sat at a new table by volunteering at an agency in our community that sponsors African refugees. There she answered the phones and helped organize donations. She worked side by side with a refugee from Sierra Leone. Her knowledge of colonialism and imperialism helped her better understand their conversations about his country's violent past. Further, she recognized the role of globalization and multinational companies, and she knew that the diamond industry was a major player in the war in Sierra Leone. Further, Nina's conversations allowed her to see how violence in Sierra Leone impacted men, an issue with troubling consequences that is often ignored by policymakers. As Pamela Scully asserts, "This silence surrounding male victims of sexual and other violence combined with an emphasis on female vulnerability leave the male subject standing alone as the default citizen of the post-conflict state" (2009, 120).

Nina's work at this agency also taught her the complicated nature of refugee agencies and so-called "development" work in general. She realized that while this agency did great work in removing refugees from horribly dangerous situations, they were often understaffed and could not adequately prepare their clients for the racism and violence that also exist in the United States. Service projects where students from the United States forge relationships with people from the two-thirds world help us move away from the "add women and stir" pedagogy to the "comparative feminist model" (Mohanty, 242). Service combined with classroom discussions that encourage students to analyze activism and the language of human rights documents also provide an opportunity to consider the ways human rights are gendered and have "developed historically within a vexed relationship with national and international security agendas" (Hesford and Kozol, 4).

The guidelines for participatory action research formulated by M. E. Torre, N. Alexander, and E. Genao provide a model that can be adapted for structuring discussions in a long table classroom. First, everyone "is understood to be a carrier of knowledge and history, is capable of creating change for justice"; second, discussions will address and explore "power and difference"; third, "disagreements and disjunctures are excavated rather than smoothed over";

and finally, "individuals and groups are understood to be under construction and are expected to change and grow" (Torre et al. 2007, 227–28). Then, we move on to the macro level of discussing race, class, gender, and other isms in global contexts and consider how these issues should be considered by activists working on transnational issues (Kirk and Okazawa-Rey 2007, 65).

At the same time, we can learn from Barbara Smith and other black feminists, who have taught us that coalition building will be a challenging job. Smith reminds us of Bernice Johnson Reagon's observation that sometimes sitting at the table and doing the really hard work of dismantling systems of oppression can be excruciating: "Most of the time, you feel threatened to the core and if you don't, you're not really doing no coalescing" (Smith 2000, 528). We continually work to teach our students that, as Torre and others assert, at the long table of feminism, "disagreements and disjunctures [should be] excavated rather than smoothed over" (2007, 228). We believe that universities are places where these disjunctures must be explored and have used WSJ to create spaces or what Pratt calls "contact zones" for discussing the "scattered hegemonies that reveal themselves in gender relations" (quoted in Johnson 288; Grewal and Kaplan 1994, 17).

Admittedly, fracturing the dominant narratives of globalization is tough, but building transnational feminist alliances transforms our teaching and service projects in positive ways. Developing feminist networks beyond the Midwest and the United States gives us opportunities to show students that service starts with building relationships. Our partnership with Dr. Béa Gallimore, a Rwandan and associate professor of French at the University of Missouri at Columbia, began when a WSJ member met Gallimore at a conference and invited her to campus. Dr. Gallimore is a great model of an activist scholar. She founded Step Up!, a group that works with survivors of the genocide in Rwanda. Dr. Gallimore spoke in several women's studies classes and joined us for a discussion of *Mother's Courage: Thriving Survivors*, a documentary that highlights the voices of genocide survivors. Dr. Gallimore's own courageous story of returning to Rwanda during the genocide to find her relatives and her continued work for reconciliation inspired our students and faculty. Instead of making assumptions about the needs of survivors, our students asked what they could do to help Step Up!. Dr. Gallimore explained that we could help by fund-raising and stated that 600 U.S. dollars was enough to support one Rwandan for a whole year; thus, raising 600 dollars became one class's goal. We taught our students skills they needed to be campus activists, such as how to reserve a room on campus, how to publicize events, and how to request funds from student government. The students made posters and sent e-mails about Step Up! and asked community members to make a donation to Step Up! for Mother's Day in honor of their mothers or other special friends. Everyone who donated received a card made by the women in Step Up! and a form showing that their donation was tax deductible. We met our goal of 600 dollars, and Dr. Gallimore sends us regular updates about how the money is being used. The Step Up! project taught students how to build and maintain transnational feminist relationships.

In addition to modeling feminist activism through service projects, we encourage our colleagues in other departments to use feminist methodologies in university-wide programs, such as our school's first book program that requires all first-year students to analyze a common text. The 2003 book *Mountains beyond Mountains: The Quest of Dr. Paul Farmer, a Man Who Would Cure the World* by Tracy Kidder, presents the life and work of Dr. Paul Farmer and Partners for Health, a nongovernmental organization founded to meet Haitian health needs. As WSJ members reviewed the book, we realized that Kidder failed to include the resilient voices of Haitian women. Thus, WSJ decided on a program highlighting both women's voices and the deeply troubled transnational relationships between Haitians and Dominicans on the island of Hispaniola. Further, our programs have asked participants to consider the impact of U.S. neoliberal economic policies on Haiti, thus following Grewal and Kaplan's model of exploring the narratives of "how people in different locations and circumstances are linked by the spread of and resistance to modern capitalist social formations even as their experiences of these phenomena are not all the same or equal" (5).

The events in our series "The Challenges and Victories of Haitian Women" demonstrated the vital role Haitian women play in the transnational economy. Dr. Rose Marie Chierici of Haiti, an associate professor of anthropology at SUNY Geneseo, spoke about the interactions of gender and globalization in Haiti. To continue our efforts to counter stereotypical image of the voiceless "other" woman, we hosted a screening of *Poto Mitan: Haitian Women, Pillars of the Global Economy* (2008), which was followed by a discussion with one of the documentary's producers, Dr. Mark Schuller. Films are a great way to bring the voices of economically disadvantaged women and men into our classrooms and communities. As well, some scholars, such as Dr. Schuller, have used documentaries to give back to women who helped them complete their research. "Citing the Haitian proverb, 'hearing and seeing are two different things,' the women [who participated in his research] implored Dr. Schuller to share their stories with people in the U.S., people who have the power to make change" (*Poto Mitan*).

Poto Mitan features the lives of five Haitian women in their own voices and "explains neoliberal globalization, how it is gendered, and how it impacts Haiti" (2008). By giving a human face to women in Haiti, WSJ hoped to inspire the audience to consider ways they could join Haitian women to create a more just global economy. However, questions during each session showed that building solidarity is a complicated task. The film depicted truckloads of U.S. crops being distributed to hungry Haitians. Some audience members questioned how U.S. farm subsidies may have contributed to world hunger. This was a tough transnational question for some students from the heartland, whose farms may have profited from these policies. The lessons learned from the *Poto Mitan* women continue to inform our community as we critique the response of the international community to the recent earthquake in Haiti. Through additional screenings and discussions of *Poto Mitan*, we have called on our community to listen to the voices of the Haitian women as they rebuild their communities and to interrogate the patronizing image of the powerless woman or girl in need of saving, which can lead to horrible outcomes, such the actions of missionaries who trafficked Haitian children into the Dominican Republic, marring legitimate aid efforts.

As we worked to develop community connections for the *Poto Mitan* program, we decided to expand our table by inviting staff and community members with connections to Haiti to be our guests at all the dinners before the events. Guests at our transnational table began speaking in several languages: English, Creole, and Spanish. The table was filled with the sound of Haitian students who laughed at Anglo Schuller's ability to joke with them in Creole, as well as more serious conversations in Spanish and English from Dominican and Haitian students who said that being at this table and at school together had allowed them to engage in a deep friendship that would not be possible between Haitians and Dominicans in their homelands.

Its 2009 event allowed WSJ to extend its table of inclusivity in a different way. Joining other campus organizations in a year-long discussion of migration, WSJ invited Dr. Mary Romero to speak on the ways conservative groups attempt to criminalize immigrant mothers. This topic gave us an opportunity and responsibility to host a bilingual event and to provide interpretation. We realized that in order to model transnationalist feminist discourse, we needed to encourage students to learn additional languages and to expose our community to a multilingual environment that privileged speakers of languages other than English. We consulted with our school's theater department, who put us in touch with a local company that provides headsets and other technology necessary to host a bilingual event.

While planning the migration program, a WSJ member came across a trailer for the film *In the Shadow of the Raid: La Redada De Mayo*, which illustrates how the raid of a meat-packing plant in Postville, Iowa, impacted two villages in Guatemala and community members in Postville. The largest immigration raid in U.S. history, this event occurred just a few hours away from our university, and some of our students watched the event unfold right in their own backyards. We purchased the film and agreed that the filmmakers Jennifer Symaszek and Greg Brosnan deftly illustrated the complex links between the demise of Postville and the economic misery it created in two villages in Guatemala. We decided to host the film as part of our migration series.

Two new members of WSJ networked with Latina community groups in our area and also in Postville. After the screening, we hosted a panel discussion that featured Rosa Zamora, a Guatemalan woman arrested during the raid; Father Paul Ouderkirk and Paul Rael, of St. Bridget's Church, who worked with immigrants in Postville; and filmmakers Jennifer Symaszek and Greg Brosnan. Our experience hosting a bilingual event in the fall gave us the confidence to host this event and allowed us to give Ms. Zamora the chance to speak about how the raid had impacted her family in Postville and in Guatemala. We provided childcare for the event, which we contend is another vital part of feminist programming. Offering childcare allowed Ms. Zamora to bring her two young children to the event and to focus her attention on telling her story. We followed the film and panel discussion with an opportunity for participants to write letters to their elected officials about changing immigration policies.

The achievements of WSJ have encouraged transnational dialogues among campus and regional entities; however, we also need to pay attention to the impact these enriched conversations have had on our central objective, the academic experience of our students. Although we hope to educate our students about the roots of global problems and encourage them to become activists, bringing the long table of feminism into the classroom poses challenges. In many classes, such as African History and the Cross-Cultural Introduction to Women's Studies, students begin by thinking about their own identities and social locations (Kirk and Okazawa-Rey 2007, 71). Peggy McIntosh's essay "White and Male Privilege" (2003) shows our students that racism affects everyone in different ways. We try to create an atmosphere where it is acceptable to discuss issues of race and class. As Dr. Patricia Hill Collins noted in her keynote address at the 2008 National Women's Studies Association conference, many of our students (especially white students) have learned that it is rude to talk about race. This creates what Collins calls a "colorblindness" that can perpetuate racism because issues of race and other "isms" are ignored, though they are still very present. We try to break down this barrier and to teach our students to talk about differences and "isms" in a respectful manner, goals that can be accomplished through variations on the long table model.

Though our successes encourage future planning, the work of transforming a campus through the dynamics of transnational feminism is not without challenges, and we realize that our model is far from perfect. Our committee is composed of mostly Anglo, heterosexual women and we continue to work on recruiting committee members from diverse backgrounds. Of course, Anglo teachers can and should teach about racism and other forms of prejudice and be models of antiracist activism; it is everyone's responsibility to work for justice. However, we also feel that it is our duty as women of privilege to expand our table to include the voices of women who have often been silenced. As Mohanty asserts, an analysis "anchor[ed] in the lives of marginalized communities of women provides the most inclusive paradigm for thinking about social justice" (231).

Our work with WSJ has led us to take Audre Lorde's advice seriously: we must examine our own positions and fight for justice on our own campus (Lorde in Collins 2003, 65). Our faculty is predominantly white, which leads us to ask who sets the long table and invites others there? Who indeed busses the tables at our dinners? The segregated power structure that Collins has written pushes us to continue to examine and to improve our school's policies (1993, 59). WSJ members have called on our administration to recruit and retain faculty, staff, and students from diverse backgrounds. Those of us who are program directors have put our money where our mouths are and have spent thousands of dollars advertising in publications that reach diverse applicant pools. Our women's studies program is working with the coordinator of Intercultural Life and Leadership to create a mentorship program for students of color on our campus, and we are also planning more activities to partner with a local community group that supports lesbian, gay, bisexual, transgender, and questioning (LGBTQ) issues. We have advocated that our administration pay fair wages to all who work at our school, and our university's strategic plan now includes a provision that all university employees should receive a living wage. We have recently noticed some pay-inequity issues in our WSJ events. In some cases, we have paid prominent white women presenters more than indigenous activists of color. We realize this isn't fair and plan to change this. Addressing some of these challenges requires significant effort, but the quest for a long table of feminism nourishes our teaching and is personally gratifying to us as scholars and activists.

To conclude, we would like to envision and then devise mechanisms by which, together with our students and colleagues, we can sit at tables with the women survivors from Rwanda, the grandmothers of Plaza de Mayo, the president of a remote village in Ecuador who has transformed her peoples' lives, or the Poto Mitan women of Haiti. Some of these conversations could be accomplished virtually; others merely call for restructuring the roles of speakers brought to campus; some call for better access to more effective study-abroad programs. Surely time is much better spent at such conversation tables than at the conference table or in the lecture hall, especially if we are to move our students toward transformative learning. Let's start with table conversation in which "they" don't become "us," but rather "they" and "we" become social peers who share and respond to each other's histories, questions, and dreams.

Works Cited

Alexander, M. J. 2005. *Pedagogies of Crossing. Meditations on Feminism, Sexual Politics, Memoir, and the Sacred*. Durham and London: Duke University Press.

Antrobus, Peggy. 2002. Foreword. *Defending Our Dreams: Global Feminist Voices for a New Generation*. Eds. Shamillah Wilson, Anasuya Sengupta, and Kristy Evans. London: Zed. xii–xvi.

Collins, Patricia Hill. 2008. Keynote address, National Women's Studies Association 29th Annual Conference, Cincinnati, OH. June 19.

———. 2003. "Toward a New Vision: Race, Class, and Gender as Categories of Analysis and Connection." *Women's Voices. Feminist Visions: Classic and Contemporary Readings*. Eds. Susan M. Shaw and Janet Lee. Mountain View, CA: Mayfield Publishing, 1993. 57–65. Previously published in *Race, Gender and Class* 1(1) (1993):25–45.

Eck, Lisa. 2008. "Thinking Globally, Teaching Locally: The 'Nervous Conditions' of Cross-Cultural Literacy." *College English* 70(6):578–98.

Ehrenreich, Barbara. 2001. *Nickel and Dimed: On (Not) Getting by in America*. New York: Macmillan.

Good Intentions Are Not Enough. http://goodintents.org/. Last accessed March 30, 2010.
Grewal, Inderpal. 2005. Foreword. *Just Advocacy? Women's Human Rights, Transnational Feminisms, and the Politics of Representation.* Eds. Wendy Hesford and Wendy Kozol. New Brunswick and London: Rutgers University Press.
Grewal, Inderpal, and Caren Kaplan. 1994. *Scattered Hegemonies. Postmodernity and Transnational Feminist Practices.* Minneapolis and London: Minnesota University Press.
———. 2006. *An Introduction to Women's Studies: Gender in a Transnational World.* Boston: McGraw-Hill.
Hesford, Wendy, and Wendy Kozol. 2005. *Just Advocacy? Women's Human Rights, Transnational Feminisms, and the Politics of Representation.* New Brunswick and London: Rutgers University Press.
hooks, bell. 2003. *Teaching Community. A Pedagogy of Hope.* New York and London: Routledge.
———. 1994. *Teaching to Transgress. Education as the Practice of Freedom.* New York and London: Routledge.
Johnson, Helen. 2002. "Feminisms Cross-culturally: Exploring Women's Worlds." *Encompassing Gender: Integrating International Studies and Women's Studies.* Eds. Mary M. Lay, Janice Monk, and Deborah S. Rosenfelt. New York: Feminist Press. 287–300.
Kidder, Tracy. 2003. *Mountains beyond Mountains: The Quest of Dr. Paul Farmer, a Man Who Would Cure the World.* New York: Random House.
Kirk, Gwen, and Margo Okazawa-Rey, eds. 2007. *Women's Lives: Multicultural Perspectives,* 4th ed. Boston: McGraw-Hill.
Lay, Mary M., Janice Monk, and Deborah S. Rosenfelt. 2002. Introduction. *Encompassing Gender: Integrating International Studies and Women's Studies.* Eds. Lay, Monk, and Rosenfelt. New York: Feminist Press. 1–18.
McIntosh, Peggy. 2003. "White and Male Privilege." *Women's Voices. Feminist Visions: Classic and Contemporary Reading.* Eds. Susan M. Shaw and Janet Lee. Mountain View, CA: Mayfield Publishing. 78–86. Previously published in Working Paper #189 (Wellesley College Center for Research on Women, Wellesley, MA, 1988).
Mohanty, Chandra. 2003. *Feminism without Borders: Decolonizing Theory: Practicing Solidarity.* Durham: Duke University Press.
Mothers' Courage: Thriving Survivors. 2005. DVD. Dir. Leo Kalinda. Productions Via le Monde, Montreal, Canada: National Film Board of Canada.
Naples, Nancy A. 2002. "The Dynamics of Critical Pedagogy, Experiential Learning, and Feminist Praxis in Women's Studies." *Teaching Feminist Activism: Strategies from the Field.* Eds. Nancy Naples and Karen Bojar. New York: Routledge. 9–21.

Poto Mitan: Haitian Women, Pillars of the Global Economy. DVD. Dir. Mary Becker, Renee Bergan and Mark Schuller. Santa Barbara, CA: Center for Black Studies Research.

Rosenfelt, Deborah S. 2002. "Teaching Globalization, Gender, and Culture." *Encompassing Gender: Integrating International Studies and Women's Studies*. Eds. Mary M. Lay, Janice Monk, and Deborah S. Rosenfelt. New York: Feminist Press. 168–79.

Scherman, Naomi B. "On Swamps, Helicopters, Corkscrews, and Cooking: Reflections on Internationalizing Feminist Thought and Theory. *Encompassing Gender: Integrating International Studies and Women's Studies*. Eds. Mary M. Lay, Janice Monk, and Deborah Rosenfelt. 233–34.

Scully, Pamela. 2009. "Vulnerable Women: A Critical Reflection on Human Rights Discourse and Sexual Violence." *Emory International Law Review* 23(1):113–23.

Smith, Barbara. 2000. "Introduction to *Home Girls: A Black Feminist Anthology*." Amy Kesselman, Lily D. McNair, and Nancy Schniedewind, eds. *Women Images and Realities*, 3rd ed. Boston: McGraw-Hill. Previously published in *Home Girls: A Black Feminist Anthology*, ed. Barbara Smith. New Brunswick, NJ: Rutgers University Press. xxi–lviii.

Taylor, Diana. 2007. "Remapping Genre through Performance: From 'American' to 'Hemispheric' Studies." *PMLA* 122(5): 1416–30.

Torre, Maria Elena, Michelle Fine, Natasha Alexander, and Emily Genao. 2007. "Don't Die with Your Work Balled Up in Your Fists: Contesting Social Injustice through Participatory Research." *Urban Girls Revisited: Building Strengths*. Eds. Bonnie J. Ross Leadbeater and Niobe Way. New York University Press. 221–42.

Wax, Emily. 2005. "A Place Where Women Rule: All Female Village in Kenya Is a Sign of Burgeoning Feminism Across Africa." *Washington Post*, July 9. www.washingtonpost.com/wp-dyn/content/article/2005/07/08/AR2005070801775.html. Last accessed March 30, 2010.

Contributors

Orit Bashkin is assistant professor of modern Middle Eastern history at the University of Chicago. Her publications include articles on the history of Arab-Jews in Iraq, on Iraqi history, and on Arabic literature. She has coedited a book with Israel Gershoni and Liat Kozma, which includes translations into Hebrew of seminal works by Egyptian intellectuals: *Sculpturing Culture in Egypt: Cultural Planning, National Identity and Social Change in Egypt, 1890–1939* (Tel Aviv: Ramot Press, 1999). Her book *The Other Iraq: Intellectuals, Pluralism and Culture in Hashemite Iraq, 1921–1958* was published by Stanford University Press.

Jessica Franklin is a PhD candidate in the Department of Political Science at McMaster University in Hamilton, Ontario, Canada. She is currently completing her dissertation titled "Building From and Moving Beyond the State: The National and Transnational Dimensions of Afro-Brazilian Women's Activism." Her research interests include racial and gender identity formations, black feminisms, and Afro-descendant and women's social movements in Latin America. Her most recent publication is a chapter titled "Afro-Brazilian Women's Identities and Activism: National and Transnational Discourses" in the edited volume *Latin American Identities after 1980* (Waterloo: Wilfrid Laurier University Press, 2010). Her field research has been supported by the Canada-Latin America and the Caribbean Research Exchange Grant (2007).

Beatrice Jacobson is professor of English at St. Ambrose University. In addition to women's studies courses ranging from the introductory to the seminar level, she teaches courses in early American, African American, and women's literatures. Recent publications include studies of contemporary novelist Alice McDermott and nineteenth-century educator Mary Lyon. Current research includes a study of literacy in the lives of Ecuadorian women weavers. In additin, she serves on the board of Centro de Estudios Interamericanos in Cuenca, Ecuador, where she teaches and directs study-abroad programs.

Anna Kłosowska is Professor of French at Miami University. She is author of *Queer Love in the Middle Ages* (Palgrave Macmillan, 2005) and editor of *Violence Against Women in Medieval Texts* (University Press of Florida, 1998) and of *Madeleine de l'Aubespine, Selected Poems and translations* (University of Chicago Press, 2007). She published some thirty articles on queer theory and pre-modern literature. She received the 2009 Nancy Lyman Roelker prize from the Sixteenth Century Society for "Erotica and Women in Early Modern France: Madeleine de l'Aubespine's Queer Poems" (*Journal* *of the History of Sexuality*). She is currently working on a monograph on l'Aubespine, author of one of the earliest openly bisexual poems in French.

Bernardita Llanos is professor of Spanish and women's studies and chair of the Department of Modern Languages at Denison University. She has published extensively on Latin American women writers, Chilean literature, and culture. Among her recent publications are the edition of a collection of essays on writer Diamela Eltit, *Letras y proclamas: la estética literaria de Diamela Eltit* (2006) and the book *Passionate Subjects/Split Subjects in Twentieth-Century Literature in Chile* (Brunet, Bombal, Eltit, 2009).

Gul Aldikacti Marshall is assistant professor in the Department of Sociology at the University of Louisville. Her teaching and research interests are in the areas of gender, social movements, social policy, and mass media. Currently she is analyzing the dynamics of national and international activism of feminist groups whose advocacy efforts are shaping gender policies in Turkey.

Irene Mata is an assistant professor in the Women's and Gender Studies Department at Wellesley College where she teaches courses in Chicana/Latina literature and culture. Her research interests include the analysis of labor and immigration representations in contemporary cultural productions and the ways in which current globalization projects have impacted the lives of women on the U.S./Mexico border area.

Clara Román-Odio is professor of Spanish and Hispanic American literature at Kenyon College. She is author of *Octavio Paz en los debates críticos y estéticos del siglo XX* (Galicia, Espana: tresCtres Editores, 2006) and coeditor of *Global and Local Geographies: The (Dis)locations of Contemporary Feminisms* (*Letras Femeninas* 33(1), 2007). She is currently working on a book titled *Sacred Iconographies in Chicana Cultural Productions: Feminism and Empowerment in Transnational Networks*. Forthcoming publications include "Queering the Sacred: Love as Oppositional Consciousness in Alma Lopez's Visual Art" (Alicia Gaspar de Alba, ed., University of Texas Press, Chicana Matters Series, 2011) and "Globalización de-centrada: feminismo transnacional, política cultural y la Virgen de Tepeyac en el arte visual de las chicanas" (Patrice Giasson, ed., CECMA, 2011).

Marta Sierra is associate professor of Spanish at Kenyon College. She has published extensively on the literatures and cultures of Latin America, the Argentinean avant-gardes, poetry and film of the 1990s Argentina, and feminist conceptualizations of space in the literatures and cultures of Argentina and Chile. She is the coeditor of *Global and Local Geographies: The (Dis)locations of Contemporary Feminisms* (*Letras Femeninas* 33(1), 2007). Her book *Gendered Spaces in Argentinean Women's Writing* has been accepted for publication by Palgrave Macmillan.

Katy Strzepek is the director of women's studies at St. Ambrose University and teaches the Cross-Cultural Introduction to Women's Studies, Women in Africa, and other seminars. Her research focuses on the intersections of feminist pedagogy and social praxis. Her article "Activist Girls in Culture of Apathy" (in progress), analyzes interviews with activist teen girls in the Midwest in order to determine how their activism helps them develop positive self-identities and critique systems of social control in their schools and communities. She is a proud community organizer, who advises several student groups and local organizations that focus on human rights.

Katherine Van Blair is director and associate professor of social work at St. Ambrose University. She teaches courses including Feminist Social Work, Empowerment Social Work in Mental Health, and Couple and Family Therapy. Her scholarship focus is on feminist administration, social justice in university systems, and feminist family therapy, and extends into local boards and social service agencies.

Kimberly A. Williams earned her PhD in women's studies from the University of Maryland and is currently an assistant professor at Mount Royal University in Calgary. Her research interests include transnational feminist and queer theories and movements and feminist theories of nationalism, militarization, and international relations. Her forthcoming book, titled *Imagining Russia: Making Feminist Sense of American Nationalism in U.S.-Russian Relations*, was awarded the 2009 SUNY Press Dissertation/First Book Prize in Women's and Gender Studies.

Index

Adams, Rachel, 71n24
Afghanistan, 203, 208–9, 211, 216n6
Afro-Brazilian women, 13, 142–3, 146–60, 160n2
Afro-Latin American, Afro-Caribbean and Diaspora Women's Network, 152
Agamben, Giorgio, 197
agency panic, 185–8
Agosín, Marjorie, 116n6
Alberdi, Juan Bautista, 85
Albright, Margaret, 116–17n9
Alexander, Jacqui, 14, 16, 213, 216n4
Alexander, Natasha, 231
Allende, Salvador, 115
Alvarez, Sonia, 147, 153–4
Alwyn, Patricio, 116n4–5
Amargi, 173
Ambrose Women for Social Justice (AWSJ), 16
Amnesty International, 184, 198n5, 227
Andermann, Jens, 96n8
Anderson, Benedict, 5
anti-Semitism, 183–4, 188–9
Antrobus, Peggy, 223
Anzaldúa, Gloria, 6–7, 17n2, 24–5, 28, 31, 40, 46, 55, 60, 69n3
'Aqrawi, Matta, 132
Arendt, Hannah, 197
Argentina, 10, 16, 77–94, 95n2–3, 96n8–10, 100, 108, 154
Arlt, Roberto, 86
artivism, 25, 31
Association for Support and Education of Women Candidates, 170
Azltán, 25, 41n6

Bac, Muftuler, 165
Bairros, Luiza, 159
Balbul, Ya'qub, 11, 119–20, 124–35, 135n1
"An Accurate Portrait," 124–9, 131–3, 135
al- Jamra al- ula, 11, 119
"The Return," 130–5
Barraza, Santa, 25–6
Barros, Pia, 95n5, 101
Bartra, Roger, 86–7
Bashkin, Orit, 11
Belgrano Rawson, Eduardo, 92, 96n10
Bellessi, Diana, 92, 96n10
Bhavnani, Kum-Kum, 6
Biden, Joe, 209–11
bildungsroman, 102, 115
Bond, Johanna, 144
Border Industrialization Program (BIP), 48
border thinking, 7
borderlands, 4, 6–12, 16, 26, 28, 31–5, 40, 55–6, 66, 80, 86, 94, 166
Bordertown (film), 45
Bourdieu, Pierre, 167
Brazil, 141–60
Brazilian Women's Articulation (AMB), 154–5, 160–1n4
Brosnan, 235
Brysk, Alison, 12
Bunch, Charlotte, 141
Burton, Antoinette, 208
Bush, George W., 203, 208
Bush, Laura, 208
Bustamante, Jorge A., 48–9, 69n4

Caldwell, Kia Lilly, 150
Carneiro, Sueli, 148, 151–2, 155–7

Carrasco, Ana María, 109
Carreño, Rubí, 106–7
Carroll, Lewis, 82
Castañeda, Mary, 42n10
Chapman, Anne, 89
Chatwin, Bruce, 86
Chierici, Rose Marie, 233
Chile, 11, 92, 95n5, 96n10, 99–117
Clinton, Bill, 116–17n9
Cohn, Roy, 181
Collins, Patricia Hill, 24, 236
colonial difference, 7
colonialism, 7, 15, 24, 121–2, 131, 133–4, 204, 215, 222–3, 226, 230–1. *See also* neocolonialism
communal option of democracy, 189–90, 196–8
conspiracy theory, 14, 181–90
contact zones, 224, 232
contestatory writing, 100–1
Convention on the Elimination of All Forms of Discrimination against Women (CEDAW), 169, 173
Cortázar, Julio, 81, 83
Cotera, Marta, 41n3
Covin, David, 158
Crenshaw, Kimberle Williams, 144
Criola, 142, 151, 157

da Silva, Benedita, 149, 155–6, 159
da Silva, Joselina, 157
Dąbrowska, Maria, 194
Darwin, Charles, 86
Darwish, Shalom, 124
de la Rúa, Fernando, 95n2
Deleuze, Gilles, 14, 81, 83, 179–80
Dell, Heather S., 214
dissensus, 14, 188, 190, 196–8
diversity feminisms, 17n3
Dobrowolsky, Alexandra, 8
Document of Brazilian Women, 154–5

Dole, Bob, 116–17n9
Dominican Republic, 233–4
Durán, Fray Diego, 28, 17n2
Dycki, Eugeniusz Tkaczyszyn-, 194

Echeverría, Claudia Martínez, 101
Eck, Lisa, 221
Ehrenreich, Barbara, 227–9
El Paso, Texas, 46–7, 56–8, 61, 66, 71n20
Electorat, Mauricio, 116n7
Eltit, Diamela, 101, 103
Encounter of Black Women, 153
Ensler, Eve: *Vagina Monologues, The*, 15, 203–16, 216n5
Epple, Juan Armando, 113
Estonia, 14, 180, 195
ethnocentrism, 15, 23, 204–5, 209, 212–16

female genital mutilation, 206, 208–10, 213, 230
feminism, U.S. Third World, 9, 12, 14, 24, 27n14, 41, 179, 187, 208–9
feminism without borders, 16, 93
feminists of color, 9, 23–4, 41n2
Fernández, Nona, 101
Fernández-Kelly, María Patricia, 49–50Figueiredo, Joao, 148–9
First Biennial of the Ends of the World, 10, 77–8, 80, 84, 86, 88, 93
Flying Broom, 169–70, 174
Foran, John, 6
Forcinito, Ana, 94, 108
Fragoso, Julia Monárrez, 51, 59, 70n13
Franklin, Jessica, 13–14
Fregoso, Rosa Linda, 51, 59, 71n21
Freire, Paulo, 13
Freud, Sigmund, 179, 188
Freyre, Gilberto, 146
Fuguet, Alberto, 116n7

Gache, Belén, 11, 78–84, 88–94, 94–5n1, 95n4
  Book of the Ends of the World, The, 82–3, 93
  Diario de la Luna Caníbal, 78–9, 83–93
  El libro del fin del mundo, 78
  Escrituras Nómadas. Del libro perdido al hipertexto, 78, 81–3, 93
Gallimore, Béa, 232–3
García Canclini, Néstor, 4, 26–7, 77, 88
Gaspar de Alba, Alicia, 30, 70n17
  Desert Blood, 10, 45–7, 53–69, 70n15, 71n24
Geledes, 142, 151, 155, 157
Genao, Emily, 231
geopolitics, 205–6, 209–12, 214–15, 217n9
Giardinelli, Mempo, 86
globalization, use of the term, 26–7
Goffman, Erving, 189, 198n9
Goksel, Diba, 165
Gonos, Goerge, 71n26, 72n31
Gonzalez, Leila, 148–9
graffiti, 61–5, 71n26–7, 72n31, 72n34
Gramsci, Antonio, 167
Grewal, Inderpal, 4–5, 12, 80, 145, 210–11, 226–7, 233
Gruszczyńska, Anna, 191
Guatemala, 235
Guattari, Félix, 14, 81, 83, 179
Gunes, Rana, 165
Guralnik, Sonia, 116n6
Gusinde, Martin, 89

Haiti, 233–4, 237
Hegel, Georg Wilhelm Friedrich, 179
hegemony, 4–5, 7–9, 16, 40, 53–4, 80, 93, 100, 166–8, 176, 195, 232

Hernández, Ester, 9, 24–6, 37–40, 42n7
  La Virgen de Guadalupe Defendiendo los Derechos de los Xicanos, 42n7
  La Virgen de las Calles, 38–40
  Libertad, 42n7
Hernandez, Ibis, 88
Hirsch, Marianne, 104, 114
Hockney, David, 194–5
Holocaust narratives, 105
homophobia, 14, 54, 61, 179–98
hooks, bell, 14–15, 213, 216n2, 216n4, 222, 227
Hortiguera, Hugo, 86, 95n2
Hughes, Karen, 208
human rights, 12, 206, 211–12, 222, 229, 231
  in Brazil, 13, 141–60
  in Chile, 114–15, 116n5
  LGBT community and, 186, 190, 194, 196–7
  in Turkey, 165–7, 175
  See also Women for Women's Human Rights/New Ways
Hunt, Michael, 216n3
Huyssen, Andreas, 100, 105, 112
hypertext, 78, 81–4, 93–4, 94–5n1

In the Shadow of the Raid: La Redada De Mayo (film), 235
Iparraguirre, Sylvia, 92, 96n10
Iraq, 9, 11, 119–35, 135n1–3, 209, 211

Jacobson, Beatrice, 16
Jamali, Fadhil, 132
Jameson, Frederic, 186
Jeftanovic, Andrea, 11, 101–10, 115–16
  Escenario de guerra, 11, 101–10, 115
  Geografía de la lengua, 106
Jewish intellectuals, 11, 119, 123–5
Johnson, Helen, 224

Juárez, Mexico, 10, 45–66, 69n1–2, 69n4, 70n13, 71n30
Jung, Krzysztof, 194–5

Kaplan, Caren, 3–6, 23, 38, 46, 233
Kardam, Nuket, 166
Kemal Ataturk, Mustafa, 176n4
Kemalist women, 168–75, 176n4, 176–7n5, 177n6
Kenya, 229–30
Kidder, Tracy, 233
Kim-Puri, H. J., 27–8
Kirkwood, Julieta, 109
Klingman, Avigdor, 72n34
Kłosowska, Anna, 14
Kochanowski, Jacek, 198
Konopnicka, Maria, 194
Kosovo, 108, 116–17n9
Kurian, Priya, 6
Kushigian, Julia A., 115
Kymlicka, Will, 12

Landow, George, 81
Latorre, Guisela, 25, 31
Latvia, 14, 180, 195–6
Lay, Mary M., 224
Lazzara, Michael, 114
League of Nations, 120
Leno, Mavis, 208
Leóon-Portilla, Miguel, 42n9
lesbian, gay, bisexual, and transgender (LGBT) population and rights, 14, 180–98, 198n5, 199n11, 236
Lewis, Hope, 144–5
Lithuania, 14, 180, 190–5
Llanos, Bernardita, 11
Lolosoli, Rebecca, 229–30
long table model, 15–16, 222–37
López, Alma, 9, 24–31, 42n8
   California Fashions Slaves, 28–31
Lorde, Audre, 24, 236
Los Alamos National Laboratory (LANL), 35

Lowe, Lisa, 68
Lukashenka, Alyaksandr, 182
Lula da Silva, Inacio, 158–9

MADRE, 229–30
al-Mala'ika, Nazik, 127
Mallarmé, Stéphane, 82
Manifest Destiny, 29–30, 33
Mansilla, Lucio V., 84–5, 92
"*maqila* culture," 50, 70n10
maquila industry and *maquiladoras*, 10, 37, 42n10, 45, 47–53, 56–9, 64, 68, 69n4, 69n6, 69n8, 70n10, 70n18, 71n20–1
Maria Mulher, 142, 157
Marshall, Gul Aldikacti, 13–14
Martinez, Marion C., 9, 24–6, 35–7
   Shrine to Guadalupe, 36–7
Masiello, Francine, 95n3
Massey, Doreen, 37
Mata, Irene, 10
Mato, Daniel, 42n8
Maturana, Andrea, 101
McCallum, Cecilia, 150
McCarthy, Joe, 181
McIntosh, Peggy, 235–6
Melley, Timothy, 14, 182, 185–90
Melville, Herman, 86
Menem, Carlos, 95n2
Meruane, Lina
   Cercada, 11, 101–3, 110–16
mestiza consciousness, 10, 24–6, 31, 33, 35, 38, 40–1, 42n7, 55, 60, 69n3
Mexico, 7, 10, 26–41, 45–69
Mignolo, Walter, 7, 78
Minh-ha, Trin, 24
Mixed Tech Media, 26, 35
Moghadam, Valentine M., 12, 41
Mohair Berets, 183–4
Mohanty, Chandra, 5–6, 14, 16, 17n1, 93, 179–80, 184, 187, 195, 230, 236

Monk, Janice, 224
Moraga, Cherrie, 6–7, 71n25
Moreno, Francisco, 85
Mort, Jo-Ann, 29–30
Mother's Courage: Thriving Survivors (documentary), 232
Motta, Athayde, 152
Moulian, Tomás, 103, 112
Movimento Negro Unificado (MNU), 147, 158
Mulenkei, Lucy, 229–30
Mulkern, Virginia, 71n26, 72n31

Nagy, Stanislaw, 189, 199n10
Naples, Nancy, 222
Narayan, Uma, 217
Nascimento, Abidas do, 149
National Conference of Representatives of Black Women's Organizations, 156
National Feminist Network of Health and Reproductive Rights (Brazil), 151
nationalism, American, 15, 203–5, 209, 211–12, 215–16
Nava, Michael, 55
Navarette, Carolina Andrea, 109–10
Nelson, Theodor, 94–5n1
neocolonialism, 10–12, 26, 31, 42n7, 116, 205, 207–8, 212, 215–16
nepantla, 7, 17n2, 28, 33, 42n9
Network of Black Brazilian Women's NGOs, 157
nomadic memory, 11, 108
nomadic writing, 78, 81–3, 93–4
nomadism, 78, 81–3, 93–4, 179
North American Free Trade Agreement (NAFTA), 48
North Atlantic Treaty Organization (NATO), 108, 116–17n9
Nouzeilles, Gabriela, 85

O'Sullivan, John, 30
Obama, Barack, 209

object books, 82–3, 95n5
Oliver, Kelly, 208–9
Oliveria, Marta, 155
Ong, Aihwa, 49–50, 70n10, 70n12
oppositional consciousness, 9–10, 24–6, 42n8, 60–1, 68
oppositional narrative, 10, 45, 52, 68, 147
oppositional technologies of power, 47
Ostolski, Adam, 199n10–11
Outlawed (film), 184, 198n5

paranoia, 185, 188–90
Patagonia, 10, 80, 84–7, 89–94
Pearlman, Abigail, 72n34
pedagogy, 3–4, 9, 14–16, 17n3, 203–7, 212–15, 231
Penley, Constance, 25, 93
Pérez, Laura, 32, 41n5
Pérez, Rosie, 206
Pérez-Torres, R., 40
permission fees for plays, 216n5
phantom acceptance, 189
Pinochet, Augusto, 95n5, 99–100, 102, 111–12
Poland, 14, 180–98
Portillo, Lourdes, 52–3, 59
postmemory, 11, 100–4, 108, 115, 187
postmodern subjectivity, 187
Poto Mitan: Haitian Women, Pillars of the Global Economy (documentary), 233–4
Poushnisky, Nicholas, 71n26, 72n31
Pratt, Mary Louise, 224, 232
Pravaz, Natasha, 146
Putnina, Aivita, 195–6

Qur'an, 129

Rabin, Yitzhak, 72n34
racial democracy, myth of, 13, 143, 145–9, 155, 157, 160

Radio Maryja, 183
Ramirez, Catherine S., 35
Rancière, Jacques, 14, 190, 196–8
Rascon, Arturo Gonzales, 51, 72n32
Reingarde, Jolanta, 191
rhizome, 78, 81, 83, 95n6, 179
Rice, Condoleezza, 208
Richard, Nelly, 111
Riedemann, Clemente, 92, 96n10
Río, Ana María del, 101
Ríos, Palmira N., 49–50
Riveros, Juan Pablo, 92, 96n10
Roca, Julio Argentino, 87, 96n9
Rocha, Carolina, 86, 95n2
Rodriguez, Ralph E., 53, 55, 62, 71n28
Roland, Edna, 151, 158
Roman-Odio, Clara, 9, 166, 198n1, 204, 208, 216n4, 222
Romany, Celina, 144
Romero, Mary, 234
Rose, Gillian, 90–1, 93
Rosenfelt, Deborah, 224
Ross, Andrew, 25, 93

Saffioti, Heleieth, 155
Sandoval, Chela, 9, 23–5, 31, 46–7, 57, 60–1, 67
Sant'Anna, Wania, 155
Santa Cruz, Guadalupe, 101
Scherman, Naomi, 223
Schmidt Camacho, Alicia, 70–1n18
Schuller, Mark, 233–4
Schulman, Barbara, 145
Scully, Pamela, 231
Señorita Extraviada (documentary), 52–3, 59
September 11, 2001, attacks of, 203–4, 213, 217
Sha'ul, Anwar, 124
Shafir, Gershon, 12
Shalev, Ronit, 72n34
Shawkat, Sami, 121–2, 133
Sierra, Marta, 10, 166, 198n1, 204, 208, 216n4, 222

Sierra Leone, 231
Silva, Marina, 159
Silva, Nilza Iraci, 155
Silverman, Kaja, 90–1
Sinacore, Ada L., 17n3
Smeal, Eleanor, 208
Smith, Barbara, 232
Soja, Edward, 95
Solanas, Pino, 86
Soviet Union, 193, 195–6
Special Secretariat for the Promotion of Racial Equality (SEPPIR), 158
Step Up!, 232–3
Stern, Steve, 102–3, 110–11
Strzepek, Katy, 16
Susa, Ahmad Nissim, 132
Sweeney, Susan Elizabeth, 54
Symaszek, Jennifer, 235

Tastsoglou, Evangelia, 8
Taylor, Diana, 222
Third World, 4–6, 14, 17n1, 27, 30, 32, 37, 212, 230. *See also* U.S. Third World feminism
Thurmond, Strom, 211
Tiano, Susan, 70n14–15
Tocci, Nathalie, 166
Torre, M. E., 231–2
Trafficking Victims Protection Act, 210–11
transnational feminist methodologies, approaches to, 4–6
transnational feminist pedagogies, 14–15
Treaty of Guadalupe, 30, 33, 41n6
Tripp, Aili, 40
Turkey, 165–76
Turner, J. Michael, 156

Underwood, Consuelo Jiménez, 9, 24–6, 31–5
Virgen de las Red-Hot Tortillas, 33–5
Virgen de los Caminos, 32–3

United Nations:
 Commission on the Status of Women (CSW), 172
 Conference against Racism, 13, 143, 156–7
 Conference on Human Rights, 153
 Conference on Women, 13, 143, 152–3, 225
U.S.-Mexican War, 30
U.S. Third World feminism, 9, 12, 14, 24, 27n14, 41, 179, 187, 208–9

V-Day, 15, 203, 206–7, 209–10, 212, 215, 216n6
Vagina Monologues, The, 15, 203–16, 216n5
Van Blair, Katherine, 16
Vidal, Hernán, 104, 116n5
violence against women, category of, 204–15
Violence Against Women Act, 209–11
Virgin of Guadalupe, 25, 28, 31, 33, 35–6, 38, 40
Virgin of Juárez, The (film), 45
virginity, 126, 171, 175

war on terror, 208, 211, 216
We, Brazilian Black Women, 157
Weaver, Lois
 "The Long Table," 15–16, 222. *See also* long table model
Wien, Peter, 120
Williams, Kimberly A., 15
Williams, Raymond, 6
Wilson, Barbara, 54–5
Women, Culture, and Development (WCD), 6
Women for Social Justice (WSJ), 223, 227–37
Women for Women's Human Rights/New Ways, 169–74
women's studies, 15–16, 23, 203–5, 212–15, 221–37
World Bank, 6
Wowereit, Klaus, 183

xenophobia, 205, 209, 212–13, 216

Zamora, Rosa, 235
Zdanevičius, Arnas, 191
Zeballos, Estanislao, 85
Zerbe Enns, Carolyn, 17n3
Zhao, Michael, 37
Zionism, 122–3